The Modern Period Room

... des one ... trospec- ... range ... recon- structions from a variety of different viewpoints. Beneath the conceptual and physical strategy of the representational technique of the modern period room lie numerous conflicting intentions.

This collection of essays by design historians, architects and curators engages with these tensions. The authors explore themes and examples by architects such as Frank Lloyd Wright, Truus Schröeder and Gerrit Rietveld, Ernö Goldfinger and others in a bid to reveal the specific cultural encoding of presented interior spaces.

The book's critical engagement with the issues and conventions that surround the modern period room will allow historians and theorists of architecture, design and social history to investigate the contexts in which this representational device has been used. The various models of period room enable the reader to understand just how dynamic, contributory and ultimately interventionist the presentation of the period room is in the process of architectural and design history making.

Penny Sparke is Pro Vice-Chancellor (Arts) and a Professor of Design History at Kingston University, London. She has published widely in the field of twentieth-century design with a particular focus on the relationship between design and gender. Her publications include *As Long as It's Pink: The Sexual Politics of Taste* (Pandora, 1995) and she has recently published a book about the pioneer American interior decorator, Elsie de Wolfe (Acanthus Books, 2005). Her current research is on the relationship between modernity and the interior.

Brenda Martin is Curator at the Dorich House Museum, part of Kingston University, London. Her publications include 'A House of Her Own, Dora Gordine and Dorich House' in *Women's Places: Architecture and Design 1860–1960,* eds B. Martin and P. Sparke (Routledge, 2003) and *Dora Gordine: Sculpture Collection at Dorich House* (Bond and Coyne, 2005). Current research interests are identity and the interior and twentieth-century furniture design.

Trevor Keeble is Head of the School of Art and Design History at Kingston University, London. A graduate of the V&A/RCA MA in the History of Design, he completed a Ph.D. entitled *The Domestic Moment: Design, Taste and Identity in the Late Victorian Interior* at the Royal College of Art. He continues to research, work and teach upon aspects of nineteenth- and twentieth-century interior design history.

The Modern Period Room

The construction of
the exhibited interior
1870 to 1950

**Edited by
Penny Sparke, Brenda Martin
and Trevor Keeble**

Routledge
Taylor & Francis Group

LONDON AND NEW YORK

First published 2006
by Routledge
2 Park Square, Milton Park, Abingdon, Oxon OX14 4RN

Simultaneously published in the USA and Canada
by Routledge
270 Madison Ave, New York, NY 10016

Routledge is an imprint of the Taylor & Francis Group, an informa business

Typeset in Univers by
Florence Production Ltd, Stoodleigh, Devon
Printed and bound in Great Britain by
TJ International Ltd, Padstow, Cornwall

British Library Cataloguing in Publication Data
A catalogue record for this book is available from the British Library

Library of Congress Cataloging in Publication Data
The modern period room: the construction of the exhibited interior 1870 to 1950 /
edited by Trevor Keeble, Brenda Martin and Penny Sparke. – 1st ed.
p. cm.
Includes bibliographical references and index.
1. Period rooms.   2. Interior decoration – History – 19th century.   3. Interior
decoration – History – 20th century.   4. Museum exhibits.   I. Keeble, Trevor.
II. Martin, Brenda.   III. Sparke, Penny.
NK2125.M56   2006
747.09'034074 – dc22   2005029750

ISBN10: 0–415–37469–3 (hbk)
ISBN10: 0–415–37470–7 (pbk)
ISBN10: 0–203–09961–3 (ebk)

ISBN13: 978–0–415–37469–9 (hbk)
ISBN13: 978–0–415–37470–5 (pbk)
ISBN13: 978–0–203–09961–2 (ebk)

Contents

Contents

Illustration credits

The authors and publishers gratefully acknowledge the following permissions to reproduce material in this book.

Chapter 1
From *Homes Sweet Homes*, John Murray, London, 1939: 1.1
Metropolitan Museum of Art, New York: 1.2
Courtesy of the Museum of Art, Rhode Island School of Design. Photograph by Del Bogart: 1.3
V&A Picture Library: 1.4, 1.7
MAK – Austrian Museum of Applied Arts/Contemporary Art, Vienna. Photograph © Gerald Zugman/MAK: 1.5
Steve Brosnahan Collection of the Lower East Side Tenement Museum: 1.6
Reproduced by kind permission of Skansen: 1.8
Reproduced by kind permission of Heal & Son Ltd: 1.9

Chapter 2
MoDA: 2.1, 2.2, 2.5
© Paul Antick: 2.3
Imad Ahmed: 2.4

Chapter 3
© Linley Sambourne House: 3.1, 3.2, 3.3, 3.4, 3.5, 3.6, 3.7

Chapter 4
© Sarah Chaplin: 4.1, 4.2, 4.3, 4.4, 4.5, 4.6

Chapter 5
© Paul Overy: 5.1, 5.2, 5.3, 5.4, 5.5

Chapter 6
Courtesy Walker Art Center: 6.1, 6.2, 6.3, 6.5
Rolphe Dauphin for Walker Art Center, Minneapolis: 6.4

Chapter 7
From *Rhythme* magazine, 1949: 7.1

From *La Maison* magazine, 1946: 7.2

Exposition Internationale du Logement (catalogue), Brussels: Art et Technique, 1946: 7.3

Louis-Herman De Koninck archive, AAM, Brussels: 7.4

Internationale Tentoonstelling Urbanisme et Habitation, Belgische Afdeling, Parijs 1947 (catalogue), Brussels: Art et Technique, 1947: 7.5

AMVC, Antwerp: 7.6

Chapter 8

George Kennethson, © Kettle's Yard, University of Cambridge: 8.1

Paul Allitt, © Kettle's Yard, University of Cambridge: 8.2, 8.3, 8.4, 8.5

Chapter 9

Crafts Study Centre (2005): 9.1

Plischke-Nachlass/Plischke Estate: 9.2, 9.3, 9.4

© Crown copyright, NMR: 9.5

Chapter 10

Harriet McKay: 10.1, 10.2, 10.3, 10.5

The National Trust: 10.4

Chapter 11

Brenda Martin: 11.1

© English Heritage/NMR: 11.2, 11.3, 11.4, 11.5

Bernard Howarth, Loom Dorich House Archives: 11.6

Contributors

Jeremy Aynsley is Professor of Design History at the Royal College of Art where he leads the graduate programme run jointly with the Victoria and Albert Museum. He is also Director of the Arts and Humanities Research Council (AHRC) Centre for the Study of the Domestic Interior. He is currently writing a book on the culture of design in twentieth-century Germany.

Sebastiano Barassi is Curator of Collections at Kettle's Yard and Director of Studies in History of Art at Fitzwilliam College, University of Cambridge. His main research interests are the history of modern and contemporary art and the theoretical aspects of its preservation, with a particular emphasis on the implications of museum practice.

Sarah Chaplin is a qualified architect with a Masters in Architecture and Critical Theory. Now Head of the School of Architecture at Kingston University, she has published widely on aspects of contemporary architecture and urbanism, digital culture and technology, feminism, and Japan. Her publications include *Visual Culture: an Introduction* (Manchester University Press, 1997), co-authored with John A. Walker, and *Consuming Architecture* (Academy-Wiley, 1998), co-edited with Eric Holding.

Fredie Floré graduated in 1997 as an engineer-architect at the Department of Architecture and Urban Planning, Ghent University (Belgium). She is preparing a Ph.D. on the mediation of modern domestic ideals in post-war Belgium. She is co-editor of two books and author of several articles in international and national magazines. Recently, she published the paper 'The representation of modern domesticity in the Belgian section of the Brussels World's Fair of 1958' in the *Journal of Design History*, 4, 2003, pp. 319–40 (co-authored with Mil De Kooning).

Eleanor Gawne, MA (RCA), RMSA, studied the History of Design and has worked in a number of design archives, including Arthur Sanderson & Sons and the Archive of Art & Design, Victoria and Albert Museum. She joined the British Architectural Library, Royal Institute of British Architects in 1995, becoming archivist in 2000.

Lesley Hoskins was Curator at MoDA (Museum of Domestic Design & Architecture) Middlesex University from 1998 to 2005. Her publications include *Living Rooms. 20th-Century Interiors at the Geffrye Museum* (Geffrye Museum Trust, 1998), and, with Charlotte Gere, *The House Beautiful: Oscar Wilde and the Aesthetic Interior* (Lund Humphries in association with the Geffrye Museum Trust, 2000). She has recently returned to full-time study prior to working on a research project on Homemaking and Material Culture in the 19th Century, instigated by Queen Mary College in conjunction with the Geffrye Museum.

Trevor Keeble is Head of the School of Art and Design History at Kingston University, London. A graduate of the V&A/RCA MA in the History of Design, he completed a Ph.D. entitled *The Domestic Moment: Design, Taste and Identity in the Late Victorian Interior* at the Royal College of Art. He continues to research, work and teach upon aspects of nineteenth- and twentieth-century interior design history.

Mil De Kooning is Full Professor at Ghent University, Belgium. He has published a number of books and articles on post-war architecture in Belgium including *Horta and After: 25 Masters of Modern Architecture in Belgium* (Ghent: Department of Architecture and Urban Planning, Ghent University, 1999). He is currently writing books on the architecture of the World's Fair of 1958 in Brussels and on the furniture and building design of Willy Van Der Meeren. Since 1984 he has been a Director of *Vlees & Beton*, a series of monographs on the theory and history of architecture and design.

Harriet McKay was Custodian of the National Trust property, 2 Willow Road, between 1996 and 2005. She has published articles, and contributed to a number of books, on interior design. She is currently writing a doctorate at the Royal College of Art on the relationship between art and the home in Britain in the twentieth century.

Brenda Martin is Curator at the Dorich House Museum, Kingston University, London. Her publications include 'A House of Her Own, Dora Gordine and Dorich House' in *Women's Places: Architecture and Design 1860–1960*, eds B. Martin and P. Sparke (Routledge, 2003) and *Dora Gordine: Sculpture Collection at Dorich House* (Bond and Coyne, 2005). She is currently researching material for a book on the work of Dora Gordine.

Paul Overy has published two books on De Stijl (*De Stijl*, World of Art Series, Thames & Hudson, 1991), and is the co-author of books on the Rietveld Schröder House and Rietveld furniture (*The Rietveld Schröder House*, Paul Overy *et al.*, Amsterdam: Thoth, 1998). He is Reader in the History and Theory of Modernism at Middlesex University and has recently completed a book on modernist architecture and health, hygiene and light.

Daniel Robbins is a Senior Curator, Museums, with the Royal Borough of Kensington and Chelsea responsible for the Leighton House Museum and the Linley Sambourne House. He was formerly a Curator with Glasgow Museums working extensively on Glasgow Style and Charles Rennie Mackintosh.

Penny Sparke is Pro Vice-Chancellor (Arts) and a Professor of Design History at Kingston University, London. She has published widely in the field of twentieth-century design, with a particular focus on the relationship between design and gender. Her publications include *As Long as It's Pink: The Sexual Politics of Taste* (Pandora, 1995) and she has recently published a book about the pioneer American interior decorator, Elsie de Wolfe (Acanthus Books, 2005). Her current research is on the relationship between modernity and the interior.

Alexandra Griffith Winton is an independent scholar and writer specialising in the history and theory of the modern domestic interior. Her current projects include a forthcoming book about the architectural fabics of American modernist textile designer Dorothy Liebes, for which she received a grant from the Graham Foundation for Advanced Studies in the Fine Arts. She is presently a visiting professor of design history and theory at the Pratt Institute.

Preface

The eleven essays in this publication are based on papers given at a 2003 conference entitled 'The Modern Period Room'. The conference was the fifth in the Dorich House Series organised by a group of art, architectural and design historians in the Faculty of Art, Design & Architecture at Kingston University, London. Faced as we were at the time with the task of turning the university-owned Dorich House – the former home of the Latvian-born sculptor, Dora Gordine and her husband, the Hon. Richard Hare, an academic and collector of Russian art – into a museum, the 2003 conference was stimulated by questions that we at Kingston were asking ourselves. How does one turn a house containing artworks into a museum? How does one narrate the story of the lives that were lived there? How authentic can a retrospective reconstruction of interior spaces and their contents be? How does one capture a moment in time when interiors are in a state of perpetual reformulation? These and many other questions provoked the discussions and debates that are contained in the pages of this book.

For anyone confronted by the challenge of reconstructing and curating an interior in a museum setting, or refurbishing and creating displays in the context of a house museum – i.e. of re-presenting, as historicised material culture, 'period rooms' – these remain live questions. When the interiors in need of reconstruction were created at a moment that refuted the role of history, seeing itself, rather, in the context of a continuous 'modern' present, they become even more complex and difficult to resolve.

The staff involved in the creation of the Dorich House Museum felt that the best way of confronting these questions was to hear how others had found answers to them. To this end we brought together a group of people who had addressed them from a range of different perspectives. We were delighted that so many of the academics/curators who have contributed to this book were able either to provide 'case studies' of actual reconstructions with which they had been involved, or papers that offered rich contextual information relating to the concept of 'the modern period room' in more general terms. In their varied ways they all contributed to the fascinating debates and discussions that emerged and in so doing opened up hitherto unexplored territory.

Since 2003 the art, architectural and design historians at Kingston University have remained committed to the themes that arose from the discussions about the 'modern period room'. Indeed, they have become central to the work of the university's Modern Interiors Research Centre, launched in 2004, which plans to host more conferences and seminars, and generate more publications, addressing the multiple museological, historical, theoretical, professional and pedagogical issues that are raised by this fascinating subject.

I would like to thank everybody who made this book possible, especially Brenda Martin, the curator of the Dorich House Museum, and Caroline Mallinder and her team at Routledge. I hope that readers will enjoy and benefit from the debates and discussions presented here and that they will help to stimulate yet more fruitful research into the problematic and paradoxical concept of the 'modern period room'.

Professor Penny Sparke
Pro Vice-Chancellor (Arts Division)
Director, Modern Interiors Research Centre
Kingston University, London

Introduction

Trevor Keeble

There is no cohesive body of writing on the subject of the period room. Where it has been discussed, it has simply been viewed as a means to an end in the dissemination of a museum's collection or a social historical tool in the representation of particular thematic histories.[1] Why, then, is it worth considering the role of the period room and, to be more specific, the modern period room? The editors of this collection would like to suggest that critical engagement with the issues and conventions that surround the modern period room will allow historians and theorists of architecture, design and social history to interrogate the contexts in which this representational device has been used and that it foregrounds issues of authenticity, time, space and place, allowing for a very specific analysis of how, as historians, we use these concepts in our work. Examination of the various models of the period room enables us to understand just how dynamic, contributory and ultimately interventionist the presentation of the period room is in the process of architectural and design history-making.

The essays assembled in this collection aim to tease out the threads of a debate that is located across and within various contexts, institutions and organisations, including the National Trust, local authority museums, university museums and art galleries. Given the diversity of contributing authors, and the differing contexts of their examples, this collection of essays is the first of its kind to establish the terrain of this discussion.

The period room has emerged as a key representational device of social history, and of the history of architecture and the fine and decorative arts. At the outset of this collection of essays it is worth considering how the conventions of the period room, as presented within these disciplines, propose certain historical and methodological conditions. Primarily, it has been used to demonstrate two of the strongest guiding principles of what might best be described as the 'old' art history – namely, dependence on the concepts of high style and authenticity.

In *Authentic Décor: The Domestic Interior 1620–1920*, Peter Thornton explained his understanding of the term 'period' as follows:

> Each period of history has its own way of seeing things – its own 'period eye', as it were – which, by some strange process, seems to affect pretty

well everyone. This in effect means that people in circles that react to fashion, even when it is only to quite a limited extent, possess a common way of viewing rooms – and, indeed, much else. It means that a certain degree of density in the arrangement of the furniture is regarded as generally acceptable at that moment. It means that at some periods a larger number of objects can be tolerated *en masse* in a room than at others.[2]

These few lines from Thornton's masterly survey of the history of interior decoration are worth reconsidering within the context of the essays assembled in this collection, as contained within them is a complex of truth and contradiction. Perhaps the most important of these propositions for a collection entitled *The Modern Period Room* is that each age has a common way of viewing. This basic assumption acknowledges the paradox at the heart of all period room presentations. Like all historical constructions, the period room comments on at least two different periods: that of its chronological gestation and that of its presentation. As if this layering of one age through the optic of another were not complex enough, many period rooms – indeed, several commented on in this collection – undergo successive 're-presentations' and hence potentially complexify the understanding of period even further. While this challenge might be made to any form of history making, it is particularly pertinent to the period room and the assumed authentic 'factualness' of its materiality. Because the period room relies so heavily on the notion of authenticity, of being a re-presentation of 'how things really were', it could be argued that the curatorial hands of its authorship are rendered somewhat invisible to the viewer and that spectators looking on the period room understand it only as a hermetically sealed capsule, uncontaminated by the passage of time.

In his seminal essays 'The Photographic Message' and 'The Rhetoric of the Image', Roland Barthes proposed that photography constituted 'a message without a code'.[3] By this he meant that photography, as an analogue medium, creates a visual representation 'to the letter' of its subject, and because of this, the photograph acts as a 'literal message' unencumbered by any apparent codification.[4] Barthes suggested that the invisibility of this process denied photography the 'duality' that was common to all other modes of representation – i.e. 'The duality of representation is evident in all reproductions other than photographic ones: there is no drawing, no matter how exact, whose very exactitude is not turned into a style.'[5] While it would be misleading to suggest that the presentation of period rooms was without convention or manner, the most common of which is the tendency to reduce the space of the room to merely a three-walled picture plane, it must be acknowledged that the period room constitutes the most literal of messages, diminished only by the knowledge that some of its aspects are not necessarily original or authentic.

Perhaps the single most important decision that any curator of a period room must take is when to locate its specific historical moment of truth. With an emphasis on authorship, art historical traditions have led the curator to seek out the moment of a room's creation in order to best represent the characteristic qualities of that particular space. This is largely due to the fact that period rooms have tended to be used to allude to the 'best' examples and representative moments of high style and luxury. The architectural and art historical canon has dictated that, if a design emanates from the hand of any esteemed creator, then it is worthy of representation and display. This specific approach, although no longer as orthodox as it once was, imposes a dimensionless quality on the period room that arrests it within a single moment of its history.

This propensity to strip back the period room to its most 'authentic' moment of origin is an impulse that has coloured much of the history of interior decoration and design. Explaining his approach to the history of the interior, Thornton suggested 'the reason for including so many architects' and upholsterers' designs is that these do actually provide a sure indication of taste at the moment they were executed; they are not overlaid with later accretions'.[6] Given Thornton's emphasis on the history of high style, this is perhaps an appropriate proposition. Thornton constructed a history of 'legitimate' taste, a taste defined clearly through the lens of production which chose to ignore suggestion of the interior as a social and material lived reality. An emphasis on production as the determining factor in the character of an interior leads to the explicit rejection of the diachronic qualities of the interior such that all 'accretions' – objects brought into the interior after the date of its production – are interpreted as undermining the intended design. By rejecting 'the addition of external matter or things', this art historical approach to the period room has resulted in a denial of its 'consumption' as a creative part of its definition.[7] The effect of this has tended to undermine further the diachronic characterisation of the period room's evolution and history.

Paradoxically, the alternative to this approach is fraught with other problems. If the emphasis of the art historical period room is authorship, authenticity, uniqueness and stasis, then the guiding principle of the social historical period room is an emphasis on the commonplace and the everyday. This tendency towards a generalised representation of 'how things were' has its own set of complications, not the least of which concerns the concept of authenticity. Whereas a museum object may be presented in isolation as simply a chair, a table or a lamp, when brought together and grouped to form a period room, these objects assume a 'relative' authenticity that relies on the coherence of the display as an authentic whole. Of course, this tendency towards generalisation is not confined to the social historical period room; it is also a part of the art historical presentation.

Returning once again to Thornton, it is worth noting that in a bid to explain the emergence and development of particular styles, he too sought to generalise from specific examples. Dwelling on his understanding of the 'period eye', he explained the subtlety of its vision in such a way as to reveal how it might illuminate a bygone age:

> the characteristics in question are not simply a question of how the walls are decorated, of what furniture is present, and of the pattern of the

carpet. It is something much more subtle and I can at present only define it as a matter of density.[8]

In the absence of any particular defining characteristic, this concept of 'density' suggests a general characteristic that is specific to a particular era and, in spite of Thornton's previous position, it might also be interpreted as an acknowledgement of the central role 'accretions', and their acquisition over time, actually play in the creation of an interior. This strategy to 'pin down' the intangible characteristics of historical interiors allows them to be accounted for in terms of their individual taste and style, while also characterising them as relatively homogenous representations of their age.

In what sense, then, might the period room be thought to be modern? In order to answer this question, it is necessary to reflect on the context in which the word 'modern' is used. The period room is identified by the essays in this volume as an emblem of modernity. As a selective representation, it emerges as an explicitly modern trope concerned to demonstrate that modernity. Ultimately, through its qual-ification and record of the past, the period room becomes the barometer with which the fleeting nature of modernity and the loss of the past might be measured, embraced or lamented. Yet paradoxically, it is for these very same reasons that the conventions of the period room became the means through which the cultural responses to that fleeting modernity – namely, modernism – might also be devel-oped. Having been established by its viewer as a 'model' of a bygone age, the convention of the period room was used repeatedly through the twentieth century to anticipate a modernist future. Just as the still 'snapshot' quality of the period room became the measure of modernity, the loss incurred in it also became the means through which polemic visions of 'how life might still be lived' were presented. From the perspective of the twenty-first century, few conceptions of modernism allow us to historicise and understand the chronology of its development as fully as the often polemic and utopian model spaces that materialised its ideals and values. In this manner, paradoxically, the explicitly 'representational' aspect of these modernist conventions allow us to periodise modernism in precisely the manner that it sought to resist. If the period room was a means by which the spaces of the past might be represented, then so too, the spaces of a modernist present and future, and because of this period rooms must be understood to act as truly modern performative entities.

The essays in this collection show that the use and consideration of the period room forces historians and curators to engage critically the extent to which they perpetuate knowledge and understanding in an explicitly performative manner. Because of its tendency to lead the viewer towards an understanding of generalised 'representativeness', few modes of historical representation are as potentially open to misinterpretation as the period room.

In recent years considerable attention has been paid to the ways in which space has been produced and understood within modern Western societies. Much of this research owes a debt to Henri Lefebvre's *The Production of Space*, published in English in 1991.[9] The significance of Lefebvre's study is that it reveals the ever-changing nature of spatial experience and suggests that key to this change is the role of 'representation'. Lefebvre suggested three specific 'modes' for spatial analysis – *representations of space*, *representational space* and *spatial practice* – to describe the different ways that space was lived in, perceived and conceived by its inhabitants.[10] Importantly for Lefebvre, these modes of experience articulated the condition of modernity and described the dynamic relationship between space and meaning. Significantly for this discussion of the modern period room, Lefebvre's analysis emphasised the role of the individual in the construction of meaning through experience. As the essays in this collection demonstrate, with regard to the modern period room 'the individual' could be construed in many and various ways: as architect, homemaker, artist, connoisseur, family, curator or visitor. Given the explicitly representational nature of the modern period room, this call to articulate and qualify the meaningful 'position' from which a period room presentation might be created or experienced is described in all the essays in this collection and goes some way towards elaborating a critical position for the historian concerned with the development of past spaces and, in particular, period rooms. The authors of this collection suggest that by considering the dynamic role of the individual within space we understand how the modern period room acts as a historical document today.

Many of the essays in this collection focus on specific modern period rooms. The first two, however, provide a contextual overview of the emergence of the period room as a representational device and a consideration of the challenges and demands of contemporary museological practice concerning the objects and décor of the domestic interior in general. Jeremy Aynsley's chapter, 'The Modern Period Room – A Contradiction in Terms?', provides a historical overview of institutional approaches and uses of the modern period room. By problematising these examples and unpacking some of the ways that they have been made meaningful, his essay provides a critical insight into the emergence of the period room and the uses to which it has been put. The themes of change and development are expanded by Lesley Hoskins in her essay 'Interiors Without Walls'. As the first curator of the Museum of Domestic Design & Architecture, Hoskins provides a unique insight into the processes of curatorial decision-making. Through reference to the requirements and guidance of professional bodies, such as the Museums, Libraries and Archives Association, she demonstrates how curatorial attitudes towards and strategies relating to the presentation of historic material change and develop according to the 'perceived' needs of a museum-going public.

Several essays in this collection focus on modern period rooms that have been judged significant because of the individuals who created and lived in them. Daniel Robbins' case study of Linley Samborne House provides a unique example of a 'period' house that is notable not because of its inhabitants and creators, but because of its survival since the 1870s. Although Linley and Marion Sambourne might have been considered 'artistic' within their circle, the significance of their home lies in its ability to represent the 'middling sorts' of late nineteenth-century London.

The importance of authority and authorship, however, is key to many of the examples considered by the contributors of this volume. In 'The Double Life: The Cultural Construction of the Exhibited Interior in Modern Japan', Sarah Chaplin contextualises a highly significant period room by Frank Lloyd Wright. Chaplin reveals the intimate sensibility with which the period room has been used to mediate experiences of cross-cultural modernity and change, and demonstrates the significance of 'authorship' in this process.

Like a number of other contributions to this collection, Chaplin's essay is concerned with interiors and spaces that have become 'representative' moments in the history of modernism.

Paul Overy's essay considers the role that Gerrit Rietveld's polemical domestic buildings of the 1920s now play in historicising a specifically Dutch narrative of modernism, while Fredie Floré and Mil De Kooning's essay considers the way that modernity was 'modelled' and promulgated through the construction of mass housing in postwar Belgium. Both of these essays deal with examples of modern architecture and design that embody a highly visible and symbolic response to the modernity of mid-twentieth-century Europe. An American response to this modernity is considered by Alexandra Griffith Winton in her essay, 'A Man's House is his Art'. Through a case study of the Walker Art Center's *Idea House* Project, this essay demonstrates the explicitly representational strategies used to promote and market contemporary modes of domestic living. Through Dutch, Belgian and American examples, these authors reveal the extent to which the 'model' room became a means by which cultural and technological authority might be demonstrated, represented and spread.

Because authorship seems so central to an understanding of the modern period room, a number of essays in this collection reveal and explore the complex ways in which this might be interpreted, enforced or construed. Eleanor Gawne's essay, which focuses on the apartment of Lucie Rie, suggests the importance of maintaining the creative spirit of its inhabitant. Although dislocated from its architecture and transported from one country to another, this modern period room has been 'preserved' to record and embody its dead inhabitant in such a way as to suggest that traces of Rie still exist in the slightly mundane surroundings of her home. In sharp contrast, through an examination of the curatorial polices of Kettle's Yard, Sebastiano Barassi in his essay 'Kettle's Yard: Museum or Way of Life?' explains the extent to which some present-day curators are still bound to the explicit vision of a house's creator and inhabitant. Unlike so many other examples of period rooms where curators have been forced to read between the lines of previous inhabitation, Kettle's Yard represents the vision of one man, Jim Eade, who left not only his collection and home for posterity but also clear instructions on how it was to be presented. Each of these examples represent approaches to the modern period room that seek to 'still' the presentation to a single moment of the room's history.

Two other case studies in this collection offer an alternative position that suggests the importance of inhabitation and acknowledges that past spaces were transitional and always subject to change. As the first custodian of 2 Willow Road,

Hampstead, the home built and lived in by the modernist architect Erno Goldfinger and his family, Harriet McKay in her essay 'The Preservation and Presentation of 2 Willow Road for the National Trust' reveals the Trust's innovative aims in representing this particular building and space. These focused on showing the house as it had been lived in by the Goldfingers over half a century. While the moment of the house's construction and creation was important, the diachronic development of it as a home became the principal means through which it was represented. A significant factor of this approach was that Ernö and Ursula Goldfinger's children and friends were still alive and able to characterise and explain how this house had been lived in.

This was certainly not an opportunity for Brenda Martin, Curator of the Dorich House Museum. Martin's essay entitled 'Photographs of a Legacy at the Dorich House Museum' explains how, by the time of the sculptor Dora Gordine's death in 1991, there was relatively little living memory of how she and her husband, the academic and collector Richard Hare, had occupied the house they had built during the mid-1930s. Martin describes how photographs taken for publication in popular magazines provided an invaluable representation of Dora and Richard within their home and became a key source in the attempt to 'reconstruct' and 'narrate' a sense of the life that had taken place in it.

The chapters in this book provide many different ways of considering the interior spaces of the past. Some emphasise issues of high style and authenticity, some the role of inhabitation and lived experience. Yet all of them testify to the continuing significance of interior spaces in the historicising of culture and society, and the overwhelming public interest in those spaces.

Notes

1 A. Peck, *Period Rooms in the Metropolitan Museum of Art*, New York: Metropolitan Museum of Art Publications, 2004; E. N. Kaufmann, 'The Architectural Museum from Worlds Fair to Restoration Village' in *Assemblage. A Critical Journal of Architecture and Design Culture*, no. 9, June 1989.

2 P. Thornton, *Authentic Décor. The Domestic Interior 1620–1920*, London: Weidenfeld & Nicolson, 1984, p. 8.

3 R. Barthes, 'The Photographic Message' in *Image Music Text*, London: Fontana Press, 1977, pp. 15–31.

4 R. Barthes, 'The Rhetoric of the Image' in *Image Music Text*, London: Fontana Press, 1977, pp. 32–51.

5 Barthes, 1977, p. 18.

6 Thornton, 1984, p. 13.

7 *Oxford English Dictionary* definition of 'accretion'. *OED* (9th edition, 1995).

8 Thornton, 1984, p. 9.

9 H. Lefebvre, *The Production of Space*, Oxford: Blackwell, 1991.

10 Lefebvre, 1991, pp. 38–9. Translated from the original French, the precision of these terms in describing Lefebvre's concepts is contested. See Shields, R. *Lefebvre, Love & Struggle. Spatial Dialectics*, London: Routledge, 1999, pp. 153–7.

Chapter 1

The modern period room –

a contradiction in terms?

Jeremy Aynsley

*what he did with was
try to connect people's choice
of interiors
with the lifestyle.*

In 1939, the British cartoonist Osbert Lancaster (1908–86) published *Homes Sweet Homes*. This book confirmed, if confirmation were needed, that conventions of interior decoration were fully understood and the idea of a period room could become a topic of humour broadly understood by the general public. As his well-known illustrations reveal, Lancaster was keen to connect people's choice of interior design with lifestyle – there was an assumption that manners and interiors could be associated and in so doing, he demonstrated their comic potential. In the context of the outbreak of the Second World War, Lancaster wrote:

> For the history of the home provides the most intimate, and in some ways the most reliable, picture of the growth and development of European culture; at all periods the average man (or for that matter abnormal man) has revealed most clearly his prejudices, his standards and his general outlook in the ordering of his most intimate surroundings.[1]

Lancaster's gender bias aside, his choice of categories can be taken as symptomatic of a broader understanding of how the domestic imagination could be captured in an assured and acutely rendered graphic style for popular consumption. In his book, Lancaster took familiar period styles such as Rococo, Regency and Art Nouveau, and combined them with more finely tuned terms, such as Greenery Yallery, a term that poked fun at the Aesthetic Movement, the Earnest Eighties and those of his own

1.1
**Osbert Lancaster, 'The Earnest
'Eighties'.**
From *Homes Sweet Homes*, John
Murray, London, 1939

invention, such as Stockbrokers' Tudor, coined for the first time in this volume. And in terms of the modern, he had no problem bringing his series up to date with 'the modernistic', 'the functional' and what Lancaster called 'the even more functional', which in this case, was an air-raid shelter (Figure 1.1).

So, if by the mid-twentieth century the period room had become a common reference point in popular publishing, what were its origins? Traditionally, the term 'period room' has been associated with the conventions of presenting ensembles of furniture, fittings and decorative schemes within the context of a museum. Museological practice has established ways of understanding such interiors for their contribution to a history of style, in a system that elevates authenticity and connoisseurship to paramount and guiding principles. Yet throughout the twentieth century, period rooms also existed in a number of other settings. For instance, they could be seen in the great exhibitions and department stores, on the pages of magazines, as well as at specialist design and home exhibitions. It is the inter-connections between these various forms of display that this chapter seeks to explore.

Initially, I think it is important to distinguish between three broad categories of representation of room. First, there are the ensembles constituted from a previous context, as in the form of the period room transposed to a museum. This tradition is most closely associated with decorative arts museums that were entrusted with responsibility for the care, preservation and display of endangered specimens of what we now call interior design. Here, great effort is made to transpose the fabric of an interior from its original setting to its new context as an object of museum display. While the public usually takes the imaginative leap to believe in these interiors, different levels of reconstruction inevitably take place in such instances. For example, the infrastructure of these newly constituted museum interiors replaces that of the original, as new lighting, museum signage and previously impossible juxtapositions with other museum objects affect their overall context and alter the experience of such rooms.

Second, there are those interiors that have been preserved *in situ*, as part of historic houses where they remain integral elements of an original architectural setting. Among these, a modern example would be Leslie Martin's 1970 extension to Kettle's Yard in Cambridge, the private home and gallery of curator Jim Eade, now open to the public on a regular basis (discussed by Sebastiano Barassi in Chapter 8). Originally, the principle of opening houses to visitors was associated with stately homes and houses of the elite, as the history of the estates owned and supervised by the National Trust in Britain reveals.[2] Furthermore, the initial impetus of such house collections was not solely on the interior; rather, as Clough William-Ellis's book *On Trust for the Nation* of 1947 indicated, a great emphasis lay on both their built form and grounds as contributions to the national landscape.[3] In the last twenty years at least, however, changing priorities in historical interpretation and popular taste, together with a particular fascination for the home in its many guises, have turned the impetus towards making accessible a broader range of houses to an ever-increasing public. Curated houses with period rooms now include examples across all social classes and many design styles, from modernist and *moderne* to traditional suburbia.[4]

Finally, a third kind of period room is the representation of an interior as an imaginary or imagined space, whether realised or not. This is a potentially vast field, particularly in the twentieth century, a time of mass publications. Representations of imaginary period rooms, for instance, occurred throughout furniture retail catalogues. They also took the form of exhibition installations, illustrations in children's picture books and other kinds of imaginative fiction, as well as in the substantial body of home interior decoration and design publications. In recent years, they have even featured in television interior make-over programmes. Such representations form a more diffuse yet important and evocative set of references that impinge on any understanding of the period room today.

Museological conventions

In the field of museums, the period room ended the twentieth century with an ambivalent press. For example, in his introduction to the volume *Period Rooms in the Metropolitan Museum of Art* in 1996, the museum's director Philippe de Montebello wrote:

> What may not be clear is that their very existence is subject of debate.
> Some scholars and experts in the field of the decorative arts do not agree
> on their appropriateness in an art museum setting, their purpose and their

degree of authenticity. But others feel that the careful combination of architectural elements rescued from condemned buildings with contemporaneous works of decorative art and furniture serves a number of important functions, not the least of which is preservation.[5]

In this extract, we immediately encounter the two key issues that recur in the commentaries on the period room – authenticity and preservation. Extending this commentary, Christopher Wilk, Keeper of the Collection of Furniture, Fashion and Textiles at the Victoria and Albert Museum (V&A), has suggested that the acquisition of period rooms by the museum has been informed by a number of impulses [6] Broadly, these fall into four categories, not mutually exclusive; first are those rooms that demonstrate histories of style, or conform to the collecting trends in the decorative arts, usefully demonstrating characteristics in other furniture forms in a total arrangement. Second, the museum has acquired rooms saved from structures about to be demolished or threatened by their owners. A third category Wilk outlined are those rooms that tell national stories; so, for example, the history of the English interior at the V&A. Finally, certain rooms illustrate particular decorative techniques, such as gilding or panelling, which are of special interest to decorative arts specialists.

The earliest room collected by the then South Kensington Museum, the Serilly Cabinet of 1778 from the Hôtel de Serilly of the Marais district of Paris, was acquired in 1869. It complemented the museum's interests in assembling examples of high-style French furniture and woodwork at the time. By contrast, collecting of rooms started at the Met in 1903 with the acquisition of the Pompeii bedroom, the Bosco Reale Room of 40–30 BC. This was followed by a wood-panelled chamber from Flims in Switzerland with its magnificent stove, and an eighteenth-century bedroom from the Palazzo Sagredo in Venice, notably all important interiors of significant European origin.[7]

In the area of the modern period room, both the Metropolitan Museum of Art and the V&A coincidentally have interiors by Frank Lloyd Wright as their most recent examples of complete interiors on display. The American Wing at the Met opened in 1924, initially concentrating on Colonial and Federal styles. It was not until 1982 that the Frank Lloyd Wright room, clearly of modern provenance and in a recognisably modern style, was put on display in this sequence. In the words of the museum, this room 'completes the American wing's survey of domestic spaces and provides visitors with the opportunity to experience a Wright-designed interior'.[8] It was the living-room from Northome, the summer residence of Mr and Mrs Francis W. Little of Wayzata, Minnesota. The house had been torn down in 1972 and the Met subsequently purchased the room, while a number of other architectural elements were distributed to various other museums. The room is installed as a free-standing pavilion, which is intended to evoke its original site, but instead of the Minnesota landscape, its windows now look out on to Central Park (Figure 1.2).

The Littles were important patrons for Wright. Among other things they helped to fund the Wasmuth portfolio of 1910–11, which was responsible for

1.2
**Frank Lloyd
Wright designed
Northome, the
summer residence
of Mr and Mrs
Francis W. Little
of Wayzata,
Minnesota, in
1902. The living-
room is now
displayed at the
Metropolitan
Museum of Art,
New York.**

introducing Wright to Europe.[9] The museum's commentary on the room stresses that it is an example of late-Prairie style and that it exemplified the architect's intentions. The room, it continues, represents 'an example of dynamic spatial continuity, and open planning, in which outer and inner spaces are unified'.[10] Formal and stylistic interests in design are therefore foregrounded. Some of the furniture was made specifically for Northome, other pieces had been created to Wright's designs for the main Little home in Peoria in 1902. The display is considered important for illustrating Wright's unified conception of exterior and interior design, and his approach to furnishings. A photograph from Henry Russell Hitchcock's 1942 survey *In the Nature of Materials* was used to determine the arrangement of the furniture. It also followed the architect's original floor-plans.[11] Perhaps crucially, it is not arranged as it was when the owners, the Littles, lived in it.

In the case of this room, museological conventions include respect for the architect's original intentions and his 'authorship' by seeking a close match to the original design through historical accuracy. Familiar questions arise in such an instance: which historical year should be chosen for the reconstruction; whether to stop with the fabric of the room itself or to include furniture, and which elements of a room to re-create and which to omit. For example, in the case of Northome, sculpture in the form of a replica of the Victory of Samothrace is included, whereas more everyday paraphernalia is not. This, as we shall see, distinguishes the period room in the context of a museum from the historic house museum.

Interestingly, the Met was not the first museum to have an American wing dedicated to American interiors and the decorative arts. Instead, this is considered to have been Rhode Island School of Design (RISD) Museum in Providence, where Pendleton House, a purpose-built extension to the museum, opened in 1906.[12] The house was arranged to display Charles L. Pendleton's remarkable collection of eighteenth- and nineteenth-century furniture. Interestingly, as the first collection of American furniture to be assembled, it was set out as a sequence of period rooms. The Art Museum at RISD was a teaching museum, established according to South Kensington principles of design reform, intended to instil good taste through example. Pendleton's contribution was to allow a reconstruction of his own home, Edward Dexter House of 1799, to be added to the museum's collections. Under its historical exterior, transformed from weatherboard to brick, the new house was actually a modern fire-proofed reconstruction of the original home in concrete and steel casing. It was unusual for the time to display the collections as room settings, which

1.3
The dining-room from Pendleton House, Rhode Island School of Design Museum in Providence, originally arranged in 1906 as the first American house museum.
Photo: Courtesy of the Museum of Art, Rhode Island School of Design. Photograph by Del Bogart

reflected Pendleton's own earlier rooms. A contemporary newspaper review indicated that Pendleton House fulfilled its stated aims, commenting: 'The Pendleton Museum illustrates the most perfect embodiment of colonial architecture. It offers to every member of our profession a lesson in good taste, history and civic pride'[13] (Figure 1.3).

As the above examples generally indicate, in the context of the United States, but also in parts of Europe such as Germany and Switzerland, the acquisition of period rooms by museums in the early twentieth century functioned on what might be seen as the flip-side of modernity. Their installation may have depended on the latest technologies and they reflected a contemporary concern to record American decorative arts. Nonetheless, the overall conception was historicist and deeply traditional. Aesthetically and culturally, these rooms indicated a turn away from modernity towards the historical idyll of the age of refinement. Moreover, the approach taken was at odds with the modern industrial systems that formed the financial base by which they were funded. Indeed, a significant lineage of American history museums founded in the early twentieth century that incorporated houses and rooms, largely of colonial and federal periods, continued to operate across this contradiction. To take the most prominent, benefactors included automotive pioneer Henry Ford at Dearborn Historical Museum and Greenfield Village, Michigan; oil magnate and philanthropist John D. Rockefeller jnr at Colonial Williamsburg, and director of the chemical conglomerate, Henry Francis Du Pont at Winterthur Museum.[14] All three founders were modernisers in business who established museums that interpreted a pre-twentieth-century polite American past.

Modernism and historic house museums

In terms of representational strategies, the orthodoxy of the museum period room is to look on to the interior, as if the fourth wall were removed, which is also often actually the case. As such, it betrays its origins in the nineteenth century, when realism was a dominant cultural force. Few museums allow the visitor to enter every room and in this sense the experience of looking on to a naturalist setting of an unpeopled room is not totally removed from viewing its representation on the published page.

Not all interpretations of the domestic interior have been bound by such traditions. Within modernism in particular, alternative presentational strategies were developed that were concerned to display contemporary room settings without an interest in the past. Just as in painting and sculpture, Cubism and Constructivism broke the picture plane and challenged conventional perspective through recourse to abstraction, so too experimental exhibition design has challenged the illusionism of the conventional room display. Such was the case, for example, in the installation of the German Werkbund contribution to the exhibition of the Société des Artistes Décorateurs Français at the Grand Palais in Paris, 1930.[15] Amid a sequence of ensemble room installations by other exhibitors, the designers, former Bauhaus staff Herbert Bayer, Marcel Breuer and Laszlo Moholy-Nagy under the direction of Walter Gropius, developed an alternative mode of display in which they stressed furniture as a serial object and an exactly repeatable idiom. In its abstraction, the display attempted to connect the exhibited objects with the everyday world of the factory and the shop. The full display, which included room settings for a modern apartment block, incorporating a collective social space and gymnasium equipped with tubular steel furniture manufactured by Thonet, indicated their resolve to move away from the conventional Victorian bourgeois interior. The most striking section featured chairs suspended from the wall in vertical series. These serial design objects were arranged in ways that found parallels in strategies current in modern window displays and avant-garde film. As the catalogue proposed,

> The presentation of the Deutscher Werkbund at the invitation of the Société des Artistes Décorateurs Français, should thus be considered as proof that there is a close relationship between all modes of artistic expression; in the fields of architecture, housing, theatre, objects of everyday life, and the social and industrial life in which we live. No object can escape this rule.
>
> The exhibition will therefore show pieces produced in series and through a scientific conception, which nonetheless show a concern for beauty. The exhibitors believe that they have reached a milestone in the alliance between aesthetics and technology.[16]

In several respects this display was an antecedent to the many experimental exhibition designs of domestic landscapes that would occur in the 1950s, especially in contexts such as the Milan Triennale[17] (Figure 1.4).

Within the history of modernist design, the Bauhaus master houses claim a significant place as designed interiors. The question is whether and how they fit the category of period room. They were designed by Walter Gropius for himself and other masters, Wassily Kandinsky, Paul Klee and Laszlo Moholy Nagy, and in many respects stood as idealised displays, furnished by Bauhaus furniture to promote the overall aesthetic of the time. Through the photography of Lucia Moholy they became well known, as featured in the *Bauhaus* magazine, the various Bauhaus books, the 1938 exhibition at the Museum of Modern Art, New York, and most subsequent publications on the school. In fact, the master houses as depicted were only lived in for eighteen months, before the original occupants moved on – Klee to Düsseldorf, Gropius and Moholy to Berlin and Kandinsky to Paris. Yet the original image of these interiors remains the dominant one and has now been used as the measure for their reconstruction.[18]

During the period 1948–89, the ambivalent position that modernism held under the German Democratic Republic regime, together with the shortage of materials for their repair, meant that the houses became a faded shadow of their former selves. Over the years, one was used as a kindergarten and another as a vet's

practice. Since the reunification of Germany, the architectural reconstruction of the houses is complete and the exterior fabric restored to its 1926 state. The houses are open to visitors and interpreted as an expression of architectural space. In the exact reconstruction of the interiors, research into the original colour schemes of the Klee/Kandinsky house has been a priority. Investigation into paint samples has revealed how the interiors, far from the stereotypical idea of the white box, were varied in colour. The Kandinsky dining-room, for example, was in a strident orange and black, which is not apparent in the original black-and-white photographs. By contrast, Kandinsky's studio was only in monochrome black, white and grey because the painter considered he did not want the interference of colour as a background to his own paintings. Apart from fitted furniture that is being gradually restored, few objects appear in the rooms and they remain largely empty. The project concentrates on the abstract idea of external and internal space, design philosophies and concepts, driven by architectural priorities, rather than the semblance of the house as a social space and home.

A second instance of a modernist icon, the Frankfurt kitchen, raises other interesting questions about the priorities of the material reconstruction of a room

1.4
Herbert Bayer, Deutscher Werkbund display from the Société des Artistes Décorateurs exhibition at the Grand Palais, Paris 1930 where new techniques of display broke the illusion of a conventional historical room.
V&A Picture Library

within a museum. The room, well recognised within architectural and design litera-ture as a highly significant development, has been the subject of an historical reconstruction in the museum für angewandte Kunst in Vienna.[19] The kitchens were designed by Margarete Schütte Lihotzky, the first woman architect to join the Frankfurt am Main municipal planning department in the 1920s. Lihotzky was informed by the planning ideas of Christine Frederick, who in turn adapted principles of scientific management to the arrangement of the home and, in particular, the kitchen. Through time-and-motion studies, the organisation of space, the measure-ment of fittings and their relationship with women's bodies, the separation and specialisation of preparation, cleaning and cooking activities all became topics of consideration. Historical photographs showed the kitchens equipped with ceramics and glassware, and emphasised the kitchen as a laboratory, a functioning workplace that assisted women as home-keepers. A film was also made of the kitchen in use (Figure 1.5).

      The reconstruction in Vienna was executed in 1990 under the direction of the architect Gerhard Lindner with advice from Schütte Lihotzky herself. Interestingly, the rebuilding of the kitchen hovers somewhere between a copy and an original. Remaining kitchens had been changed, redecorated and reduced, and

1.5
The Frankfurt kitchen, originally designed by Grete Schütte Lihotzky in the mid-1920s, as reconstructed by the Museum für Angewandte Kunst, Vienna.
Photo: MAK – Austrian Museum of Applied Arts/Contemporary Art, Vienna. Photograph by Gerald Zugmann/ MAK

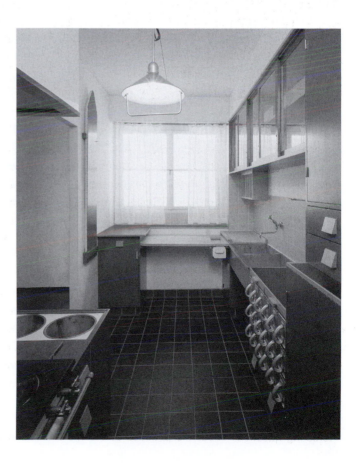

were considered too far removed from the original to be installed as authentic objects. In the absence of plans for the actual fittings and details of their materials and execution, only architectural drawings of the kitchen layout, the reconstruction was guided by reference to extant kitchens and archival photographs.

Lindner explained that it was Lihotzky's concern to give a general impression rather than an exact reconstruction. Not all kitchens had been identical but they were laid out according to a comprehensive ergonomic system. At the time of their production, the wish to assemble them according to prefabricated systems could only be realised in certain aspects – a large part of the making was carried out by hand, so that variations occurred. A number of small structural differences between 1928 and 1990 exist that would not usually be noticed by the museum visitor. For instance, they include the type of wood used in the bottom of drawers, which today is plywood and previously was a softwood. Also, the colour of the floor tiles changed from white to ochre; the draining-board, from lead to beech wood; and other details such as the shift from the original two drawers to one on the window cabinet.

The priorities of decorative arts and design scholarship in art museums tend to separate the room from its use and afterlife. It is perhaps ironic that it is the kitchen – the room that usually excites most interest in visitors to country houses and is so dependent on all the senses – that is denied such context in this instance. The modern is captured as a frozen moment – the ways that occupants customised and adapted an architect's work are not incorporated into the reconstruction. This, it would seem in this instance, remains the project of the photographer or ethnographer or the house museum.

Authenticity and the popular imagination

By the 1980s, in the British context, a popular movement towards people's history prompted a proliferation of museums and heritage sites. This had important and often damaging implications for the period room. Patrick Wright and Robert Hewison led the critical reception of the museum boom respectively in *On Living in an Old Country* (1986) and *The Heritage Industry* (1987).[20] Mounting what was largely a Leftist political critique of the cultural phenomenon of heritage, they took the preoccupation with the past, which was evident in a broad range of cultural forms beyond the museum at that time, to be emblematic of Thatcherism and the failings of post-industrial society. In particular, both authors were disparaging about people's relation with the past, criticising those responsible for stifling the culture of the present by distorting the past through nostalgia. Ironically, the touchstone Hewison and Wright used to assess the new museums, which were largely living museums dependent on interpretation and experiential approaches, was authenticity. Of such museums, Hewison wrote:

> Beamish Open Air Museum, just south of Newcastle upon Tyne has a
> more ironic relationship to the region whose life it memorialises.

. . . The buildings are genuine enough, but they have all come from somewhere else. The Georgian terrace comes from Gateshead, the miners' cottages stood in Hetton-le-Hole until 1976, the Co-op shop comes from Anfield Plain. . . .

The paradox of Beamish is not that it is false, the exhibits are as genuine as they possibly could be, but that it is more real than the reality it seeks to recall.[21]

The counter-attack to what was seen by some as this heritage-baiting was also to come from the Left eight years later with Raphael Samuel's *Theatres of Memory*. In this, the social historian argued that the pleasure and specific knowledge or memories people bring to such sites represent a genuine engagement with life and history. This is not lessened by the postmodern distraction that so concerned Wright and Hewison. Samuel challenged the idea that the past was a plaything of the present. Instead, through reference to museums, historical television drama and heritage sites, he suggested that we live in an expanding historical culture, one that is newly alert to the evidence of the visual. It is, he went on, more democratic than earlier versions of the national past and much more hospitable to hitherto stigmatised minorities. Samuel pointed out:

Arguably it is not the traditionalism but the modernism and more specifically the postmodernism of heritage which offends. Aesthetics condemn it for being bogus: a travesty of the past, rather than a true likeness, let alone – the preservationist's dream – an original. In other words, in spite of the charge that heritage is imprisoning the country in a time-warp, and the accusation that it is sentimentalizing the past, heritage is being attacked not because it is too historical but because it is not historical enough. It lacks authenticity. It is a simulation pretending to be the real thing. It is not because heritage is too reverent about the past that it provokes outrage, but on the contrary fact that, in the eyes of the critics at least, it seems quite untroubled when it is dealing with replicas and pastiche.[22]

In reality, heritage sites exhibit a very broad spectrum of approaches to authenticity. As a Social History house museum, the Tenement House Museum in Lower East Side, Manhattan, could be seen to epitomise Samuel's more positive point of view. This museum is located in a set of apartments of a typical block, in the former garment district of New York. This district has been home to many newly arrived immigrants from when it was built until today, when its residents are largely of Chinese origin. The museum takes the understanding of the condition of migration as its mission. Accordingly, the period rooms are used to engage with the experience of modernity, depicting the conditions of poor immigrant labourers in an urban, cosmopolitan setting. At the start of the tour, a guide, dressed in ordinary clothing of today, asks visitors where they are from. The idea of mobility and identity are therefore asserted from the start. The tour then moves in to the dark hallway of

a tenement block, where commentary gives details of the levels of occupancy of newly arrived German, Italian and Polish families in such buildings. The guide draws attention to the poor conditions of sanitation, lighting and heat, as well as the noise and over-crowding of the neighbourhood. Conditions of family life, work, health and childcare are emphasised in the commentary, and reinforced through the arrange-ment and details of the rooms. An emphasis on people and social relations means that objects are rarely specifically interpreted unless as a result of a question from members of a visiting group and the family stories are indicative rather than actual. One room is left bare to indicate the basic poor quality of the built fabric of the block. Others are presented as *mis-en-scène* for the accounts of particular family lives to take place (Figure 1.6).

As critic and philosopher Walter Benjamin warned in the essay *The Author as Producer* of 1934, there is potential for everything to be rendered aesthetic. He wrote at the time of the National Socialists' appropriation of radical aesthetics for political ends, but his argument applies to more general issues of cultural represen-tation. Writing about photography and what he called the 'photographic effect', Benjamin suggested:

> (And) the result is that it can no longer depict a *tenement block* (my italics) or a refuse heap without transfiguring it. It goes without saying that photography is unable to say anything about a power station or a cable factory other than this: what a beautiful world! A Beautiful World – that is

1.6
The Gumpertz room, displayed at the Tenement House Museum, Lower East Side, New York, suggests an emphasis on the everyday and the home as workplace.
Photo: Steve Brosnahan
Collection of the Lower East Side Tenement Museum

the title of the well-known picture anthology by Renger-Patzsch, in which we see New Matter-of-fact photography at its peak. For it has succeeded in transforming even abject poverty, by recording it in a fashionably perfected manner, into an object of enjoyment.[23]

To resist transforming even mundane things into beauty, Benjamin's answer was to call for captioning, to anchor meaning in the photograph. In the same spirit, to counter the potential aestheticisation of the distressed material fabric of the building and objects at the Lower East Side Tenement Museum – something all too easily done in a world of interiors magazines – the visit is 'anchored' by the guide's commentary. Linda Young commended the Tenement House Museum for drawing attention to the gendered division of labour, displaying as it does the place of women's part-work at home, through the presence of objects such as the sewing-machine and other props.[24] She also warned, however, that 'Introducing the consumption systems that produced, say, a dining room, or the sexual politics that governed a bedroom, requires more of a display than furniture and more of visitors than passive gazing.'[25] The author went on to question whether the Social History house museums can ever be successful in achieving their goal of presenting people's lives, quoting another commentary: 'Even though premised on presenting the history of the marginal, (they) do so by covertly promoting them to the heroic, but vernacular, status: common men and women made great through the display of their domestic environments.'[26]

The question therefore remains whether such a 'museum effect', to use Svetlana Alpers' term, is an inevitable consequence of putting rooms on display and one that is essentially unavoidable.[27] At the Tenement House Museum, visits are organised around the names of families – the Levines, Gumpertz, Baldini and Confinos – re-created to different years. There is a quality about the various constructed family narratives, themselves a result of painstaking research that means we bring to them our own sense of other cultural forms, both real and imaginary, personal and public. The average visitor may have seen too many television sit-coms or costume dramas to avoid reading-in such personalised meanings, projecting a filmic narrative on to these staged scene settings that may have little bearing on historical events.

Period rooms in exhibitions

For the upper and middle classes of the early twentieth century, the practice of viewing the interior offered a continuum between the magazine, the department store, the trade catalogue and the exhibitions. To develop this idea, I would like to dwell on the St Louis Purchase Exhibition of 1904, an international exposition where room displays were presented in a variety of guises.[28] At this exhibition, individual US states contributed a house of grand proportions, as, for example, the Connecticut State Building, which was a reproduction of the colonial mansion of the Sigourney family, furnished with appropriate colonial furniture. In contrast to the pavilions of the host nation, the interiors of the Japanese pavilion were enacted through the performance of a tea ceremony, while in the case of Pacific island villages, a whole people was put on display and expected to perform everyday life rituals for a visiting public, outside the home.

Pavilions from contributing European countries often used the trope of the domestic and within this, the period room became a symbol of national character. For example, the British pavilion contained a series of room settings that stressed style, history and authenticity, in which the room stood for home and nation. Its main room was a reproduction of the banquet hall at Kensington Palace.[29] A carefully constructed lineage of England's history was presented to the visitor as a sequence of rooms. They passed from an Elizabethan oak breakfast room, through a Georgian dining-room with Chippendale mahogany furniture, then into an Adam room, set out as an English tea-room, and finally into a Queen Anne reception room. As the commentary in the official guide read:

> In addition to the handsome banqueting hall of the Orangery, England's quaint and interesting building, there are four rooms, breakfast, dining and tea rooms and a magnificently appointed reception room of the period of Queen Anne for whom the Orangery was built. The room adjoining the banquet hall is the Elizabethan breakfast room, a perfect gem of old English furnishing. The ceiling is an exact copy of the one in the breakfast room at Holland House, Kensington, a palace in which several noted men have resided, chief among whom, at least in American interest, was William Penn. All the fittings are of the early seventeenth century and several pieces are genuine antiques. Two of the cabinets were made in the year 1621, and the table, carved chairs and small cabinet are copied from furniture now in the possession of Sir William Maxwell. The other pieces of real antique furniture are four embroidered breakfast chairs, excellent examples of an elaborate style that was very much in vogue during the reign of Queen Elizabeth. These and the handsome old armour, with which the room is adorned and which serves to add the real Elizabethan touch, are from the collection of the late Earl of Egmont.[30]

As might be expected in such a context, the displays stressed the links with royalty, aristocracy and leading historical figures in ways that mirrored the preoccupations with the homes and personalities of the wealthy in a journal such as *Country Life*.[31] The visitor was guided through the room, not encouraged to distinguish between genuine and fake in the construction of a fictional and material national past.

By contrast, the Swedish pavilion at St Louis emphasised the intact craft traditions of a rural and skilled population. A tendency persisted at the international exhibitions for countries considered among the second nations of the world, such as those of Scandinavia and Eastern Europe, to be presented as a people, their lives alluding to an idealised country life of a pre-industrial era. The catalogue stated:

A group of fine, hearty Swedes, shown here is the most interesting part of the exhibit Sweden has made at her national pavilion . . . In this roomy yellow house, modelled after the Swedish country house, these bright-faced young people, in peasant costume rich in colour and picturesque design, give life and animation to a scene already full of suggestion. Wares made by these Swedes are sold there, and the decoration of the building itself is all home products. In fact, the very building was made in Sweden and shipped here. Pottery, rugs, beaten metal and other articles of use and adornment all attest (to) the skill and patriotic pride of these people.[32]

1.7

'A group of fine, hearty Swedes' - exhibitors outside the Swedish pavilion at St Louis Purchase Exposition, 1904.
V&A Picture Library

As historians of National Romanticism have discussed in relation to these displays, the tendency was to present such cultures in an ethnographic continuous present, rather than the historically specific and evolutionary evocation, of, say, the British pavilion above[33] (Figure 1.7).

Further connections can be made between such displays at the great exhibitions and those that were emerging in a new form of museum – the living,

GROUP OF SWEDES—SWEDISH BUILDING.

The group of fine, hearty Swedes shown here is the most interesting part of the exhibit Sweden has made at her national pavilion on the north side of Administration Avenue, between the buildings erected by Austria and Holland. In this roomy yellow house, modeled after the Swedish country-house, these bright-faced young people, in peasant costume rich in color and picturesque in design, give life and animation to a scene already full of suggestion. Wares made by these Swedes are sold there, and the decorations of the building itself are all home products. In fact, the very building was made in Sweden and shipped here. Pottery, rugs, beaten metal and other articles of use and adornment all attest the skill and patriotic pride of these people. Here in America we are familiar with the Swedes, and no class of immigrants has proved to be better citizens. They bring with them their steady, thrifty habits, and add to our national strength. Sweden is well represented at the Exposition in the Palace of Fine Arts and in other departments.

— 11 —

1.8
Skansen, the original open-air museum founded by Artur Hazelius in 1891 in Stockholm, placed emphasis on the interpretation of folk customs and ways of life.
Photo: reproduced by kind permission of Skansen

open-air museum that originated in Sweden. Skansen, the first open-air museum of its kind, which was also a zoological park specialising mainly in Nordic fauna, is located on the island of Djurgården, a royal park near the centre of Stockholm. It was founded in 1891 by Artur Hazelius (1833–1901) for the purpose of showing how people had lived and worked in different parts of Sweden in earlier times. Hazelius' academic background was as a philologist and linguist interested in the development of the Swedish language. In 1872 he had begun his collection of Scandinavian ethno-graphical objects as a small private museum. By 1901, this had grown into 90,000 objects, on which he worked with 30 assistants and over one hundred employees.[34]

For his original museum, Hazelius created folk life pictures and tableaux of daily life which he took to the great exhibitions of Philadelphia in 1876 and Paris in 1878.[35] His objective was to collect, preserve and treat scientifically Swedish thought, customs, creeds and manner of living in the face of 'advancing civilization and the disappearance of those manners and customs which typify a people'.[36] Hazelius realised the need to rescue relics and traditional associations by which it would be possible to salvage a continuity in Swedish civilisation. For him, Sweden was defined by the 'life of the working people and the deeds of peace'.[37] Over the years, about 150 historic buildings have been moved to Skansen from nearly every part of Sweden. Most of them date from the eighteenth and nineteenth centuries. From its foundation, visitors to the houses and farmsteads at Skansen were met by hosts and hostesses in period costume who demonstrated domestic occupations such as weaving or spinning, artisanal skills or performed traditional music. The settings are intended to show how people in different social classes lived, worked or were housed. The model became adopted internationally as the paradigm for open-air museums (Figure 1.8).

While Skansen clearly was concerned to collect and interpret houses that were a product of the past, its activities deserve mention in this context of a consideration of the modern period room for their implications for future design. As was the case for similar national museums that developed in other parts of Europe at this time, Skansen's emphasis on everyday life and the democratic, non-elite character of the Nordic home held an important resonance for the design identity that Scandinavian countries would develop in the twentieth century. A lineage can be traced between Skansen and the picture of the Swedish home created by Karin and Carl Larsson in Sundborn, which gained notoriety through the publication of water-colours in the book *Ett Hem* of 1899, and finally to the Home Exhibition held in Stockholm in 1917. This was in many respects the first modern Swedish design exhibition.[38]

Period rooms in a commercial context

Many overlaps and interconnections existed between the exhibited interior and another category of room, the commercialised and commodified period interior – that which was for sale. It is clear from looking at a range of trade journals and popular magazines that the idea of viewing or purchasing a complete historical interior was a familiar one in the late nineteenth and early twentieth centuries and it is from here that the last examples of period rooms come.

To take one instance, in November 1925, the 'Things I Have Seen' column in the British magazine *Ideal Home* reported on a new shop in London,

> The Old World galleries have opened new premises exactly opposite Selfridge's, at 449, Oxford Street, W1. Your first impression is that time has gone back 300 years, and a wonderfully peaceful feeling steals over you as you enter the crazy paved old courtyard and linger to admire the sundial, the old bow oriel windows with quaint tile roofs, then you peep into the windows, of which there are six, and your eyes are gladdened by a beautiful old hall with some fine pieces of Queen Anne furniture, one of the features being the stone fireplace mellowed with age, giving out its welcome glow. It is impossible to describe the numerous

rooms which are there, fifteen in all! Every room has been carefully thought out to the minutest detail. There are bedrooms of all periods, dining-rooms, boudoirs, drawing-rooms in Italian, French and English styles. Then there are cosy dens for the male sex to smoke in, and even the children are not forgotten. The public is cordially invited to inspect this wonderful place without being under any obligation whatever to buy.[39]

Quite how such interiors sold or even whether they did, is a subject for further research. It is clear from the tone of the commentary that a visit to such a retail space involved more than shopping and included many experiences more often associated with leisure spaces. Another London company from this period, Oetzmann and Co. advertised themselves as buyers and sellers of 'genuine antique furniture' and illustrated interiors in evocative depictions reminiscent of copper-plate scenes from an early nineteenth-century novel. And even Heal's, a company associated with a restraint informed by Arts and Crafts ideals and early Modernism, ran ranges catering for historical and period effect. A catalogue of the early 1920s announced: 'Old Fashioned Fabrics being careful reproduction from the best examples of early English fabrics in printed linens and cretonnes by Heal and Son.'[40] The text of the catalogue went on to outline the reasons for making available this line of fabrics and indicated the close connection between furniture stores and decorative arts museums. It said:

> To go with Old English Furniture
> The charm of a room furnished in an old fashioned style is frequently spoilt by the lack of harmony in the curtains and coverings with antique furniture, glass, brasswork, and so on.
> The reproductions of typical old English examples, some from South Kensington Museum, others from private collections, – and will overcome the difficulty that has always presented itself 'to get anything to go with old furniture'.[41]

The list of names ranged evocatively from Tudor Rose, Queen Anne, Knole, The Nosegay and Jacobean, to Adam and Sheraton (Figure 1.9).

The debate on the appropriateness of period effect continued in the immediate post-war period in Britain. By 1951, the latest style, 'Contemporary', was the topic of discussion in *The Daily Mail Ideal Home Yearbook*. This opened with an article on the Queen's interior at Marlborough House and continued with 'What is Queen Anne Furniture?'. Amid advertisements for modern furniture and fittings, and articles on renovating nineteenth-century terraced houses, there was a distinct preoccupation with historicism and period rooms. This was perhaps understandable in a period of reconstruction, continued rationing and relative lack of new buildings. In the article 'Mixing to Taste' in this volume (see Figure 1.10), Roger Smithells confronted the question head-on:

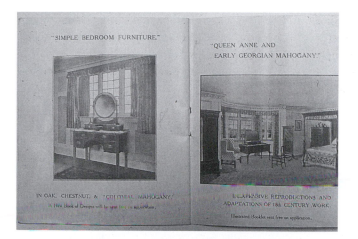

1.9
A double-page catalogue spread announced the historical interiors of Heal's, the London furniture company, available in the 1920s.
Photo: Heal and Son

MIXING TO TASTE

ROGER SMITHELLS

1.10
The article, 'Mixing to Taste' from the *Daily Mail Ideal Home Book*, explored the issue of period styles available for home decoration in the immediate post-war period, a time when the modern style of Contemporary was also in vogue.

> In furnishing, as in other milieux, no doubt, there are various magic words. Regency . . . Antique . . . Georgian . . . Period. Solemnly uttered, they are not always understood but always make their effect. Especially *Period*. Poor Period, it is grandly bandied about and sometimes even appears to indicate a period all by itself. 'Hmm . . .' they say in a pondering, weighting sort of voice, 'Contemporary furniture is all very well, no doubt. But I prefer *Period* . . .' It would be unkind to say what period![42]

Then the author took the more audacious step of collapsing the distinction, suggesting:

> And even worse to suggest Contemporary could be a period too. Unless we are condemned to pass into history un-named, without a face or style of our own.
>
> Yes, Contemporary may be called a period as much as Jacobean, Georgian and all the rest of the neat little labels.[43]

In its light-hearted way, this article brought up to date Osbert Lancaster's earlier list of historical styles for the domestic interior in *Homes Sweet Homes* by offering the apparently oxymorous 'Contemporary Period'. The modern(ist) interior had become another period.

The installations of period rooms, like all representation, inevitably reflect the principles and priorities of their time of making and prevailing practices of heritage conservation, rather than achieve an accurate reconstruction of the past. But within this broad review of the various kinds of curated and re-presented rooms in this essay, where do we stand in relation to the ideas of modernity and the modern, in particular? In the Baudelairean tradition, the modern was defined as coming from the 'ephemeral, the fugitive and the contingent'. However, as constructed spaces, the strength of period rooms lies in making available to the visitor ideas of form and structure; they are arguably less effective in offering those of function.[44] The impulse to locate the interior in time, to animate it through the lives lived, which takes it towards a consideration of function, goes against the abstracted, disinterested gaze associated with so much museum and gallery visiting. And even when attempts to turn the period room into a performative space are made, this often depends on our sense of 'then' and 'now', which only reinforces the sense of time passed, difference and historical distance. In this way, I would conclude, the modern period room remains a site of many paradoxes and possibly even a contradiction in terms.

Acknowledgement

I am extremely grateful to Tracey Avery (University of Melbourne), Christopher Wilk (V&A Museum) and members of the AHRC Centre for the Study of the Domestic Interior, London, for comments on earlier versions of this essay. I would also like to thank Harriet McKay for assisting with picture research.

Notes

1   Osbert Lancaster, *Homes Sweet Homes*, London: John Murray, 1939, p. 10.

2   See Peter Mandler, *The Fall and Rise of the Stately Home*, New Haven, CT: Yale University Press, 1997.

3   Clough William-Ellis, *On Trust for the Nation*, drawings by Barbara Jones, Paul Elek, London, 1947.

4   National Trust acquisitions have included The Homewood, a modernist house by Patrick Gwynne in Surrey in 2004, and Mr Straw's House, a semi-detached Edwardian house of a well-to-do grocer's in Worksop, Nottinghamshire, in 1990. DOCOMOMO specialises in the protection and conservation of canonical modern movement buildings on an international scale. See the journal *International Working-Party for Documentation and Conservation of Buildings, Sites and Neighbourhoods of the Modern Movement*, DOCOMOMO, Eindhoven, 1993–, and Catherine Cooke and Dennis Sharp (eds) *The Modern Movement in Architecture: Selections from DOCOMOMO*, Rotterdam: 010 Publishers, 2000.

5   Philip de Montebello, Introduction, in Amelia Peck, James Parke, William Rieder *et al.*, *Period Rooms in the Metropolitan Museum of Art*, Metropolitan Museum of Art, New York: H. N. Abrams, 1996, p. 9.

6   Christopher Wilk, unpublished paper, *Period Rooms in the V&A: Changing Patterns of Acquisition and Interpretation*, presented at The Museum and the Period Room, a conference held at the V&A Museum, 14–15 November 1997. Wilk was curator responsible for the display of the Kaufmann Office by Frank Lloyd Wright in the museum (see Christopher Wilk, *Frank Lloyd Wright: the Kaufmann Office*, London: Victoria and Albert Museum, 1993). He also directed the installation of the historic British period rooms, part of the redisplay of British Art and Design Galleries at the V&A Museum in 2001.

7   Amelia Peck, op. cit.

8   Text from the Metropolitan Museum website in 2004, www.Metmuseum.org/worksofart/vr/wright/wright/-main.asp.

9   Amelia Peck op. cit. p. 282. The publication was *Ausgeführte Bauten und Entwürfe von Frank Lloyd Wright*, Berlin: Ernst Wasmuth AG, 1911.

10 Amelia Peck, ibid., pp. 275–83.

11 Henry-Russell Hitchcock, *In the Nature of Materials. The Buildings of Frank Lloyd Wright 1887–1942*, Duell, New York: Sloan and Pearce, 1942.

12 Christopher P. Monkhouse and Thomas S. Michie, *American Furniture in Pendleton House*, Providence, RI: Museum of Art, Rhode Island School of Design, 1986.

13 J. Randolph Coolidge, 1907, quoted in ibid., p. 38.

14 For an interpretation of the formation of museums in the United States, see Steven Conn, *Museums and American Intellectual Life, 1876–1926*, Chicago: University of Chicago Press, 1998, in particular Chapter 5, 'Objects and American History: the Museums of Henry Mercer and Henry Ford'.

15 For a detailed account of this exhibition, see Paul Overy, 'Visions of the Future and the Immediate Past: The Werkbund Exhibition, Paris 1930' in the *Journal of Design History*, Oxford: Oxford University Press, December 2004, Vol. 17: pp. 337–57.

16 This is reprinted in English translation in Yvonne Brunhammer and Suzanne Tise, *French Decorative Art, the Société des Artistes Décorateurs, 1900–42*, Paris: Flammarion, 1990, p. 182.

17 Richard P. Lohse, *Neue Ausstellungsgestaltung*, Erlenbach-Zurich: Verlag für Architektur, 1953.

18 For the Bauhaus master houses, see Hans Engeland and Ulf Meyer, *Bauhaus-Architektur Bauhaus Architecture*, Munich, London, New York: Prestel, 2001. For photographs of the original interior installations, see Rolf Sachsse, *Lucia Moholy: Bauhaus Fotografin*, Museumspädagogischer Dienst, Berlin: Bauhaus Archiv, 1995.

19 On the museum installation, see Peter Noever, *Die Frankfurter Küche von Margarete Schütte-Lihotzky*, Berlin: Ernst & Sohn, 1992. For an interpretation of the room, see the essay by Susan R. Henderson 'A revolution in the woman's sphere: Grete Lihotzky and the Frankfurt Kitchen', in Debra Coleman, Elizabeth Danze and Carol Henderson, *Architecture and Feminism*, New York: Princeton Architectural Press, 1996.

20 Patrick Wright, *On Living in an Old Country: The National Past in Contemporary Britain*, London: Methuen, 1985 and Robert Hewison, *The Heritage Industry: Britain in the Climate of Decline,* London: Verso, 1987.

21 Hewison, op. cit. p. 93.

22 Raphael Samuel, *Theatres of Memory, Vol. 1: Past and Present in Contemporary Culture*, London: Verso, 1994, p. 266.

23 Walter Benjamin, 'The Author as Producer', in *Reflections*, ed. Peter Demetz, pp. 229–30.

24 Linda Young, 'A Woman's Place is in the House ... Museum: Interpreting Women's Histories in House Museums', *Open Museum Journal*, Vol. 5: Interpreting Historic House Museums, July 2002, Australian Museums and Galleries. Available at http://amol.org.au/omj/journal-index.asp/.

25 Ibid., p. 8.

26 Ibid., p. 8. The quote comes from Charlotte Smith, *The House Enshrined: Great Man and Social History Museums in Australia and the United States*, unpublished Ph.D. thesis, University of Canberra, 2002.

27 Svetlana Alpers, 'The Museum as a Way of Seeing' in Ivan Karp and Steven D. Levine, *Exhibiting Cultures: The Poetics and Politics of Museum Display*, London and Washington: Smithsonian Institution Press, 1991, pp. 25–33.

28 This and other examples are taken from *The Greatest of Expositions Completely Illustrated, Official Publication,* The Official Photographic Company of the Louisiana Purchase Exposition, St Louis, MI, 1904. The idea of presenting room displays at the expositions began at Paris, 1867 and Vienna, 1873.

29 Ibid., p. 81.

30 Ibid., p. 82.

31 *Country Life*, Country Life Ltd, London, 1897, weekly.

32 *The Greatest of Expositions*, op. cit. p. 73.

33 Nicola Gordon Bowe (ed.) *Art and the National Dream: The Search for Vernacular Expression in Turn of the Century Design*, Dublin: Irish Academic Press, 1993.

34 On Skansen, see Axel Nilsson, *Guide to Skansen, The Historical and Ethnographic Department of Skansen*, Stockholm: Nordiska Museet, 1911 and Ralph Edenheim and Inga Arnö-Berg *Skansen. Traditional Swedish Style*, London, Wappinger Falls, NY: Scala Books, 1995.

35 Barbara Kirshenblatt-Gimblett, 'Objects of Ethnography' in Karp and Levine, op. cit., pp. 401–43.

36 Unpublished manuscript, 'Artur Hazelius, the founder of the Nordiska Museet and Skansen in commemoration of the hundredth anniversary of his birth', National Art Library, London, MSL. 1933.9.19.

37 Ibid.

38 Cilla Robach, 'Design for Modern People' in *Utopia and Reality, Modernity in Sweden, 1900–60*, New Haven and London: Bard Center for Studies in the Decorative Arts, Design and Culture, New York and Yale University Press, 2002.

39 'Things I have Seen', *The Ideal Home*, Vol. VIII, No.5, November 1923, p. 345. I am grateful to Rebecca Preston for introducing me to this article.

40 Catalogue *Heal's Old Fashioned Fabrics*, London: Heal & Son, 'n.d. *c.*1920'.

41 Ibid.

42 Roger Smithells, 'Mixing to Taste', in *Daily Mail Ideal Home Book 1951–2*, ed. Margaret Sherman, London: Associated Newspapers Ltd, 1952.

43 Ibid.

44 The French philosopher Henri Lefebvre uses these distinctions in *The Production of Space*, translated by Donald Nicholson-Smith, Oxford: Blackwell, 1991. He wrote, 'like any reality, social space is related methodologically and theoretically to three general concepts: form, structure, function. In other words, any social space may be subjected to formal, structural and functional analysis. Each of these approaches provides a code and a method for deciphering what at first may seem impenetrable.' (p. 147).

Chapter 2

Interiors without walls

Choice in context at MoDA

Lesley Hoskins

Museums and other exhibiting institutions offer narratives, usually constructed by, with and around objects. The same object or series of objects can be used to support a range of different narratives, but any one institution is able to present only a limited number of interpretations at any one time. Museums (or rather the decision-makers within those institutions) have to choose their narratives and they make those choices in the context of institutional, professional, financial and personal factors, all of which relate to the broader social, cultural, political and economic climate.

This chapter looks at the ways that one museum – the Museum of Domestic Design & Architecture (MoDA) at Middlesex University – has chosen to represent the domestic interior, and suggests that a congruence in the distinct discourses of professional museum practice and of academic attention to the domestic environment has supported interpretations that focus on the demotic and, increasingly, on personal experience.

MoDA offers a particularly clear-cut case study for two main reasons. First, it is a 'blank-screen' museum. Unlike most historic houses, it has no obligation to present a particular domestic environment and although MoDA's collections can readily be related to the domestic, they offer many other potential avenues of inter-pretation. Second, it is a new museum, relatively untrammelled by expectation or tradition, and the reasons for its decision to focus on the domestic interior and for its particular approaches can be readily excavated.

The Geffrye Museum, located in the East End of London, is similarly a blank screen. In their discussion of the Geffrye's varied representations of the domestic interior since the instigation of its first period room in 1930, Julia Porter and Sally MacDonald highlight the personal interests of the responsible curators as contributing to the changes in approach.[2] While the expertise and interests of individual staff always have an effect, as does a museum's specific institutional and financial situation, the present discussion puts more emphasis on the professional and academic agendas within which MoDA's staff operated. At the time of writing, MoDA has been open to the public for almost five years, and planning for the displays started about two years previously. But, even during that relatively short time, ideas about processes of learning and the function of museums in British society (both of which have been incorporated into professional standards for museums) and the academic approach to the domestic interior have developed. MoDA's close engagement with those ideas and approaches has prompted continuing shifts in the narratives offered and the means of delivery.

MoDA opened in a specially designed new building in October 2000, with substantial support from the Heritage Lottery Fund (HLF) and Middlesex University. The HLF required that the museum's environmental conditions and security arrangements should meet the standards set by the Museums and Galleries Commission, the body at that time responsible for standards in the profession. MoDA was provided with two exhibition spaces (one for a permanent display and one for temporary exhibitions, both 9m × 16m) and with a range of other facilities, including a study room and a lecture theatre.

MoDA's core holding is the Silver Studio Collection, the archive of a commercial design practice that was active from 1880 to the mid-1960s. The Silver Studio produced designs, mainly for domestic wallcoverings and textiles, which it sold to a wide variety of manufacturers, merchants and retailers at most levels of the market. At the top end, the Studio's customers included Liberty's, Warner's and Sanderson's; at the lower end, there were huge companies such as John Hawkins, which sold large quantities of cheap goods through catalogues and whose slogan was 'From the Mills to the Multitude', and the Calico Printers Association. The collection includes thousands of pieces of original artwork, textile and wallpaper samples of Silver Studio origin, many more wallpapers and textiles collected by the Studio for design reference purposes, books, magazines, newspaper cuttings and business records such as sales books and design logs.

MoDA's second most important group of material is its Domestic Design Collection, composed largely of trade or retail catalogues, and books and magazines relating to the design, decoration and management of the home. This collection, which was set up to support the Silver Studio material, relates largely to the UK during the period 1870–1960.

Until 2000, these and four other associated collections had been available as an inadequately housed and poorly resourced reference resource in Middlesex University.[3] There was no in-house display space, but the small staff had mounted a number of travelling exhibitions and issued several publications. The most popular of these had been the *Little Palaces* exhibition and accompanying book

(Turner, M. *et al.*, 1987, London: Middlesex Polytechnic), which looked at the 1930s suburban house.

The 1996 application to the HLF for support in the building of a public-access museum to house and exhibit the collections did not define the contents or themes of the displays; this was not addressed in detail until 1998, two years before opening, although the architecture and thus the general shape and size of the display areas had already been finalised. At this point, MoDA underwent, coincidentally, an almost complete change of staff; the new team, with relatively little personal attach-ment to curatorial past history, had great freedom with regard to what it might display and present. There were certain constraints and considerations; the period covered most adequately by the collections was 1900–60; conservation and security require-ments meant that all items from the collections were to be cased and that lighting levels were low; a restricted budget meant that display and lighting were relatively basic and that highly technological displays were out of the question; the space was small. It was decided that the permanent display would be based on MoDA's existing collections (almost entirely of two-dimensional items), which had previously been poorly accessible and which it was felt deserved a public showing. There was, in any case, little budget for new acquisitions.

These collections could have been interpreted in a number of ways: the focus could, for example, have been on the Silver Studio itself, looking at its design methods and its contribution to British design, or on the design and production of wallpapers and textiles, or on stylistic changes. But, for a number of reasons, the decision was taken to interpret them through the history of the demotic domestic interior, particularly the living–dining–eating parts of the home. The collections already had a reputation in this field because several previous exhibitions had presented the material in this context.[4] The new curator had experience in this area. The collections could be utilised for this theme because the Silver Studio had designed mostly for middle-class homes. MoDA is located in an area of 1930s suburban housing. MoDA believed that this approach would appeal to visitors, and there was an existing and growing museum and academic interest in demotic design and demotic ways of life.

A number of writers have discussed the relationship between museum practice and contemporary political and social agendas.[5] Bennett argues that in the nineteenth century, museums became major organs of the state, dedicated to the instruction and edification of the public in general. In the broadest sense, this remains the essence of museums today. But the means of instruction and the subjects of edification have shifted and are currently in a self-conscious and active state of change.

Bennett shows that while late nineteenth-century museums were open to 'the people', they generally presented elite or bourgeois cultural artefacts, whether objects or systems of knowledge. However, almost as soon as this type of museum was firmly established, there arose a partial challenge from a small number of new institutions whose intention was to collect and display artefacts relating to the daily lives of non-elite social strata. The first of these opened at Skansen in Sweden in

1891, displaying traditional customs, crafts, objects and buildings. This was soon followed by a number of other continental European and North American folk sites. But it was not until about 1970 that a similar approach gained strength in the UK, when the North of England Open Air Museum at Beamish, Ironbridge Gorge Museums, and the Weald and Downland Open-Air Museum all opened around the same time. Bennett argues that although the intentions of Beamish and Ironbridge included representing the industrialisation of their respective geographical areas, 'the cultures and values of non-elite strata are subordinated to bourgeois culture and values just as effectively as they were in the great public museums which developed in the nineteenth century'.[6] However, he admits that they nevertheless did acknowledge the everyday lives of ordinary working people. And this acknowledgement in museums and similar institutions gathered ferocious pace thereafter; Robert Hewison could cite the existence of 41 heritage centres by 1987.[7] Hewison and Patrick Wright propose that this development was driven by nostalgia in the face of the UK's declining industrial power and world standing. Wright suggests that the 'saving' of Calke Abbey in 1984 is an example of high culture's colonisation of an ordinary past. Calke was the home of the politically and socially inactive and unimportant Harpur-Crewe family, who had spent very little on maintenance for the previous hundred years and who had retreated from large areas of the house, leaving them to moulder untouched. It was considered of interest precisely because '*nothing had happened there*'.[8] The lives of rather ordinary people were represented by the time-capsule interiors.[9]

And from much the same time, scholarly attention to interiors began to include the demotic. The new subject of design history that emerged in the mid-1970s encouraged an interest in everyday items. It broke away from a traditional art historical approach, which focused on special designers and the finished appearance of exemplary designed objects, and turned its attention to processes. It looked, for example, at the processes of designing, taking into account the interrelated contributions of economic, manufacturing, business and market factors, rather than concentrating on an individual designer's personal input. And these processes were just as interesting whether they were concerned with cheap mass-produced goods or with fine Hammersmith carpets made by William Morris. A history of the development of the new subject notes the central part played by Middlesex Polytechnic.[10] MoDA's own development is rooted in this tradition by virtue of its location in Middlesex University.

In the field of the domestic environment, this interest in the non-exemplary and the non-elite supported the publication of two books for a cross-over academic/popular market. *Semi-Detached London,* by A.A. Jackson (1973), and *Dunroamin: the Suburban Semi and its Enemies,* by Oliver *et al.* (1981), both dealt with the mass suburban interwar housing that had previously attracted little, fully considered, external notice.

The new design history was also interested in the processes of use – not only the practical processes of consumption, but also the social use of objects as a means of identifying with (or disassociating from) other people. Bourdieu's *La distinction,* 1979 (published in English in 1984), was very influential.[11] This large-scale French sociological study correlated people's cultural and aesthetic preferences with their economic, social and educational histories, and established regular patterns of 'taste'. This notion of taste (later sometimes discussed as 'propriety' – having what is appropriate for membership of a particular social grouping), not as a system of absolute values, but as a fluid system of establishing differences, supported design history's cultural relativism and further legitimised the study of mass culture and artefacts. This relativist approach began to influence even museums that had been set up with a traditional absolutist remit to educate and improve the public's aesthetic judgements. The Whitworth Art Gallery's collecting policy for its wallpapers has, since about 1990, included a commitment to the regular acquisition of best-sellers with a view to representing everyday consumption as much as 'good design'.

La distinction was such a large-scale survey that it could be authoritative about what different categories or classes of people typically owned, did or liked. But such quantitative information relating to the domestic interiors of the past is not available. The problem of representing 'the typical' was one of the issues discussed at *Into the Interior,* a conference for both academics and heritage professionals held at Ironbridge Gorge Museum in the late 1980s. One solution was the use of personal oral testimony. Social and local history curators were familiar with working in this way (and with the associated methodological concerns), but it was unusual in museums that concentrated on objects. This approach informed at least two exhibitions (*Household Choices*, a joint venture between the V&A and Middlesex Polytechnic, and *Putting on the Style* at the Geffrye Museum, both in 1990 and both with accompanying publications), which relied on oral testimony to present in-depth case studies that focused on the process of making domestic environments, as well as their appearance. *Putting on the Style* at the Geffrye Museum dealt with setting up home in the 1950s. It presented 'five different rooms in an attempt to demonstrate the impossibility of defining the typical', although the displays were intended 'to suggest common practices and preferences amongst a variety of social groupings'.[12] It represented domestic interiors in terms of the conscious, individual choices of the people who made and inhabited them, at the same time explicating some of the economic, social, cultural and aesthetic factors that constrained or stimulated those choices.

These shifts towards the demotic, towards cultural relativism and the personal, which had been visible in the wider world, in academic work and in museum practice for some considerable time, have also more recently crystallised in museums' professional agendas. This can be traced in the differences between the UK Museums Association's definition of a museum in 1984 and 1998 (see Table 2.1). Definitions are disseminated in professional publications, such as *Museums Journal* and *Museum Practice*, and through regulatory schemes, professional training, conferences and workshops. The latter definition remains in force at the time of writing.

Table 2.1 UK Museums Association's definitions of a museum

1984	1998
A museum is an institution which collects, documents, preserves, exhibits and interprets material evidence and associated information for the public benefit.	Museums enable people to explore collections for inspiration, learning and enjoyment. They are institutions that collect, safeguard and make accessible artefacts and specimens, which they hold in trust for society.

Source: Museums & Galleries Commission, *Registration Scheme for Museums and Galleries in the United Kingdom: Registration Guidelines*, London: Museums & Galleries Commission, 1995, p. 3 and MLA, *The Accreditation Scheme for Museums in the United Kingdom: Accreditation Standard*, London: MLA, 2004, p. 6.

In the 1984 version, a museum '. . . exhibits and interprets material evidence and associated information for the public benefit'. This implies that a museum knows what the public benefit *is* and does something *for* the public. In the 1998 version, this phrase is developed into two statements: a museum '*makes accessible* artefacts and specimens'; and it '*enables . . . people . . .* to explore collections . . . for *inspiration, learning and enjoyment*' (my italics).

The 'benefit' of the earlier version was thus subsequently defined as 'inspiration, learning and enjoyment'. And, instead of the museum giving something ready-made to the public, its role was changed to that of an 'enabler', making it possible for 'people'· (a much friendlier term than 'the public') actively to explore (to engage with) collections themselves.

The means of engagement are not specified, although examples of good practice are provided in professional literature, illustrating the understanding that museum users are more readily engaged if they can see themselves (or groups with whom they might identify) and their own histories represented, either directly or indirectly. One such exemplary project was *Every Object Tells a Story,* established in 1998 at the Castle Museum, part of Nottingham City Museums. Here, in one gallery, decorative art objects were interpreted in a variety of ways, both traditionally by medium or style, but also socially and economically. Thus, finely wrought silver items used for dealing with sugar were shown as dependent on slavery, highlighting the relevance of such objects not just to the wealthy owner, but also to the underprivileged slave classes. There was also a 'People's Choice' section in which local people chose objects from the collections for display and gave their reasons for doing so.

It was in this context of academic interest and museum practice that the curatorial team at MoDA began to formulate plans for its permanent display.[13] They decided to focus on the modest domestic interior, but wished to avoid several of what they saw as problems that are common in representing interiors in museums. First, how could MoDA represent interiors without either explicitly or implicitly suggesting that what the visitor saw was representative or typical of all living-rooms of the period in question? A specific re-creation of particular historic interiors would have the advantage of demonstrable truth to reality, but was not considered to be appropriate to the general nature of the collections. Second, how could the presentation avoid making or suggesting value judgements as to the quality of design or taste of the styles and methods of furnishing being displayed? A third issue was the desire to dispense with a domineering curatorial voice and to encourage visitors to take authority and draw their own conclusions. This, too, was part of a general shift in museum practice, which was already observable in the early 1990s and which subsequently became crystallised in professional agendas. Eilean Hooper-Greenhill (who has been influential in developing those agendas) observes that 'at the birth of the public museum, a division was drawn between the private space where the curator, as expert, produced knowledge (exhibitions, catalogues, lectures) and the public space where the visitors consumed those appropriately presented products' but that more recently 'conceptually, some curators are inclined to see themselves as facilitators for learning rather than as sole dispensers of knowledge'.[14]

To meet these issues, it was resolved to interpret the interior through consumer choice. The display should indicate that a wide variety of new furnishings was available at any one time for different tastes and markets without prioritising any particular types or styles. It should show that people could choose from the range of what was available, but that their choice operated within constraints, either conscious or unconscious. Personal circumstances, social grouping, life stage, family size, available funds, social mores, generally accepted standards of housing and domestic technology are just some of the issues that affect choices regarding the decoration and furnishing of the home. (Geographical differences are also important, but the display did not intend to address these, concentrating instead on the North London suburbia of the museum's location.) And the exhibition should allow for the fact that, for a variety of reasons, people very often furnished with a mixture of old and new items.

In terms of presentation and tone, visitors to the museum would be offered some evidence both about how rooms of the past looked and why they might have done so, but they were not to be offered generalised conclusions. The title of the exhibition, *Exploring Interiors: Home Decoration and Furnishing 1900–60,* was intended as a signpost, and it was hoped that visitors would respond to the implicit questions of how people decorated and furnished their homes, what choices they had and why they chose one item rather than another.

The display was divided into four sections. Three were chronological – pre-World War One, the interwar period and post-World War Two – and reflected significant differences in social, cultural and economic conditions. The fourth section was devoted to the kitchen, which underwent major changes in technology and use during the period.

Each section offered a compilation of three categories of evidence:

1   *Examples of new furnishings as potential purchases.*
     The collections are rich in wallpaper and textile samples. These were displayed in a manner reminiscent of a shop window, to encourage visitors

2.1
**Illustration from
Catesby's catalogue,
about 1938, one
of the exhibits in
*Exploring Interiors.***
Photo: MoDA

2.2
**Unknown interior,
1911, shown in
*Exploring Interiors.***
Photo: MoDA

to respond like 'consumers', both expressing their present preferences and perhaps imagining what their responses might have been in the past. Trade and retail catalogues indicated other available items of household furnishings. Their images, text and graphic presentation usually offer additional information – for example, about prices, room layouts, styles and associated lifestyles (Figure 2.1).

2   *Examples of determinants on consumer choice.*
The textual presentation (in the curatorial voice) of information about matters such as new domestic technologies, changes in room differentiation and use, prices, incomes, occupations and housing types was intended to suggest the parameters within which people made their furnishing choices. Short personal quotations brought this to life and highlighted the social context of many choices.

3   *Photographs of interiors* (preferably with a known provenance and accompanying contextual information).
Most images of inhabited demotic interiors show how unusual it was for a room to be newly furnished throughout. Many of the interiors shown do not comply with the stylistic tenets that have been subsequently attributed to a particular period and that tend to be based on the upper part of the market (Figure 2.2).

This was MoDA's main exhibition when it opened in 2000. But in the five years since then both professional agendas and academic approaches to the domestic interior have developed, along paths that in different areas of discourse demonstrate a remarkable congruence in centralising people's experience and their relationship with objects, rather than objects themselves. And, once again, MoDA's activities reflect that.

When MoDA was initially planning its displays, the Registration Scheme for Museums and Galleries in the UK was in place. This was a minimum standards scheme that conferred registered status on museums that met those standards. It was a voluntary scheme, but with the substantial incentive that registration was a necessary prerequisite for many funding opportunities; by 2003, more than 1,860 museums and galleries had joined the scheme. The Registration Scheme employed the 1984 Museums Association definition of a museum and was largely concerned with the safety, care and documentation of collections. Standards were also set for 'the public face of the museum', but were seen mostly as physically facilitated by, for example, adequate opening hours, public services and visitor facilities.[15] As more and more museums were able to meet those basic standards, the new Museum Accreditation Scheme of 2004 (administered by Museums, Libraries and Archives (MLA)) set further targets. Accreditation adopted the more recent Museums Association definition of a museum and, on the assumption that basic physical standards had been met, now also focused on learning as 'a core purpose of museums' and on 'interpretation of the collections in ways which support users' learning and enjoyment'.[16] The use of the word 'learning', rather than 'education', implies a pedagogical process in which museums facilitate users in developing their own pre-existing knowledge and understanding through an active and reflective engagement with a museum's collections, exhibitions and events. Help in meeting this aim is offered by the MLA's *Inspiring Learning for All* web resources and training sessions.[17]

The increasing replacement of the term 'visitor' with 'user' in discussions of learning also signals the changing balance of power and knowledge between staff and public, refusing the passive connotations of 'visitor'. The emphasis on engagement further encourages the presentation of themes or objects that learners can relate to their own experience. Hooper-Greenhill describes how, historically, museums have participated in using and producing the contemporary episteme (structures of knowledge and knowing) and writes that currently 'the main themes of knowledge are people, their histories, their lives, and their relationships' and that 'this focus on themes, ideas, and relationships can be identified as one of the guiding forces of the modern museum'.[18] She agrees with Trudel's statement about the Musée de la Civilisation that 'Artefacts, however important they may be, are only so because of their meaning and use. They are seen above all as evidence of human activity.'[19] Many museums recognise this by offering visitors the opportunity to put themselves in other people's shoes through activities such as dressing in clothing of a previous era or participating in a Victorian school session. The popular Channel 4 television series *The 1900s House*, aired in 1999, also achieved this. By following a family attempting to live in the domestic conditions of a previous age, viewers could identify with the experience of those conditions.

In the academic world, the revival of interest in the domestic interior over the past six years or so has been so intense that it is not possible to give a comprehensive overview here. Some of this work has considered how the domestic environment reflects and forms social relations; some uses ethnographic techniques, biography and personal testimony to discuss how people form and transform their environments; some has focused on the symbolic, metaphorical and personal meanings of home. But in general, it can be said that much new work has focused on people, in their relationship with objects and spaces in the domestic environment.[20] These developments, alongside those in the museum agenda, influenced MoDA's subsequent practice.

An evaluation of *Exploring Interiors* by a museum consultant (who was personally much involved in developing the new learning agenda) led to a number of small changes intended to encourage user engagement. The previously implicit questions were made explicit; large graphics ask visitors questions such as 'What factors do you think affected people's choices in the 1930s?' and encourage personal identification with the displays by asking 'Do you prefer the patterns to your right or to your left?' and 'What would you have chosen at that time?'. Visitors' written replies and other comments are displayed as part of the exhibition, increasing the sense of active participation and dialogue, both with the museum and with other visitors.

Temporary exhibitions and displays have provided the opportunity for a variety of approaches and, although a number have pursued more traditional object- or designer-centred topics, several, of which some examples are given below, have directed attention towards the personal relationship between occupant/user/maker and the domestic environment or objects.

The focus of study of *Bungalow Blitz: Another History of Irish Architecture*, 2001, was the self-build bungalows that have become a feature of the west coast of Ireland since the 1960s. There were four elements to the exhibition. One element offered an overview of the economic and planning structures that allowed for and encouraged the spate of building, and presented the popular pattern books that many of the self-builders used. Another section represented the public response, much of it negative, to the bungalows. Both of these elements were straightforwardly historical and presented in a neutral, authoritative, curatorial manner. In a very different 'voice' were newly commissioned photographs of the bungalows and their inhabitants that vividly expressed the photographers' responses. These images were in no way neutral or documentary (Figure 2.3). The final element used yet another

2.3
Edition 13,
Plan 317, **by Paul**
Antick, shown in
Bungalow Blitz.
Photo: Paul Antick

2.4
Photograph for
What Home
Means to Me.
Photo: Imad Ahmed

2.5
Filet crochet tea-
cosy, made by
Mary T. of Ilford.
Exhibited in
Stitch! The Art
& Craft of
Homemaking.
Photo: MoDA

voice – that of the occupants themselves. They had been sensitively interviewed about why and how they had built their homes. Written extracts ranged from practical and economic aspects to more personal and emotional matters. Overall, the exhibition withheld direct judgement, allowing visitors to make up their own mind about the pros and cons of this particular form of popular culture. It was curated by Aoife MacNamara of Middlesex University's School of Art, Design and the Performing Arts and its use of personal statement influenced several subsequent displays.

What Home Means to Me, 2003, featured the personal relationship between occupant and living space even more strongly (Figure 2.4). A group of 14-year-old school students was asked to take photographs of things in, or parts of, their homes that were especially meaningful for them (whatever they understood by that) and to complement their photographs with words. Their work was put on display. Although home constitutes a large part of their world, children and young people have been very little considered in studies of the domestic. This was a small display and led to no general conclusions, but it was the activity itself that was particularly important for MoDA because it addressed the professional museum agenda of widening participation (to a socially and ethnically mixed group of teenagers).

Stitch! The Art & Craft of Homemaking, 2003, was a larger exhibition, displaying two sorts of objects: stitched items made at home, for the home; and, just as importantly, the transcribed words of the people who made or used or were given them (Figure 2.5). Directed interviews drew out the social and cultural meanings of the objects and of the processes of making, giving, receiving and keeping them. Respondents' associations included womanliness, creativity, family, tradition, identity, nurturing and privacy. Both the work and the words were ordinary; one of the intentions of putting such things on display in a museum context, where usually only the extraordinary is shown, was to confirm that the ordinary is also interesting and worth investigating. In this activity, too, MoDA hoped to encourage the direct engagement of its constituency. All the items were borrowed locally and all were such that most visitors would have direct experience of similar items. These last three displays and exhibitions all relied on solicited personal testimony, which is now not readily available for any period earlier than the 1930s but earlier evidence of people's relationship to their domestic space can be gathered from sources such as diaries and memoirs, although there is obviously limited availability.

This brief description of some of MoDA's approaches to representing the domestic interior is not intended to suggest that the museum is breaking new ground, but to demonstrate that its current interest in the personal is drawn from institutional and academic agendas that have come together very persuasively. Recent museum professional agendas reflect and reinforce a political view of museums as a potential tool in the battle against social exclusion, as well as pedagogical changes in attitudes to teaching and learning. The result is that although collections and collections' care remain essential features of museums' duties, there is a new emphasis on visitors and on personal (visitor) *experience*, both as a way of learning and as a subject of learning. This has been, and still is being, actively promoted within the profession and was, unsurprisingly, a major determinant in MoDA's approach to its themes, the content of its displays and the methods of presentation. This allows for an approach to exhibiting the domestic interior that responds to an academic approach that has, over a longer period, shifted attention away from elite or avant-garde objects towards processes, the user and the demotic.

Notes

1   See, for example, C. Saumarez Smith, 'Museums, Artefacts, and Meanings', in P. Vergo, ed., *The New Museology*, London: Reaktion Books, 1989.

2   J. Porter and S. MacDonald, 'Fabricating Interiors: Approaches to the History of Domestic Furnishings at the Geffrye Museum', *Journal of Design History* 3, 2–3, 1990, pp. 175–82.

3   The Silver Studio Collection was given to Hornsey School of Art in 1967. Hornsey was subsequently incorporated into Middlesex Polytechnic, which in 1992 became Middlesex University.

4   For example, *The Decoration of the Suburban Villa 1880–1940*, 1983 and *Textiles for the Home,* 1983, as well as *Little Palaces*, previously mentioned.

5   For example, E. Hooper-Greenhill, *Museums and the Shaping of Knowledge,* London: Routledge, 1992 and T. Bennett, *The Birth of the Museum: History, Theory, Politics,* London: Routledge, 1995.

6   T. Bennett, op. cit., p. 117.

7   R. Hewison, *The Heritage Industry. Britain in a Climate of Decline*, London: Methuen, 1987, p. 24.

8   P. Wright, *On Living in an Old Country, the National Past in Contemporary Britain*, London: Verso, 1985, pp. 38–42.

9   Domestic life and interiors of the past were certainly popular, as evidenced by the success of the BBC costume drama *Upstairs Downstairs*, 1971–5, the introduction of *Interiors* (later *The World of Interiors*) in 1981 and a National Trust membership of 1,400,000 in the mid-1980s.

10 J. Woodham, 'Designing Design History: From Pevsner to Postmodernism', in *Working Papers in Communication,* Digitisation and Knowledge, Vol. 1(1), December 2001. Available at www.aut.ac.nz/ research/research_institutes/ccr/publications/workingpaper.htm; accessed 8 July 2005.

11 P. Bourdieu, *La distinction: critique sociale du jugement*, Paris, Les Éditions de Minuit, 1979. P. Bourdieu, translated by R. Nice, *Distinction: A Social Critique of the Judgement of Taste,* London: Routledge & Kegan Paul, 1984.

12 J. Porter, and S. MacDonald, *Putting on the Style: Setting up Home in the 1950s*, London: Geffrye Museum,1990, preface.

13 It has to be noted that personal interest and experience necessarily contribute to such decisions. The lead curator at the time had studied Design History at Middlesex Polytechnic (now University) and was influenced by the practice cited. But it should also be noted that she is the author of this chapter, the objectivity of which is therefore subject to the caveats associated with autobiography.

14 E. Hooper-Greenhill, op. cit., p. 200.

15 Museums & Galleries Commission, *Registration Scheme for Museums and Galleries in the United Kingdom: Registration Guidelines*, London: Museums & Galleries Commission, 1995.

16 MLA, *The Accreditation Scheme for Museums in the United Kingdom: Accreditation Standard*, London: MLA, 2004, p. 24.

17 'Learning takes place when someone is stimulated, motivated or inspired and undergoes some kind of personal change. The term learning is used instead of "education" because it emphasises that all users and staff collaborate in and benefit from activities which increase skills, understanding, engagement and which change behavior and attitudes. It also emphasises that these activities are centred on the learner's experiences.' Available at www.inspiringlearningforall.gov.uk/utilities/glossary/default. aspx; accessed July 2005.

18 E. Hooper-Greenhill, op. cit., pp. 198 and 208.

19 Ibid., p. 208.

20 Some examples of relevant publications are given here but, in tracing the chronology, it should be noted that conferences and symposiums, which can either precede or follow publication, were as influential as printed works. Several papers in *Domestic Space: Reading the Nineteenth Century Interior*, edited by Inga Bryden and Janet Floyd, 1999, deal with social relations manifested within and by a domestic environment. Biography and personal testimony have been used to give an understanding that remote study of the interior alone would not have provided (A. Girling-Budd, 'Comfort and Gentility: Furnishings by Gillows, Lancaster, 1840–55', in S. McKellar, and P. Sparke, eds, *Interior Design and Identity*, Manchester: Manchester University Press, 2004). Work from the Department of Anthropology, University College London, has dealt with the social use of objects within the domestic sphere (D. Miller, ed., *Home Possession: Material Culture Behind Closed Doors*, Oxford: Berg, 2001). The AHRC Centre for the Study of the Domestic Interior, established in 2000, has gone outside the previously core discipline of design history and has actively developed new approaches drawn from other disciplines such as archaeology, geography and literature.

Chapter 3

Stopping the clock

The preservation and presentation of Linley Sambourne House, 18 Stafford Terrace

Daniel Robbins

On 19 April 2003, Linley Sambourne House, 18 Stafford Terrace reopened to the public after nearly three years of restoration and refurbishment (Figure 3.1). The process yielded a great deal of new information about the house and its contents, and afforded an opportunity to reconsider how it is presented and understood. This chapter presents some of these findings and considers how they informed the restoration and interpretation of the house.

No. 18 Stafford Terrace is a standard Kensington terraced house built as part of the development of the Phillimore Estate on the north side of Kensington High Street between 1868 and 1871. After a brief occupation by a widow called Mrs Bentley, the house was bought almost as new in 1875, by the *Punch* cartoonist Edward Linley Sambourne (1844–1910) and his wife Marion (1851–1914).[1] Arranged over four floors, the disposition of the rooms follows a well-established pattern – the raised ground floor contains the dining-room and morning-room. The drawing-room occupies the full width and depth of the first floor, two bedrooms are on the second floor, and the top floor originally contained the day and night nurseries and the maid's room. The night nursery later became Sambourne's studio.

It would also be worthwhile outlining at the outset the passage of the house through the subsequent generations of the family, as they will all feature in

3.1
Exterior view of Linley Sambourne House, 18 Stafford Terrace.
Photo: Linley Sambourne House, The Royal Borough of Kensington
and Chelsea

the discussion of the interiors. The Sambournes had two children Maud (1875–1960) and Mawdley (1878–1946) who perhaps unsurprisingly was always known as Roy. Following his parents' death, the house was left to Roy. He continued to live there alone, apart from the servants, until his own death in 1946, when it passed to his sister Maud. From 1905 her married home was a large house in Lancaster Gate on the north side of Hyde Park and, rather than sell Stafford Terrace, she maintained it fully staffed, calling in regularly until she died in 1960. The house was left to her three children, but ultimately taken on by her daughter Anne who, with her second husband the Earl of Rosse, used the house as their London home until its sale to the Greater London Council in 1980. It was subsequently leased to the Victorian Society which agreed to open it to the public. This arrangement continued after the house was transferred to the Royal Borough of Kensington and Chelsea in 1989 and only came to an end in December 2000. The house is now fully under the Royal Borough's care, together with the nearby Leighton House Museum, built from 1865 by Frederic, Lord Leighton (1830–96).

The surrender of the lease by the Victorian Society was an element in the development project that was completed in 2003. The trigger was a survey of the electrical services completed in 1999 that revealed an urgent need to rewire the upper floors. Bulging plastic water-tanks in the roof and the absence of any automatic fire and intruder detection immediately suggested that a more substantial programme of works should be implemented. Since this could only be done by emptying the house of all its contents, it quickly became apparent that this was, as it were, a once-in-a-lifetime opportunity to address other aspects of the fabric of the building, the conservation of the interiors and the cataloguing of the contents. A final element, the development of the basement caretaker's flat to provide new reception and visitors' facilities, was seen as critical to the future operation of the house.

Amid all this was the opportunity to re-evaluate and reconsider what the house was about. The reputation it had enjoyed since opening to the public in 1980 was straightforward and uncomplicated. Stafford Terrace was presented and enjoyed as a remarkable and unique surviving example of a 'typical' Victorian middle-class home – unchanged in its decoration and furnishings since Linley and Marion left it in 1914. The guidebook written in 1987 did not really challenge this perception, downplaying subsequent alterations and emphasising the integrity of the whole.[2]

For anyone who has visited the house, it does have a compelling atmosphere and sense of the past. But, as will be discussed, the interiors have not remained static and, even if this 'stopped clock' reading was true, the whole issue of how 'typical' or 'representative' the house is – and of what exactly – is itself far from clear. The fascination of Stafford Terrace is, in fact, how it resists easy categorisation, balanced as it is between middle-class convention and a highly personalised, not to say idiosyncratic artistic environment. Part family home, part working studio, part promotional tool, it was in certain instances literally Sambourne's own creation. He was at least partly responsible for the design of the stained- and

3.2
**Detail of door panel for
dining-room painted by
Linley Sambourne.**
Photo: Linley Sambourne
House, The Royal Borough
of Kensington and Chelsea

painted-glass panels set into the windows in the rear elevation and for painting the
doors to the dining-room, morning-room and drawing-room with illusionistic
decoration (Figure 3.2).

The re-evaluation of the interiors was greatly assisted by discoveries made
via the Sambourne Family Archive.[3] This is the collection of some 150,000 items,
including letters, diaries, bills and other material relating to the house and family that,
until 1999, was contained within the furniture of the house. With the support of the
Heritage Lottery Fund, it was catalogued during the period of the restoration and
began to provide new information relating to the evolution of the interiors. As work
progressed, the archive could be coupled with the findings of the specialist conservators working on the interiors who, through sampling and analysis, were able to
establish new chronologies for the painted decoration within the building.[4]

The key document in this regard is the full inventory and valuation of the
contents made in 1877, which included the valuation of works completed by
the Sambournes since they had taken possession of the house two years earlier.[5]

Taking the inventory and Sambourne's account books together, it becomes clear that virtually all the significant works were carried out immediately – probably prior to their moving in.[6] These included the extension of the morning-room, the installation of stained glass at the rear of the ground floor, the introduction of dado and plate rails, the hanging of Morris papers throughout and the painting of the woodwork in blue-green from the original cream. The one substantial later alteration was the extension at the rear of the drawing-room on the first floor, which was completed to provide Sambourne with studio space in 1878.[7] Sambourne clearly came with a preconception of how he wanted the house to look. The division of the wall surfaces into three, the conspicuous display of blue-and-white ceramics, and the extensive use of the Morris papers all suggest an awareness of contemporary 'aesthetic' trends in house decoration and a commitment to the creation of a progressive interior. These initial schemes remained essentially unchanged throughout Linley and Marion's lifetime and indeed are the core of what remains today.

The subsequent alterations made by the Sambournes were almost all either to do with services – electrification in 1896, complete upgrading of water-borne services in 1907 – or with partial redecoration. Through the 1880s and 1890s, they upgraded almost all the interiors, mostly replacing or covering over their original Morris papers with more expensive Japanese embossed designs. The restoration project highlighted a particularly interesting example. The removal of all the contents of the house prior to the start of restoration works confirmed what had already been surmised. The drawing-room had originally been papered in yellow Morris *Larkspur* (Figure 3.3). Then in 1884, a new embossed and gilded imitation Japanese paper was introduced, but rather than simply papering the entire wall, it was used only where it would be visible, leaving islands of *Larkspur* behind the clusters of prints and mirrors that were then rehung. Even in the exposed areas, the new paper was hung as a patchwork, with the pattern sometimes running on its side and sometimes vertically. Above the plate rail it runs laterally along the room. Sambourne was fully aware that the density of the furnishings within the interior would prevent the eye from reading the pattern over any distance and the richness of the effect would obscure the sleight of hand by which it had been achieved.

The archive confirms the sense that the house was created through an initial burst of activity during the late 1870s, followed by refinements made over subsequent decades. The accumulation of the contents followed a similar pattern. The 1877 inventory reveals the extraordinary quantity of objets that had been assembled in the immediate period after the family moved in. By 1877, 250 objets were already contained in the drawing-room. In later years, Sambourne was keen to give the impression that the contents of the house had been assembled with great discernment and care. While there certainly was a flair in the way Sambourne arranged and displayed the furnishings and objets he had amassed, the quality was mixed. The archive confirms that he would seek out purchases from a wide variety of sources. A core group of the contents were, in fact, purchased with the house from the estate of its previous owner.[8] Family gifts and inheritance accounted for

3.3
**Section of
wallpaper in
drawing-room
showing
embossed paper
over William
Morris *Larkspur*.**
Photo: Linley
Sambourne House,
The Royal Borough
of Kensington and
Chelsea

another group. On to these were grafted acquisitions from house clearances, auctions and antique shops. A final category of material came from the more fashionable retailers such as Edwards and Roberts, Liberty's and Maple & Co. By the 1890s, Sambourne was enthusiastically welcoming journalists to the house and receiving recognition as the owner of a conspicuously artistic home full of decorative flourishes, its contents showing the discernment of the artist's eye.[9]

Sambourne was well aware of the impact of the artists' houses built between 1875 and 1880 in the nearby Melbury Road. The importance of underlining his artistic credentials were perhaps particularly important to Sambourne in the early part of his career. His initial motivation in buying Stafford Terrace must have been, in part, the opportunity to socialise with the artists whose studio-houses were under construction just ten minutes' walk away. Without the financial muscle to build on this scale, Sambourne was nevertheless motivated by the same considerations as his more affluent contemporaries, conscious of the benefits that a determinedly 'artistic' home could bring in the furtherance of a career and reputation.[10]

Sambourne died in 1910 and his death initiates a definite and increasingly determined bid by the family, not to stop the clock, but to hang on to its hands as much as they could. They start, as it were, behaving oddly in the way they approach the house and its contents.

In 1911, Sambourne's widow worked with Maud to redecorate the staircase. Significantly, they took the opportunity not to change the existing scheme and simply replaced the Morris *Diaper* like for like. The instinct to sustain the appearance consciously seems to have been present from the moment of Linley Sambourne's death. No doubt the family knew how much the house and its contents meant to Sambourne and there is a sense that he is memorialised through the preservation of the interiors he created.

The next occupant, Roy, was by temperament disinclined to make changes in any aspect of his life. His well-recorded friendships with actresses of the day left him to ruminate in his diaries about whether he should marry, but he could never quite bring himself to do so.[11] His job as a City stockjobber was a constant source of anxiety and dissatisfaction, but he doggedly continued with it. He was content to remain living alone in the house, significantly only ever occupying the 'spare' room. Towards the end of 1923, his diary records a sudden spate of activity as he applies himself to the custodianship of the house. This continued intermittently until 1925, when references to the house disappear from his diary. Quite what prompted this activity is unclear, but on 22 September 1923 he records 'man calls re photographing the various rooms of this lovely house'. This was the local photographer Argent Archer who completed a full record of the principal interiors over the following months. These prints were then put into an album and remain an invaluable record of the changes made to the interiors up to that date.[12]

In the case of Sambourne's studio, installed in the former night-nursery on the top floor in 1899, Roy's photographs were the sole record of how it had appeared before it was turned into a bedroom in the 1960s and were invaluable in the restoration of the interior in 2002 (Figure 3.4). Throughout October he recounts sorting through family correspondence and papers, writing on 29 October that 'these blessed treasures bring back memories of the past'. On 3 November 1923, his attention turned to the soft furnishings: 'the cleaned chair covers look very nice. It makes me sad as I come across memories of my Father & Mother – God bless them.' Chairs are also reupholstered in his bedroom and on 5 December (1923) he shows off these changes to Maud who 'approves'. In his diary entry for the day, he writes 'Pray god I may keep my beautiful home in its original state as long as I live, & may it be cared for after I am gone.' The following spring (1924) he redecorates his bedroom. It had last been decorated in 1899 by his parents who removed the original Morris paper and hung a hand-painted and gilded Japanese paper in its place. At the same time, the fireplace and dado were painted a deep red. While retaining the paper, Roy repainted the dado and fireplace white. His enthusiasm for the house was tempered by occasional comments that he could see the attractions of a serviced flat without the difficulties he was enduring from a devoted, if troublesome housekeeper. An evocative entry in his diary recounts him having dinner alone and ends, 'my life is a wasted one with no-one to share this beautiful house of mine'.[13]

That Roy could get emotional over chair covers demonstrates the hold the house had over him. No doubt part of this was a simple nostalgia for his own childhood. But his relationship with his parents had never been entirely satisfactory in their lifetimes, as he had been a continuous source of anxiety and, indeed, something of a disappointment. His prime motivation appears, to a large degree, to be driven by a

3.4
**Studio looking
towards the south
west: Argent
Archer 1923.**
Photo: Linley
Sambourne House,
The Royal Borough
of Kensington and
Chelsea

desire to honour their memory through the preservation of their home. As a result, his entire adult life was spent living in a house where the wardrobes continue to contain his parents' clothes, their papers fill the writing desks and his father's extensive photographic collection and studio remain intact. The proximity of these objects and their associative power render even the most banal activity capable of shaking his fragile self-esteem. On 18 November 1923 his diary entry reads, 'Sort out receipts in Papa's desk. I feel more & more unworthy and deplore the way I have neglected my opportunities.' He was 45 years old at the time.

Roy's efforts were certainly supported by his more forceful sister Maud, now comfortably established in her own home overlooking Hyde Park and at Nymans in East Sussex. She regularly called and encouraged him in his efforts to preserve and restore. During this period, there clearly was some discussion of how the house might be preserved into the future. Maud's husband, Leonard Messel, was party to one such discussion recorded in Roy's diary entry for 29 September 1925, 'we sit till 10.45. Lennie says "Are you going to leave your house to the Nation?" '. The suggestion evidently pleases Roy, but it is perhaps significant that it comes not from Roy or Maud themselves, for whom emotional ties remain paramount, but from an outsider.

Following Roy's death in 1946, Maud was in a position to maintain the house empty but for the staff. And this marks the moment, 32 years after Marion Sambourne's death when Stafford Terrace stops being used as a full-time home. Maud's country home at Nymans was largely destroyed in a fire in 1947 and the house would have taken on a new significance as a link to the past. Although occasionally used by Maud's daughter Anne from the late 1950s, for the next 15 years time was, if not arrested, then substantially slowed.

The next phase from 1960 when Anne takes over the property, having bought out her siblings, sees considerable changes made to the fabric and in some senses time is sent into reverse.[14] The archive supports the view that her approach to these alterations, building a small extension to the rear to create a new bathroom and toilet facilities, and rewiring were, on the whole, completed with considerable care and sympathy.

In a number of the interiors, the later embossed and gilded papers were removed and Morris designs reintroduced – although 'Morris' is now understood and applied in a more generic 'period' sense. There is no suggestion that attempts were made to establish the exact patterns and colourways dating from the Sambournes' time and re-create them accurately. In some instances, what counts as 'Morris' is quite loosely applied. In the entrance hall, for example, the original Morris *Diaper* paper was replaced by a Cole & Son sub-Morris paper that at least made a good colour match. The dining-room was redecorated using a Morris *Pomegranate* but in a contemporary colourway. In the principal bedroom, the embossed paper was removed and rehung in a Morris *Norwich* design (Figure 3.5). The ceiling paper was

3.5
View of the Countess of Rosse's bedroom.
Photo: Linley Sambourne House, The Royal Borough of Kensington and Chelsea

3.6
**Countess of Rosse's
staircarpet purchased
from British Rail.
View looking down to
the first-floor landing.**
Photo: Linley Sambourne
House, The Royal Borough
of Kensington and Chelsea

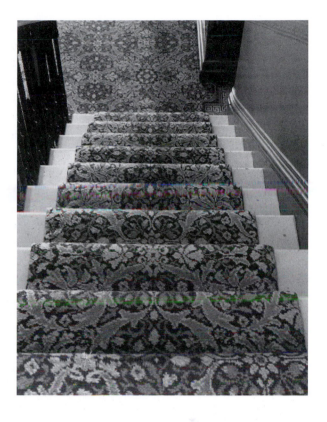

painted over in a coffee colour and a matching fitted carpet installed. On the top floor, Sambourne's studio and the servant's bedroom were both redecorated in Morris papers.

The treatment of the staircase carpet is particularly revealing of her approach to the alterations. When the house was acquired by the Sambournes in 1875, a crimson Brussels carpet was on the staircase. This was later replaced by a brown felt runner which was then replaced during Roy Sambourne's occupancy. In 1963, Anne Rosse put down the current carpet. Designed by Henry Dearle (1860–1932) who was trained by William Morris and, following his death, became Art Director of Morris & Co., she had evidently seen it in use in a station hotel and wrote to the British Transport Hotels & Catering Services to ask that if a future order was to be made some extra might be run off for use at Stafford Terrace. Her approach was successful and an opportunistic solution was found that brought a 'second generation' Morris design into the interiors, but which in fact had little to do with any of the earlier stair coverings (Figure 3.6).

So, in stark terms, of the eight principal interiors – including the entrance hall – currently open to the public, the decoration in five has been considerably altered since 1960, and if one counts the smaller alterations made by Roy and Maud, and Marion, then the number of decorative finishes through the house that can be identified unequivocally as those introduced by Linley and Marion between 1875 and 1914 are reduced to surprisingly few. Small but significant changes have also been made to furnishings. For example, the group of armchairs in the drawing-room are an arrangement from the 1960s, as is the lighting of the interior through 'country house style' table-lamps. Many of the soft furnishings have also been replaced and altered.

So, how did this understanding inform the restoration approach? Harmonising these alterations would pose a complex and hugely expensive puzzle, but the reality is that the extent of the later interventions makes a return to any particular moment virtually impossible. To return to a 1914 presentation of the house would require speculation and interpretation that would risk far more than would be achieved and in some instances require the wholesale redecoration of certain interiors. The introduction of new decorative finishes would throw out the unified appearance that has settled over time – the interventions made by Anne Rosse are themselves now more than 40 years old. Major changes made now would demand that existing tarnished and faded papers, and painted decoration would need to be restored to match. The decision was therefore made to treat all changes made by the family equally and not to alter or amend the sequencing of the interiors. Anything that post-dated the sale of the house to the Greater London Council in 1980 fell into a different category and could be considered on its own merits and retained or altered accordingly – but again the feeling was that it would only be undone if there was a strong reason to do so. Into this category fell the restoration of Sambourne's studio on the top floor – under previous operation of the house this was the shop. Partially restored in the 1980s, the interior was now put back with reference to the 1923 photograph, reassembling the contents that had been displaced into the other interiors. The adjacent maid's room – formerly a store cupboard – was also restored, although it retains its 1960s Morris *Willow* pattern wallpaper.

If applying this stance to the restoration was relatively straightforward, changing the way in which the house is understood and perceived is less so. If it is inaccurate to sell it as representing a moment in time, neither is it a document of the changing taste of three generations across a century, each making their mark on the interiors in their own way, consistent with their own time. The gaze of the latter two generations was firmly over their shoulders. Their interventions were constrained by a desire to do what was appropriate within the context of the original decoration and presentation of the interiors.

Stafford Terrace represents something more subtle than these two strands, suggesting themes around conservation and continuity. The formation of the Victorian Society at the house in 1957 emphasises the former of these two. The house does allow an exploration of what motivates preservation and the transition from emotional attachment to a more objective appreciation and perception of the value of a 'period' or style. It also allows an examination of how 'Victorian style' specifically has been reinterpreted and reinvented over the last 40 years and what the various custodians of the house have considered appropriate at different points in its history. An intriguing example of where this can lead is to be found in the

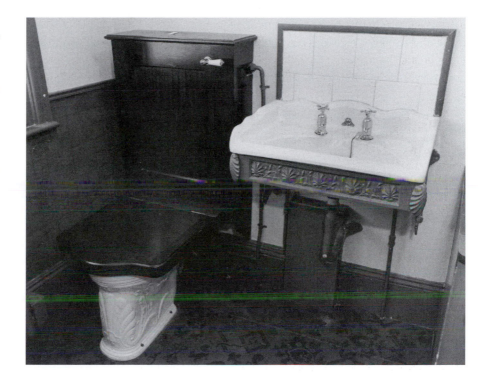

principal bathroom. This contains the original marble bath installed by Linley and Marion Sambourne modified to allow Linley to utilise the room as a darkroom. The room was extended by Anne Rosse and a standard toilet and wash hand-basin installed. In the 1980s, the Greater London Council removed them and introduced 'period' fittings, redecorating the room at the same time and 'Victorianising' this 1960s extension (Figure 3.7).

But the difficulty remains, that such themes cannot for a moment expect to compete with the 'house frozen in time', a concept that is so much more seductive, easily understood and sold – something that has been a significant consideration for us with visitor and income targets to meet. In relaunching the house, all marketing advice suggested that the message should be simple and the resulting press coverage has seen the return of familiar phrases. The house as 'time machine', 'time standing still' as you cross the threshold are very similar to the way the house was first written about when it was opened by the Victorian Society.

The museum staff, of course, have not been entirely innocent in this. Tours of the house by costumed interpreters are now available at weekends. These go further than anything undertaken previously in encouraging visitors to believe they have stepped back in time. On this level, visitor responses are highly positive and many are captivated by the house's ability to conjure the past.

But this is only one strand of the way that the house can be accessed. The intention is to establish as many opportunities as possible for the house and its collections to be used in different ways. The new guidebook and all other guided tours acknowledge the changes that have been made to the house and do address some of the themes around conservation and presentation that we would like to see given greater prominence. Specialist tours and study days where different readings and interpretations of the house can be suggested and discussed will all form part of its future.

Far from stopping the clock, perhaps our job is to ensure that it keeps ticking.

Notes

1 Mrs Bentley's lease of 18 Stafford Terrace dated 3 May 1871 is contained in the Sambourne Family Archive, ST/1/6/9.

2 Jervis, S. and Ormond, L. *Linley Sambourne House*, London: The Victorian Society, 1987.

3 The Sambourne Family Archive is held as part of the Local Studies section of the Kensington Central Library. The catalogue can be viewed at www/rbkc.gov.uk/linleysambournehouse.

4 An analytical survey of the paint finishes throughout the house was completed by Crick Smith Conservation in 2001. A copy of their report is held at Leighton House Museum.

5 The inventory, dated 1 December 1877, is in the Sambourne Family Archive, ST/1/6/18.

6 Edward Linley Sambourne's bank books, 1869–1910, in the Sambourne Family Archive, ST/1/6/68.

7 Papers relating to the extensions at the rear of the morning-room in 1875 and dining-room in 1878 are contained in the Sambourne Family Archive, ST/1/6/13.

8 An inventory of the fixtures, fittings and furnishings acquired by the Sambournes with the house dated 1875 is in the Sambourne Family Archive, ST/1/6/10.

9 For example, see 'Interesting People. A Chat with Linley Sambourne', *Winter's Weekly*, 25 August 1894.

10 For a full discussion of the artists' studio-houses of Holland Park, see Dakers, C. *The Holland Park Circle, Artists and Victorian Society*, New Haven, CT and London: 1999.

11 Roy Sambourne's diaries 1916–45 are held as part of the Sambourne Family Archive.

12 The album is in the Sambourne Family Archive, ST/8/2/15.

13 Roy Sambourne's diary entry for 5 October 1923.

14 Extensive letters and papers regarding Anne Rosse's refurbishment work at the house in 1963 are contained in the Sambourne Family Archive, ST/5/2.

Chapter 4

The double life

The cultural construction of the exhibited interior in modern Japan

Sarah Chaplin

Masao Miyoshi describes Japan's experiences with the West during the Meiji period from 1868 to 1912, when Japan opened up to the rest of the world after over 200 years of self-imposed isolation, as a 'nearly colonial encounter'.[1] While other countries were experiencing colonial domination as a consequence of having been taken over against their will, with new settlers imposing their way of life, Japan in the late nineteenth century requested and commissioned Western-style industrialisation, militarisation, education and architecture, employing experts from Britain and elsewhere to facilitate the desired changes. As a result, new concepts were introduced and assimilated, in such a way that, as Yuko Kikuchi has pointed out,

> Japanese cultural nationalism was heavily dependent on Occidental ideas. Not only were the concepts of 'nation', 'nationality', 'culture', and 'ethnic race' borrowed, but the Japanese also had to borrow Occidental ideas and 'scientific' disciplines embedded in Western historiography to evolve their own national identity. As a result, this 'nationalism' appeared in the form of an intellectual ideology involving a hybrid (*yuugoo*) of East and West.[2]

A prominent Meiji mantra that summed up prevailing Japanese ideology was *wakon-yosai*, or 'Japanese spirit, Western learning'. This formula justified to the Japanese people a new way of life that embraced a harmonious juxtaposing of domestic ethos and foreign method. Most historians concur that the Meiji period was one of Japan's most dynamic eras, a major turning point, a time of unique and rapid transformation, but some complain that there is a tendency to paint a 'larger than life' picture of the time.[3] The subsequent Taisho era, 1912–26, was similarly transitional in character, but less ideological in its orientation, and more concerned with a burgeoning cosmopolitanism, the penetration of new mass media and emerging gender roles.

Inside/outside

Against this historical backdrop, this chapter presents two contrasting contemporaneous examples of interior environments, the seeds of which occur at the end of the Meiji period, but whose realisation occurred during the Taisho period. One is the design for the Imperial Hotel in Tokyo by the American/Welsh architect, Frank Lloyd Wright, commissioned in 1912–13 and built between 1919 and 1923. The other is a Culture Village (*bunkamura*), built in Tokyo in 1922, and consisting of 14 model homes that epitomised a Western way of living. Culture Village guidelines stipulated that 'the living room, guest room and dining room must be chair-style, but other rooms are left to builder discretion'.[4]

Both examples embody the *wakon-yosai* principle, but in very different ways. While the Culture Village epitomises an attempt by Japanese architects to construct an exhibited interior based on Western precepts of inhabitation, the Imperial Hotel is symptomatic of a self-proclaimed 'organic' approach by an American architect who was trying to embrace and respond to Japanese precepts of interior design.

I am going to examine both case studies through a literary optic: the Imperial Hotel will be viewed through the eyes of the poet Nakano Shigeharu, and the Culture Village is glimpsed through the novel *Naomi*, or *Chijin no Ai, A Fool's Love*, by Junichiro Tanizaki,[5] serialised in a popular journal between March 1924 and July 1925. These two texts provide insights into the shifting Japanese response towards the meaning of modern (Western) architecture, from embracing it wholesale, to exhibiting an attitude of ambivalence, to an outright rejection, thereby allowing for a dialectical, comparative and diachronic reading.

In order to interpret their contextual meanings, it is, however, first necessary to make reference to certain normalised or naturalised constructions within Japanese cultural and social mores. The terms *uchi* and *soto* refer to conditions of interiority and exteriority, insideness and outsideness, which dominate the discourse of Japanese social and cultural history. It is immediately noticeable how much a sense of belonging to a group is ingrained conceptually and historically through even a cursory examination of the Japanese characters for country, home, wife and mother. As Chinese-derived calligraphic ideograms or *kanji*, these convey graphically notions of spatial confinement and boundedness as a condition of identity: the box enclosing a figure, the roof over the family home, and a combination of roof, enclosure and elevation above the ground is evident in the character for *oku*, the polite term for wife, which also carries the meaning of a deep interior space in a temple, and literally translates as 'honourable lady within'. In fact, the core character enclosed within this complex *kanji* is that of rice, implying a wife's household duties to provide sustenance.

It is well known that the Japanese demarcate these spatial boundaries of belonging not only in written communication, but also in conversation, venerating each other with polite forms of address, and using more humble language when speaking to or about one's own family. The foreigner, or *gaikokujin*, 'person from outside', can never transgress the familial boundary of the 'in group', to become Japanese, even if they are Korean or Chinese. Once an outsider, always an outsider. Likewise, once a Japanese, always a Japanese: leaving home, the family, the group or the country cannot ensure a departure from this commitment.

Moga

A new persona emerged in the 1920s that challenged these established boundaries – namely, that of the modern girl, or *modan gaaru*, a Taisho neologism which was shortened to *moga* as the stereotype became established. The *moga* epitomised the cosmopolitan lifestyle and, according to Akira Miura's dictionary of '"English" in Japanese', it was coined by Choogo Usui in an essay in *Josei* magazine in 1919 or 1920.[6] The way *moga* is written reveals its relative outsideness: The *katakana* script is used for Japanese words that do not derive from Chinese, i.e. foreign or 'loan' words that have been incorporated into spoken Japanese as transliterations. Many writers are critical of the notion 'loan-word', arguing that its connotations of borrowing are false: the word will not be 'returned' to its donor language. However, the idea of a loan-word preserves its status as a 'visitor' to the Japanese language and its rendering in katakana has a similar effect as placing a word in English in inverted commas – setting it apart as not quite belonging to the author.

Tanizaki's female protagonist in *A Fool's Love*, Naomi, has been identified with the image of the *moga*, in that both represented according to one writer 'a constellation of heterogeneous cultural influences, including the foreign, the passionate, the extravagant, and the individualistic, all of which militated against the hegemony of traditional social mores'.[7] Masao Miyoshi regards the publication of this novel as 'a daring experiment with the hegemonic role of the West in marginalised Japanese culture'[8] and argues that it shows how '[Tanizaki's] attitude toward both the "traditional" and the "new" Japan was from the very beginning problematic – that is, equivocal, qualified, tentative, ironic'.[9] Tanizaki's ambivalent relationship towards the West is charted in this novel, particularly evident in the way that he contextualises and satirises the contemporaneous experiment in cultural living.

Chijin no Ai is an 'I'-novel, written in the first person by a male protagonist, Joji, as an account of his affair with Naomi. He finds her working as a waitress in a popular café and is attracted to her because she looks like Mary Pickford. He invites her to live with him and attempts to transform her into an elegant Western-ised woman, providing English and piano lessons, and modern clothes. Instead she transforms herself from cute teenager to fully fledged femme fatale, and Joji's relationship with her becomes increasingly masochistic. The novel proved extremely controversial and produced an atmosphere of panic among male journalists of the day: according to Ian Buruma, the resulting concept of 'Naomism' meant 'a breakdown of traditional restraints'.[10]

In terms of Tanizaki's literary *oeuvre*, *Chijin no Ai* was published in the early part of his literary career, at a time when he was searching for an adequate response to the changes taking place around him. Miyoshi perceives a consistent characteristic in Tanizaki's early writings: 'they all saw Japan as dull and drab, and they all try to invent a space for escape in its midst.'[11] By contrast, he posits that 'as a utopian space, the West insists on intimidating and humiliating Tanizaki's own situation, which he identifies with Japan in general. In this view, the West stands for freedom, progress, and sophistication, and Japan represents restriction, stagnation, and crudity.'[12]

Culture homes

Throughout *Chijin no Ai* it is possible to map a spatial progression on the part of its main characters, beginning for both as they set up house together and embark on their ambiguous Lolita-like 'marriage' between a pubescent girl and an older man, and ending with a failed attempt at reintegration into 'normal' society. What is significant at each critical point in the novel are the detailed descriptions Tanizaki provides of the interior spaces they occupy and the effect that these different living environments have in shaping the power games that are taking place within them.

This first excerpt occurs when they take up residence in a suburb of Tokyo:

We rented a shoddy Western-style house near the tracks of the National Electric Line. Modern and simple, it was, I suppose, what people would nowadays call a "Culture Home", though the term was not yet in vogue then. More than half of it consisted of a steep roof covered in red slate. The white exterior walls made it look like a matchbox; rectangular glass windows had been cut into them here and there. In front of the entrance porch was a small yard. The house looked as though it would be more fun to sketch than to live in, which isn't surprising, as it was built by an artist who had married one of his models. The rooms were laid out in the most inconvenient way. On the ground floor was an absurdly large atelier, a tiny entryway, and a kitchen – nothing else. Upstairs, there were two Japanese-style rooms, six feet by nine feet, and nine-by-nine respectively. Hardly more than attic storerooms, they were really quite useless. This attic was reached by a stairway in the atelier. Climbing the stairs, one came to a landing enclosed by a handrail, just like a box in the theatre, from which one could look down into the atelier.

No doubt the odd design – it was like an illustration for a fairytale – appealed to Naomi's childlike curiosity, despite the impractical arrangement of the rooms. To be sure, it was just right for an easygoing young couple who wanted to live playfully and avoid the trappings of a conventional household. No doubt this was the sort of life the artist and his model had in mind when they occupied the house. In fact, the atelier by itself was large enough to satisfy the needs of two people.

There was no place to put the usual household items like cabinets and braziers in a house like this, so we were free to choose our pieces and carry out whatever design we liked. We bought some inexpensive India prints, which Naomi, with her uncertain fingers, sewed into curtains. At a Shibaguchi shop that specialised in Western furniture we found an old rattan chair, a sofa, an easy chair, and a table, all of which we set out in the atelier. On the walls we hung photographs of Mary Pickford and several other American movie actresses. I also wanted Western style bedding, but I gave up on that idea because two beds would have been expensive, and I could have Japanese bedding sent from my home in the country.[13]

This passage is important, as it must have instilled in the minds of its Japanese readers a clearly defined image of a Western-style home, which is valorised in Tanizaki's narrative as both creative and at the same time difficult to live in. Its performative possibilities are alluded to and the atelier becomes a site of playfulness in their relationship, with innocent and frivolous games of dressing up and showing off, and of riding around on each other. Indeed, Tanizaki's primary means of eroticising Naomi's body is presenting her in motion against the backdrop of this exotic and unfamiliar context. The concession regarding bed-linen also indicates the symbolic value that such aspirational foreign items carried in the 1920s and permits a spatial binary to exist between the upper floor with its Japanese rooms where they sleep separately and the Western-style atelier downstairs, thereby effecting a distinction that marks the dual character of their daily life, a constant flux from Japanese to Western-style living – the 'double life'.

The passage also functions as a piece of social history, in the sense that, as an example of a 'Culture Home', it situates their experiment as one of 'cultural living', a lifestyle espoused for a short time during the 1920s. Harry Harootunian attributes this new development to the French bestseller *La Vie Simple*, which was published in 1917. Cultural living was promoted as the height of consumer sophistication, sold as the inevitable and desired identity that was at first 'limited to the urban middle class'.[14] Harootunian argues that the purpose of the movement was to 'control the newly emerging everyday life being imagined and figured in the new popular media and beginning to be lived in cities'.[15] It was a way of packaging the everyday with its access to new media and new commodities, including 'Radio, movies, tabloids, magazines, cars, phonography, telephone, fashion, and cultural houses built for salarimen'.

Later in the novel, Joji is encouraged by Naomi to rent a house for the summer in Kamakura, although it transpires that this was a cunning plan on her part to be near her secret lover, and to conceal her affairs from her 'husband'. The house therefore functions as the spatial crux and partial denouement in the story, and signals a move on Joji's part towards needing to contain Naomi by reverting to a more private Japanese lifestyle. At this moment he also reacquaints himself with his former preference for Japanese domesticity:

> I had misgivings, but the house, once I saw it, was better than I'd expected. It was a one-storey building, separate from the main house, with two matted rooms, twelve by twelve and nine by nine respectively, an entryway, a bath, and a kitchen. It had its own entrance leading directly to the garden and the street, and there was no need to come in contact with the nurseryman's family. It was as though the two of us were setting up a new household. For the first time in a long time, I sat down on new mats in pure Japanese style. Crossing my legs in front of the brazier, I felt refreshed.[16]

It is interesting to note the role that the *tatami* mats play in forming a contrast between this dwelling and the earlier one which relegated the matted/Japanese rooms to the upper floor. Sarah Teasley in an article entitled 'The National Geographics of Design' discusses the culture life movement from a different perspective, locating the shift from floor-sitting to furnished interiors as a critical representational juncture: 'the sudden juxtaposition of vernacular forms with Euro-American equivalents elided previous distinctions to create an imagined geo-cultural opposition of *tatami* and floor-sitting practices as Japanese – against "western" hard flooring and chair-sitting practices'.[17] In her view, 'the 15-year period from 1918–33 saw a sea-change in tatami rhetoric and use', moving from 'universal element, to consciously vernacular style, to "architectural appendix"'.[18]

Teasley identifies this sea change as being characterised experientially by a kind of 'double life' which she describes as 'a lifestyle employing both traditional Japanese and newly imported western-style spaces, practices and goods'.[19] This double life is evident in many respects: inside and outside/public and private in relation to the home, upstairs and downstairs representing a shift from Japanese to Western forms of inhabitation, and this doubling also sets up the central tension in Tanizaki's novel, with its masochism and the impossibility of closure through spatial and domestic containment. By the end of the novel, 'cultural living' is represented as a slide into extreme decadence and male/Japanese inferiority.

After a breakdown in their relationship, the final solution which Joji devises is to start again and install Naomi as his wife proper in a Japanese house. The following excerpt marks his intention to end the transitional phase of their lives and re-enter society by playing more acceptable male/female roles:

> If Naomi wouldn't agree to have a child, I had another resource. We'd move out of the "fairytale house" at Omori and set up a more sedate, sensible household. I'd lived in our strange, impractical artist's atelier because I was drawn to it by the alluring idea of the simple life, but there was no doubt that the house had contributed to making our lives disorderly. It was inevitable that a young couple living without a maid in such a house would get selfish, abandon the simple life, and fall into careless ways. No more "culture homes", we'd move to a pure, Japanese-style house, suitable for a middleclass gentleman and just large enough for a husband, wife and two servants. I'd sell the Western furniture we'd been using and buy Japanese style furniture instead.[20]

After the unexpected popularity of *Chijin no Ai*, which the authorities actually succeeded in suspending from publication in 1924 because it was seen to be encouraging the adoption of Western ways too much, Tanizaki himself underwent what Miyoshi describes as an 'apparent volte-face' by the early 1930s, culminating in the publication of an essay entitled 'In Praise of Shadows' in 1934.[21] Writing by then in a more nationalistic mode, Tanizaki's personal reorientation of values can be identified as the search for a lost tradition of Japan, explored through the construction of the traditional Japanese interior.

In this later essay, which is often seen as a reactionary aesthetic manifesto, Tanizaki discusses the impact of Western technology, particularly the effect of electric light on the traditional Japanese interior, and suggests that if the Japanese had not had Western technology imposed on them, they might have developed products that were more appropriate to their needs, such as lights that were less harsh and radio that reproduced the delicate sounds of Japanese music more sympathetically.

Strangehood

Zygmunt Bauman in his book *Postmodernism and its Discontents*, discusses changing attitudes towards foreignness by citing two complementary strategies for dealing with strangers that Lévi-Strauss identified.[22] On the one hand, there is the interiorising 'anthropophagic' strategy – or strategy of assimilation – which is a case of 'annihilating strangers by devouring them, and then metabolically transforming them into a tissue indistinguishable from one's own' – that is to say, making the different seem similar.[23] This can be seen to exist at the outset of the Taisho era and at the outset of Tanizaki's *Naomi*, in which everything Western is absorbed into their everyday lives. The alternative strategy is termed the 'anthropoemic', or strategy of exclusion, which operates by exteriorising, or 'vomiting the strangers, banishing them from the limits of the orderly world and barring them from all communication with those inside'.[24] This is anticipated by Joji at the end of *Naomi*, although as a strategy it is never followed through.

However, in the second case study discussed in this chapter, Frank Lloyd Wright's design for the Imperial Hotel, there is scope to examine the effect of the anthropoemic, or strategy of exclusion, in greater detail (Figure 4.1). The following poem by Nakano Shigeharu is unequivocal in its denunciation of this interior and its deleterious effect on Japanese culture, presenting the hotel interior as one that both debases and belittles the Japanese and, in so doing, caricatures its contextualisation of Western lifestyle:

The Imperial Hotel

> Here, it's the West:
> The dogs talk English.
> Here, manners are the West's:
> The dogs invite you to Russian Opera.
> Here it's the West, the West's bazaar:
> A junkshop of Japanese fly-blown clothes and curios.
>
> Here, too, is a gaol:
> The warder twiddles his keys.
> Yes, here a dank and cheerless gaol:
> Warder and prisoner speak to no man.
> Prisoners are known by numbers:
> A warder stands by the door.
>
> Here, it's a cheap bar:
> Fat men get tight.
>
> Here, it's a whorehouse:
> Whores parade in the nude.
>
> Huge nothing
> Huge whorehouse
> Huge bar parlour
> Huge dank gaol.
> A seedy junkshop of Japan
> Squats in the heart of Tokyo
> And vomits a vile stink
> Over all our heads.[25]

4.1
**Entrance of the
Imperial Hotel,
which can be
regarded as
embodying
strategies of both
assimilation and
exclusion in terms
of its enveloping
yet forbidding
presence.**
Photo: Sarah
Chaplin

Frank Lloyd Wright worked hard to earn this commission to redesign a hotel in the heart of Tokyo. He first visited Japan in 1905 and made a number of subsequent visits, primarily to acquire woodblock prints which he exhibited in the United States in 1906 and 1908, becoming in the process a confirmed Japanophile. His attitude towards Japan was typically orientalising, and this in itself introduces a further dimension to the double life: as Kikuchi explains:

> Orientalism is not merely a one-way phenomenon. Its effect on the Orient, at least in Japan in the modern period, is complex, giving rise to the following circular mechanism. First, 'Orientalism' influenced Japan's views as to how to define its own art. Second, Japan in turn applied this 'Orientalism' not only to its own art but also to the art of other 'Oriental' countries, a phenomenon I have termed 'Oriental Orientalism'. Finally, 'Oriental Orientalism' was projected back to the Occident by Japan thereby reinforcing 'Orientalism' in the Occident.[26]

Kevin Nute in his book *Frank Lloyd Wright and Japan*, points out, 'Even in the face of what must have been plentiful evidence that Japan was fast becoming an industrialised nation, these idealised images of its recent feudal past seem to have coloured his whole perception of the country.'[27] Wright was determined to produce a design for the Imperial Hotel which would, as he himself put it, 'help Japan make the transition from wood to masonry and from her knees to her feet without too great loss of her own great accomplishments in civilisation'. Wright ambitiously called it a 'transition building', intended to bridge between East and West, and it was reputed to be popular in its time with foreigners and Japanese alike. Peter Blake describes its pretensions to being Japanese and justifies some of its apparent meanness:

> In its scale, and in its play with surprise elements, the Imperial Hotel is completely Japanese. Wright was apparently so struck by the smallest of Japanese things that he made everything in the Imperial Hotel tiny . . . There were little terraces and little courts, infinitely narrow passages suddenly opening into large two- or three-storey spaces.[28]

However, Shigeharu's interpretation, as an exponent of Marxism, is staunchly opposed to its patronising design stance, and the last line is clearly indicative of Lévi-Strauss's anthropoemic approach, rejecting it outright for espousing vulgar values. The poem exposes the inherent hypocrisy of the double life, articulated through the repetition of the word here.

Reconstruction: second life as exhibit in museum

Zygmunt Bauman remarked 'While modern strangers were earmarked for annihilation, and served as bordermarks for the advancing boundary of the order-under-construction, the postmodern ones are, joyfully or grudgingly, but by common consent or resignation, here to stay.'[29] He also notes that

> one can expect the present duality of the socially produced status of strangers to continue unabated. At one pole, strangehood (and difference in general) will go on being constructed as the source of pleasurable experience and aesthetic satisfaction; at the other, as the terrifying incarnation of the unstoppably rising sliminess of the human condition.[30]

It is this shift from a modern construction of the exhibited interior to a postmodern one that I would now like to turn to. Bauman talks about the need to disembed and re-embed cultural meanings. In the process of recontextualising the modern in the form of the Imperial Hotel, a subtle shift is effected from the 'rising sliminess' that is so palpable in Shigeharu's poem, to become instead a 'source of pleasurable experience and aesthetic satisfaction' within a postmodern paradigm of cultural consumption.

Frank Lloyd Wright left Japan before the construction of the hotel was complete, a hired foreigner who was himself initially subjected to the strategy of assimilation and later expelled as a stranger by his Japanese client. Ironically, the

Imperial Hotel survived the devastating Kanto earthquake of September 1923, but as the shift towards nationalism grew – a shift that is captured in the negativity expressed towards Western aesthetic precepts in the poem – the Imperial Hotel's valorisation changed and its popularity waned (Figure 4.2). The hotel was eventually demolished in 1968.

In 1965, a new 'Culture Village' opened, that of Meiji Mura, a private theme park 'collection' of Japanese architectural history from the Meiji period, located on the outskirts of Nagoya (Figure 4.3). In its midst the hotel, regarded by then as not only a seminal piece of Wright's architectural *oeuvre*, but also as an important part of Meiji heritage, was reconstructed, thereby altering its status to something museumified. It is only a fragment of the whole building – the foyer – which has been rebuilt here, positioned overlooking a long lake in a lush landscaped setting, at the far end of this theme park, a commanding finale to the tour (Figure 4.4).

The interior retains something of its performativity: here the manners are still the West's: visitors can order afternoon tea and sit at tables overlooking the lake as they contemplate Wright's bizarre and somewhat chunky detailing. Exploring this partial interior, one discovers that staircases lead nowhere, as in a film set or a hotel lobby designed by another émigré American, Maurice Lapidus, and if you go around the back of the building, you discover it has a scenographic status that renders it no different from a piece of pure façadism like that found in a Disney theme park, being abruptly closed off with a blank rear elevation (Figure 4.5). To emphasise this impression still further, pieces of the heavily ornate masonry structure litter the ground, ruined fragments of a past that increase the effect of its historicisation.

The double life of the Imperial Hotel is effectively a recontextualisation that brings it from the anthropophagic to the anthropoemic and back again, this time assimilating it through its representation as an exhibited interior and signalling it more-

4.2
As a reconstructed interior, visitors to Meiji Mura can now take tea in the former foyer of the Imperial Hotel, where 'manners are the west's'.
Photo: Sarah Chaplin

4.3
**The darkness of
the interior is
perhaps what
inspired the line
in Nakano
Shigeharu's highly
critical poem
'dank and
cheerless gaol'.**
Photo: Sarah
Chaplin

4.4 *(below)*
**Frank Lloyd Wright's Imperial Hotel in Tokyo, built between 1919 and 1923, was pulled down in the
1960s when part of it was re-erected at Meiji Mura, a cultural theme park near Nagoya.**
Photo: Sarah Chaplin

4.5

The scenographic quality of the Imperial Hotel's partial reconstruction is only apparent at the rear of the exhibit, where large blank concrete walls form a backdrop to fragments of the building's original masonry littering the ground.
Photo: Sarah Chaplin

4.6 *(below)*

The heavy masonry and brick construction may echo Japanese architecture in terms of its overall composition and proportioning, but its detailing owes more to Mayan or even Cambodian influences.
Photo: Sarah Chaplin

clearly as intrinsic to the nearly colonial encounter that Japan staged during the Meiji era, while at the same time placing it in inverted commas, loan architecture or *katakana* architecture, appended to Japanese history, an explicit exercise in 'cultural living' and an interior that is nevertheless an outsider (Figure 4.6).

Notes

1   M. Miyoshi, 'Against the Native Grain', *Postmodernism and Japan*, Miyoshi and Harootunian (eds), Durham NC: Duke University Press, 1989, p. 151.

2   Y. Kikuchi, 'Hybridity and the Oriental Orientalism of Mingei Theory', *Journal of Design History*, 10(4), 1997, p. 349.

3   J. Huffman, 'The Popular Rights Debate: Political or Ideological?', *Japan Examined: Perspectives on Modern Japanese History*, H. Wray and H. Conroy (eds), Honolulu: University of Hawai'i Press, 1983, p. 98.

4   S. Teasley, 'National Geographics of Design: Rhetoric of Tatami in 1920s and 1930s Japanese interiors', *De-placing Difference, Architecture Culture and Imaginative Geography Camea 3rd Symposium*, S. Akkach (ed.), Centre for Asian and Middle Eastern Architecture, University of Adelaide, 2002, p. 269, note 9: 'Takahashi Hitoshi, *Bunkamura jutaku sekkei zuzetsu* (Illustrated Plans of Culture Village Homes), Tokyo: Suzuki Shoten, 1924, p. 5.

5   J. Tanizaki, *Naomi*, a novel, translated from Japanese by Alfred Knopf, New York: North Point Press, 1985. Japanese title *Chijin no Ai, A Fool's Love*, serialised and published in issues of *Osaka Asahi* and *Josei* in 1924.

6   A. Miura, *"English" in Japanese*, Tokyo: Yohan Publications, 1985, p. 102.

7   D. W. Davis, *Picturing Japaneseness: Monumental Style, National Identity, Japanese Film*, New York: Columbia University Press, 1996, p. 57.

8   Miyoshi, op. cit., p. 130.

9   Miyoshi, ibid., p. 127.

10   I. Buruma, *A Japanese Mirror: Heroes and Villains of Japanese Culture*, London: Vintage, 1995, p. 53.

11   Miyoshi, op. cit., p. 129.

12   Miyoshi, ibid., p. 130.

13   Tanizaki, op. cit., pp. 16–17.

14   H. Harootunian, *History's Disquiet: Modernity, Cultural Practice and the Question of Everyday Life*, New York: Columbia University Press, 2000, p. 118.

15   Harootunian, ibid., p. 117.

16   Tanizaki, op. cit., p. 129.

17   Teasley, op.cit., p. 268.

18   Teasley, ibid., p. 268.

19   Teasley, ibid., p. 269.

20   Tanizaki, op. cit., p. 166.

21   J. Tanizaki, *In Praise of Shadows*, New Haven, Conn.: Leete's Island Books, 1977.

22   Z. Bauman, *Postmodernity and its Discontents*, Cambridge: Polity, 1997.

23   Bauman, op. cit., p. 18.

24   Bauman, ibid., p. 18.

25   N. Shigeharu, 'The Imperial Hotel,' *The Penguin Book of Japanese Verse*, G. Bownas (trans.), Harmondsworth: Penguin, 1964, p. 213.

26   Kikuchi, op. cit., p. 344.

27   K. Nute, *Frank Lloyd Wright and Japan*, London: Chapman & Hall, 1993, p. 144.

28   P. Blake, *Frank Lloyd Wright: Architecture and Space*, Baltimore, MD: Penguin Books, 1960, pp. 69–72.

29   Bauman, op. cit., p. 30.

30   Bauman, ibid., p. 34.

Chapter 5

The restoration of modern life

Interwar houses on show in the Netherlands

Paul Overy

In this chapter I compare two modern movement houses in the Netherlands on display to the public as 'modern period rooms' or 'exhibited interiors': the Rietveld Schröder house in Utrecht, and the Sonneveld house in Rotterdam designed by Brinkman and Van der Vlugt. I also discuss another house designed by Gerrit Rietveld with Truus Schröder which is now on show in Utrecht, No. 9 Erasmuslaan. Unlike some of the interiors discussed in this book, such as Lucie Rie's apartment, described in Chapter 9, which travelled from Vienna to London and back, these interiors are still inside their exteriors, which are also on display. Not, of course, 'their original exteriors', for such houses have been so extensively restored that it is debatable whether either the interiors or the exteriors are in any sense the originals, but rather faithful replicas.

The restoration and reconstruction process they have undergone is part of a continuing programme of preservation of what the Dutch call 'young monuments' – a phrase used to describe historic buildings of the twentieth century. This includes very large complexes, such as the Van Nelle factory in Rotterdam and the Zonnestraal sanatorium near Hilversum, but also individual houses such as those discussed here. Whereas these houses are former homes now open to the public, after restoration as modern period rooms or exhibited interiors, both the Van Nelle factory and the Zonnestraal sanatorium have been returned to professional or public use. The part of the factory already restored now houses architectural and design offices, while the sanatorium is destined to become a medical and rehabilitation centre. Although it is possible to visit these buildings by appointment, they will continue to have a life in the present beyond that of the representation of the past – unlike the houses discussed here, whose function is now entirely representational. I want to keep the idea of representation in the foreground throughout this chapter, to emphasise the fact that exhibited interiors, or period rooms, are *representations* of interiors that existed in the past. They are not those rooms or houses themselves, however much they may resemble them, or the photographs by which they are so often known.

The idea of the 'young monument' is an interesting concept in itself, one that perhaps seems more appropriate to a factory or sanatorium than to a relatively small domestic building that was once a family home, for 'monument' suggests largeness of scale and qualities of unchanging permanence, while the nature of domesticity and the home is one of continual change and renegotiation. The restoration and public display of former domestic homes, such as the two buildings discussed in this chapter, tends to produce fixed and frozen representations that cannot adequately convey the process of change.

While there seems to have been relatively little change in the Sonneveld house interior during the 20-year period its first owners lived there, the Schröder house was lived in continuously for 60 years by Truus Schröder – who was also directly involved in its design – and was subjected to considerable alterations, many of them directly supervised by Rietveld (Figure 5.1). This, of course, presents problems for its restoration and display. During the six decades Schröder lived there, it underwent several major (and many minor) changes. Although the reconstruction on display approximates to the 'original' house as it was shortly after Schröder and her children moved in, and has been stripped of later 'accretions', inevitably such a reconstruction remains layered and overlaid with other accretions – of memory, publication and its own canonic status (Figure 5.2).[1] This is further complicated by the fact that both the Schröder and Sonneveld houses are now run as dependencies of public foundations or museum-type institutions, and therefore also have to represent these as well as the buildings and homes they once were.

Situated about twenty minutes' walk from the centre of Utrecht, the Schröder house is run as an outpost of the Centraal Museum (the Utrecht municipal museum), although it is owned by an independent foundation. It can be viewed on pre-booked guided tours of about ten people. From late 2002, the interior of another slightly later Rietveld house, 9 Erasmuslaan, across the street from – or more correctly, on the other side of the raised motorway which today runs past – the Schröder house, has been on view as an extension of the guided tour. Another Rietveld house in the same row, 5 Erasmuslaan, has now been bought and converted into a visitors' centre.

Both houses on display were designed by Rietveld in collaboration with Truus Schröder. Located at what was then the edge of the city but is now a mainly residential inner suburb, the Schröder house was completed at the end of 1924 and

5.1
**Truus Schröder
with a visitor in
the dining area on
the first floor of
the Schröder
house, Utrecht,
July 1982,
designed by Gerrit
Rietveld with
Schröder in 1924,
with later
modifications by
Rietveld and
Schröder.**
Photo: Paul Overy

5.2 *(below)*
**The restoration architect Bertus Mulder in the restored dining area of the Schröder house, Utrecht
(Rietveld with Schröder, 1924), 14 February 1987, shortly before the house was opened to the
public.**
Photo: Paul Overy

occupied by the recently widowed Schröder and her three young children early in 1925. Nos 9 and 5 Erasmuslaan are part of a row of four houses built as a speculative venture by Rietveld and Schröder in conjunction with a construction company, Bredero's Bouwbedrijf. No. 9 was decorated and furnished by Rietveld and Schröder in collaboration with the Amsterdam furniture store Metz (the Dutch equivalent of Heal's) and put on display to the public as a show house between 4 and 25 October 1931. The interior has been restored as a representation of how the house looked in October 1931, furnished with original or reconstructed pieces of furniture.

The Sonneveld house was designed in 1933 for A. H. Sonneveld, one of the managers (and later a director) of the Van Nelle coffee, tea and tobacco company. The architects Brinkman and Van der Vlugt had designed the internationally celebrated modernist factory for the Van Nelle company (begun in 1926 and completed in 1931) on a greenfield site on the outskirts of Rotterdam. The house is in an enclave of luxurious upper middle-class modernist houses overlooking the Museumpark, on the edge of which the Van Boymans Museum was built in 1935.[2] Today, the area is much changed. In the last two decades, the Museumpark has been extended to include Rem Koolhaas' Kunstzaal and Joe Coenen's Netherlands Architecture Institute (or NAi), to which the Sonneveld is immediately adjacent. The house was restored and opened as an annexe of the Architecture Institute in early 2002. In contrast to the Schröder house, visitors view the Sonneveld house on their own, relying on the full captions and signs in every room, or with the help of audio-guides that are available in Dutch, English and other major European languages.

It is important to emphasise that the 'original' houses that the restored and reconstructed Schröder and Sonneveld houses represent also operated as display spaces or show houses during the time they were inhabited, and were essentially lived-in 'exhibited interiors' for much of their domestic life. Where the Erasmuslaan show house was on display for only three weeks in 1931 and was then sold like the three other houses in the row, the Schröder house was lived in by Schröder until her death at the age of 95 in 1985. Yet in certain ways it can be considered as much a 'model' or 'show' house as 9 Erasmuslaan. While the Erasmuslaan house was on display to anyone who wanted to visit it as a furnished (but uninhabited) 'model' house during those three weeks in the autumn of 1931, the Schröder house was on show as an inhabited house for 60 years to a more restricted, but influential professional audience that included architects, journalists, critics and architectural historians who visited Schröder there between 1925 and 1985. Indeed, Schröder seems to have considered the way she lived in the house – and was seen to live in the house – as essential to its acceptance and survival as an icon of modernism, and had a clear idea of how she wanted herself and her house represented to posterity.

The Sonnevelds lived in their house from 1933 to 1954, when Sonneveld (who had retired from the Van Nelle company in 1950) and his wife moved to a newly converted apartment in central Rotterdam after their two daughters left home. They took with them most of the movable and some of the built-in furniture from the house, which had remained virtually unaltered during the 20 years they lived there.[3]

Like the Schröder house, the Sonneveld house was also on display, particularly in the first years. The Sonnevelds would regularly entertain visiting clients of the Van Nelle company in the evening. The spectacular living and dining areas on the first floor with their panoramic views across the Museumpark were to a large extent intended to serve this function (Figure 5.3). Designed by the same architects in a similar style and equipped with similar furniture, the interior of the house would have reminded the Sonnevelds' business guests of the boardrooms in the Van Nelle factory where they met with the managers and directors of the firm (Figure 5.4). The Sonneveld house was also displayed through representations in magazines and periodicals. It featured in February 1934 in the magazine *Het Landhuis* (The Country House) – the Dutch equivalent of *Country Life* – with a series of spectacular photographs taken by the well-known modernist photographer and graphic designer Piet Zwart, as well as in the professional architectural and building magazines of the period.[4] The living-room of the Sonneveld house was also illustrated in the product brochure of the W. H. Gispen company, the leading Dutch manufacturer of steel furniture that had supplied furniture for both the Van Nelle factory and the house.[5] Some of this consisted of standard production models, while other pieces were specially designed by Van der Vlugt.[6]

In early 2003, shortly after it had opened to the public, the author was shown round 9 Erasmuslaan house by Bertus Mulder, the architect who restored it and who had previously restored the Schröder house in the mid-1980s. When I

5.3
The restored first-floor dining-room of the Sonneveld house, Rotterdam, February 2003, designed by Brinkman and Van der Vlugt in 1933.
Photo: Paul Overy

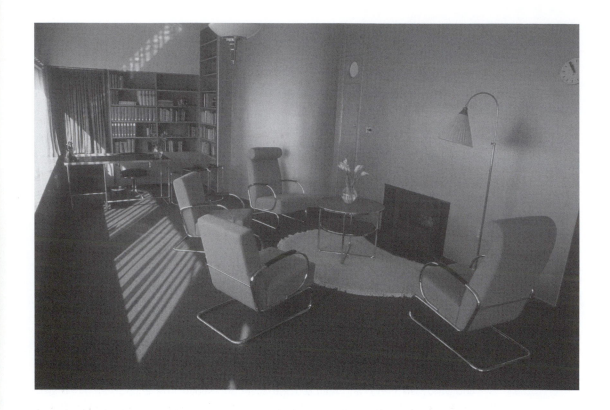

5.4
**The restored
first-floor living-
room of the
Sonneveld house,
Rotterdam,
February 2003.**
Photo: Paul Overy

mentioned that I was going on to visit the Sonneveld house in Rotterdam, Mulder said with what one sensed was a tone of disapproval: 'Now that *is* a luxury house . . .'. Luxury and austerity have always been key issues in the debates around early modernist architectural design, and this clearly must be addressed in a comparison between the Schröder and Sonneveld houses as exhibited interiors. Modernist architecture of the 1920s and 1930s can be seen at one level as an attempt to mask the privileged position of the middle classes in the political and economic climate during the aftermath of the First World War and the Russian Revolution, and the very real fear of similar revolutions in the rest of Europe. This was particularly true in the Netherlands, a country that already had a long tradition of discretion in the display of wealth and privilege by the middle classes, and where there had been a real possibility of left-wing revolution immediately after the First World War. Nevertheless, even within the Netherlands (and the spectrum of Dutch modernism between the wars) the two houses were very different, as were the clients.

Truus Schröder and her husband (who had died shortly before she commissioned the Schröder house for herself and her three young children) both came from factory-owning families. Schröder's husband had trained and practised as a lawyer, and until his premature death, the family had lived in an apartment above his office in Utrecht – a common practice among Dutch professionals at the time, as it had been of Dutch merchants since the seventeenth century. A. H. Sonneveld, on the other hand, was a self-made man who had worked his way up after joining the Van Nelle company at the age of 15, eventually becoming business director of the tobacco division. His decision to commission a house from Brinkman and Van der Vlugt was (one suspects) not unconnected to the fact that Kees van de Leeuw, the Van Nelle partner who was largely responsible for commissioning the new factory, had commissioned a house for himself from Brinkman and Van der Vlugt, while Van der Leeuw's recently married younger brother M. A. G. (Dick) Van der Leeuw (also a Van Nelle partner) had commissioned the architects to modernise the nineteenth-century family home for himself and his wife.

If one can – stereotypically, and with all the reservations that term demands – categorise these three commissions in terms of their style, Kees Van der Leeuw's house was a luxurious modernist house, the conversion for Dick van der Leeuw and his wife was in an art-deco style, while the Sonneveld house was some-where in-between. This combined a relatively austere modernist exterior with a richly coloured and luxuriously finished interior furnished with a number of specially commissioned tubular-steel pieces designed by Van der Vlugt, and curtains and upholstery chosen from designs by Bart van Leck (who had once been associated with De Stijl) and the French designer Elise Djo-Bourgeois. Many of the tubular-steel pieces were of the kind dismissed as 'macaroni monsters' by the leftist architect Mart Stam, who worked for Brinkman and Van der Vlugt at the time when the firm was designing the Van Nelle factory, shortly before he went to work for Ernst May's neue Frankfurt and subsequently in the Soviet Union with the May Brigade. (He is sometimes credited with a major share in the design of Kees van der Leeuw's house, sometimes of the factory itself.) The publication by the Netherlands Architecture Institute on the Sonneveld house is subtitled 'An Avant-Garde Home from 1933'. While the distinctions between avant-garde and modernism are an area of continuing debate, I would argue that one thing the Sonneveld house definitely is not is an avant-garde house, although the Kees Van der Leeuw house has been so characterised, as has the Schröder house.

The Sonneveld house was built on the edge of what had once been a private estate and park, very close to the centre of the city. This had recently been purchased by the Rotterdam municipal council who decided to turn part of the land into a public park and to construct the Van Boymans Museum on the edge of this, while leasing about half-a-dozen prime plots overlooking the park to wealthy members of the Rotterdam business and professional community. This was conceived as part of a carefully defined policy to attract the well-to-do middle classes back to the city centre. Like Liverpool and Manchester in the late nineteenth and early twentieth century, the majority of the prosperous bourgeoisie of Rotterdam had moved out to distant suburbs of the city, or to nearby towns such as The Hague or Wassenaar. Great efforts were made in the 1920s and early 1930s to persuade members of this class to return to the city centre as part of the modernising process to which the prosperous and rapidly expanding port city was being subjected prior to its devastation by Nazi bombing in 1940. Six plots of land were earmarked and all six villas were eventually built in modernist style to a luxurious standard, although two of these were not erected until the 1950s and 1960s.[7] The deliberate siting of select residences for leading members of the city's dominant elite opposite its major art museum is a fascinating aspect of social engineering that is beyond the scope of this chapter. Today, a different (although related) modernising process is being imposed on the city by means of far-reaching architectural and planning decisions and commissions. In the 1990s, the Kunstzaal and Netherlands Architecture Institute were built opposite the Van Boymans Museum, and today most of the luxurious modernist houses are no longer in private hands.[8]

Certainly, in terms of its site and specification, the Sonneveld house was a luxury house with its enormous well-fitted kitchen, spectacular entertaining areas, two-car garage, and bedrooms for two live-in maids with their own private bathroom and service stairs. By contrast, the Schröder house is often seen as a house that was a model for a reduced middle-class lifestyle without elaborate entertaining facilities and live-in servants, which attempted to enable a closer relationship between mothers and children by means of a more informal organisation of public and private living areas.[9] Such an aim was undoubtedly related to Truus Schröder and Rietveld's political and social views. Nevertheless, the expense and difficulty of finding servants, reduced middle-class incomes and living space, and changing perceptions of gender relationships and the relationships between parents and children, were all factors that influenced social and architectural change throughout Western Europe at this time.

Politically, both Rietveld and Schröder were what would have been referred to in Anglo-Saxon countries at the time as 'fellow travellers' – i.e. close to, but not actually members of the Communist Party. At the height of the McCarthyite era in 1956, Rietveld was refused a visa to take part in an exhibition in Washington, and he presumably must therefore have been on some CIA list.[10] In the 1930s he had been secretary of the Utrecht branch of the Filmliga, the leftist Dutch film society founded by the film critic Meno ter Braek and the radical documentary film-maker Joris Ivens to show films by Eisenstein, Pudovkin, Vertov and other Soviet directors that were banned from being shown in Dutch cinemas for political reasons. Meetings of the Utrecht Filmliga were sometimes held in the Schröder house and a projector can be seen in an early photograph of the first floor interior. Truus Schröder's sister An Harrenstein was married to a left-wing paediatrician. Rietveld redesigned the Harrenstein's Amsterdam apartment in 1926 in a style similar to that which he used five years later for the interior of the exhibited house at 9 Erasmuslaan. The apartment was destroyed in the 1970s, but the bedroom was bought by the Stedelijk Museum in Amsterdam and has often been exhibited as a 'modern period room'.

It is not clear what the Sonnevelds' politics were, although one suspects that, as leading members of the Rotterdam business community, they were not those of Rietveld and Schröder.[11] Yet, like Schröder and her family, when the Sonnevelds moved into their new house they left behind almost all the trappings of their former lifestyle, taking none of the furniture from their traditional late nineteenth-century former home. At this time modernisation, modernity and modernism could be marshalled to represent a variety of political and social fronts and positions – fascist/communist, upper middle-class villas/social housing, etc.

The Schröder house first opened to the public in 1987 after the major restoration that followed Truus Schröder's death in 1985. Until the new visitors' centre was opened at 5 Erasmuslaan in 2004, visitors entered through the ground floor of the house next door. This was one of a row of brick-built pitched-roof suburban houses erected not long before the Schröder house, to which it was somewhat incongruously attached. Here, visitors were met by the guide and could buy postcards and books about the house and related subjects, or watch a video. After putting on felt overslippers, they entered the Schröder house through a door knocked between the two houses, a symbolic entry from the old to the new – from what Theo van Doesburg called the 'brown' world of the old order to the white and primary-coloured world of De Stijl and early Dutch modernism. Today, viewing starts at the new visitor's centre at 5 Erasmuslaan, from where visitors are guided to the Schröder house, and from there to 9 Erasmuslaan, where the visit concludes, passing twice under the raised motorway built in the 1960s.

Whichever way the viewing is made, visitors enter the Schröder house via the relatively dark and intimate ground-floor spaces and climb the stairs to the first floor. Blinking in the sudden surge of blinding light, they emerge into the open space of the main living area which, when the house was first built, looked across a green farmland of polders and dykes, but now overlooks the motorway. On the other side of this, visitors can see the tops of the Erasmuslaan houses to the left, and to the right a slightly later duplex block built by Rietveld and Schröder in the mid-1930s with the new middle-class suburbs of Utrecht stretching beyond.

The Sonneveld house shares with the Schröder house the distinction of having its main living rooms on the first floor. These originally commanded stunning views of the park and lake, now partly blocked by the bulk of the Netherlands Architecture Institute. As in the Schröder house, visitors also reach the first floor from a relatively narrow and dark entrance hall via a spectacular spiral concrete staircase lined with thick and luxurious cream tiles, an experience described in the NAi publication as 'like going onto the topmost deck of an ocean liner'.[12] By comparison, the experience of climbing to the upper floor of the Schröder house is more like going up to the bridge of a tugboat. While both are planned so that the major living areas are on the first floor, one of the major differences between the two houses is that, despite its huge and spectacular living space, the first floor of the Sonneveld house is conventionally arranged into separate living, eating and sleeping rooms. By contrast, the flexible first floor of the Schröder house could be arranged in seven different combinations of spaces for living, working and sleeping by means of folding partitions.

Compared to the Sonneveld house audio-guide, the commentaries given by the human guides at the Schröder house seem to be aimed more at a specialist audience – architecture students and lecturers, practising architects, architecture and design historians, and so on – a type of audience that is perhaps indicated by the difference in price for visits to the Schröder and the Sonneveld houses. While the guides demonstrate the flexible first-floor spaces by moving some of the folding partitions and explain how these were used by various members of the Schröder family, the tone and tenor is less personalised and populist than the audio-guide commentary to the Sonneveld house, which seems aimed at a more general audience. In this context, it is interesting that the Netherlands Architecture Institute initially wanted to buy the house designed for Kees de Leeuw, but were unable to do so. This more austerely luxurious modernist (or 'avant-garde') house is some way from the NAi, as is the Schröder house from the Utrecht Centraal Museum, which houses the Rietveld archives and the major collection of Rietveld furniture. Had the NAi acquired the De Leeuw house, it would almost certainly have had fewer (if more specialised) visitors. It would undoubtedly have cost more to visit and the tone of the commentary would have been different.

Having acquired the Sonneveld house – a less iconic 'young monument' than the Van der Leeuw house, but more centrally located and conveniently next door to the NAi building – a decision seems to have been made to create a more popular experience, similar to that of visiting middle-class or upper middle-class houses from the more distant past – for example, an Amsterdam canal house or the Anne Frank house. Joris Molenaar, who restored the Sonneveld house, has written that it was decided to reconstruct this 'in its original 1933 state as if nothing had happened in the meantime, and then to exhibit it to the general public as a collection item'.[13] In contrast with the Schröder house, the Sonneveld house is presented as though the Sonneveld family might still be living there, as a kind of modernist 'Dutch heritage' experience. In the dining-room of the house, for example, one is invited to press the buzzer under the table used to summon the servants – *Upstairs Downstairs* re-presented in modernist guise. By means of the audio-guides, and the captions and storyboards found in each room, visitors are introduced to the Sonneveld parents and their two daughters Puck and Gé, and encouraged to empathise with them and their adventures in modernity. In the Schröder house, the partionable spaces on the upper floor used as bedrooms by Truus Schröder's two daughters Han and Marjan, and her son Binnert, are demonstrated and identified by the human guides at the Schröder house. But this is done in a rather different manner, attuned to a different type of audience, although as these are live guides rather than audio-guides, the presentation differs a little from guide to guide.

While it might seem that a restoration of a show house originally exhibited for only a few weeks like 9 Erasmuslaan might correspond more closely to the 'original' than the restored Schröder house, it is not without its problematic aspects, not least because what was initially a temporary show house before being occupied, is now represented as a permanent and unchanging continuous display. An identification and personalisation of the consumers or clients of modernist architecture is not possible in displaying a show house like this, although reference is made to Schröder contributions to the design of the furniture and the interior, and her role in commissioning and marketing the houses emphasised. As exhibited in October 1931, 9 Erasmuslaan had to suggest a less specific and individual mode of living than the Schröder house in order to present the furniture in a more 'neutral' environment. This relative neutrality was necessary so that people viewing the show house could imagine themselves furnishing it with the exhibited furniture designed by Rietveld and Schröder, or with their own furniture, or a mixture of the two. Alternatively, they could visualise how this furniture might look in their own houses or apartments. The show house presented a strong image of a modernist interior that gained immediate attention.[14] It was favourably received and widely published at the time, both in the local and national press, and in design and architectural magazines where it was represented as a 'key example' of international modernism. Although not all the pieces exhibited were put into production, the exhibition led to Metz commissioning a number of furniture designs from Rietveld. This helped to give the company an up-to-date image and made Rietveld's work more widely known – a successful marketing ploy in the commodification of modernism.

There are only a few extant contemporary photographs of the Erasmuslaan show house. The display aims to follow these as closely as possible, using existing pieces or remaking what does not survive, even trying to replicate the spiky plants visible on the window-sill of the living-room in one of the original photographs (Figure 5.5). As photographs do not exist for every room in the house, the first floor has been let out, initially to a young museum employee. This is in accordance with the policy of the Henrich der Keyser foundation, which now owns 9 Erasmuslaan, to encourage the use of the houses they own as lived-in, or partly lived-in, spaces wherever possible.[15]

5.5
The restored ground-floor living area of No. 9 Erasmuslaan, Utrecht, February 2003. The restoration represents the interior of one of a row of four speculative houses designed by Rietveld in collaboration with Schröder in 1931, as it was exhibited as a show house with furniture by Rietveld in October 1931.
Photo: Paul Overy

While it does not appear in contemporary photographs, the galley-type kitchen of the Erasmuslaan has been reconstructed from the plans. This was in the tradition of Grete Schütte Lihotzky's Frankfurt kitchen. Truus Schröder wrote about the Frankfurt kitchen in a feminist magazine edited by her sister An Harrenstein, *De werkende vrouw* (The Working Woman) in the early 1930s, and it seems certain that Schröder had a considerable involvement in the design of the kitchen of the show house.[16] *De werkende vrouw* was not aimed at working-class women, but at the middle-class woman who had a job, or even at those who considered household management their vocation – the 'new woman' of the late 1920s and early 1930s – the kind of woman who Schröder and Rietveld perhaps hoped would want to live in the Erasmuslaan houses. These were intended for the middle-class purchaser, but the specification was not very different from a number of designs that Rietveld had made in the late 1920s and early 1930s for social housing. They are quite closely related to the houses he was commissioned by Josef Frank to design for the Vienna Werkbund Siedlung model-housing exhibition of 1932 which were designed to a relatively tight *existenzminimum* specification.[17]

Although the Schröders and the Sonnevelds were very different kinds of people within the spectrum of the prosperous Dutch middle classes of their time, they also had a good deal in common. While in many ways typical of their class and national interests, they were also committed to wider although different kinds of internationalism: the Sonnevelds to the internationalism of world commerce and trading interests, Schröder to the notion of the international avant-garde and the international communion of ideas that briefly marked the late 1920s and early 1930s. But the differences are perhaps as great as the similarities. The Sonneveld house can be seen as a domestic building that was designed to give a modernising image to the family life of the prosperous business classes in the Netherlands. The Schröder house, however, aimed to produce a new kind of non-traditional family life by means of its flexible interior spaces that could be constantly adjusted and readjusted as time passed, relationships changed, children grew older and left home, and so on. It is significant that (as already indicated) Schröder continued to live for 60 years in her house, while after Sonneveld had retired and the children left home, he and his wife moved from their house into a newly refurbished apartment, something that Schröder's commitment to her house and its architect would not have allowed her to do.

Today, as exhibited interiors or 'modern period' rooms, the restored or reconstructed houses discussed here now signify in a number of ways that are different (although related) to the ways in which the early modernist houses they represent originally functioned. As reconstructed display spaces they are 'museums of modernism' in a 'postmodern' era, 'demonstration rooms' or show houses for the popularisation of revived modernist styles, and as 'human interest' tableaux that exploit the lives of those who lived in or designed them. These were once individual family homes (in the case of the Schröder and Sonneveld houses) or demonstrations of how a modern family home might be (like the Erasmuslaan show house) but are now annexes of museums, tableaux of 'how we lived then', or rather of how a few privileged and extraordinary people chose to live differently in the years between the wars. They are 'young monuments' that will now remain eternally young, rather than age and change like the 'real houses' they represent or those who lived in them.

Notes

1 Bertus Mulder, the architect who restored the Rietveld Schröder house, wrote that after careful discussion and deliberation:

> It was finally decided to restore the interior in such a way that the use of space and the sense of space would give an idea of how it must have been in the first years after the house was built. The qualification was added that this did not mean reproducing exactly the original state. Those elements which had been determining factors in making the house a blueprint for a new style of living and a new approach to architecture as the art of designing space, and which had been subsequently lost through alteration, would be reconstructed.
>
> (B. Mulder, 'The restoration of the Rietveld Schröder House', in P. Overy,
> L. Büller, F. den Oudsten and B. Mulder, *The Rietveld Schröder House*, London:
> Butterworth Architecture/Cambridge, MA: The MIT Press, 1988, p. 113)

2 The name of the area was changed to the Museumpark by a decision of the Rotterdam Municipal Council in 1929. Previously, it had been known as the Land van Hoboken after the family who owned the large tract of land that had been purchased shortly before by the Council. (E. Adriaansz, 'The Dijkzigt Villa Park', in E. Adriaansz, J. Molenaar, B. Laan and M. S. Thomas (eds), *Brinkman and Van der Vlugt: The Sonneveld House. An Avant-Garde Home from 1933*, Rotterdam: NAi Publishers, 2001, p. 40.)

3 B. Laan, 'A Tailor-Made Suit', in Adriaansz *et al.*, 2001, p. 31.

4 Laan, in Adriaansz *et al.*, 2001, pp. 28–9.

5 A photograph of the Sonneveld living-room by Jan Kamman was illustrated in W. Gispen, furniture catalogue, no. 52, 1934.

6 Otakar Máčel, 'Furniture: Van der Vlugt's designs for tubular steel furniture', and André Koch, 'W. H. Gispen: Working with and for Van der Vlugt: a creative evolution', in Elly Adriaansz, Joris Molenaar and Joost Meuwissen (eds), Leen van der Vlugt (*Wiederhall* 14), Amsterdam: Stichting Wiederhall, 1993, pp. 41–3 and 45–7.

7 Adriaansz, in Adriaansz *et al.*, 2001, pp. 34–44.

8 After the Sonnevelds left their house in 1954, it was bought by the Belgian government and became the residence of the Belgian Consul General in Rotterdam until the 1990s, when the proximity of Rotterdam to Brussels and the speed of modern communications and information technology made a consul general in Rotterdam unnecessary.

9 The Schröder house was originally designed with a kitchen on the ground floor, with a dumb waiter connecting to the living–dining area on the first floor and a day room next to the kitchen for a woman home help who came in by the day. The latter was quite common in middle-class modernist houses of the 1920s – see, for example, many of the houses designed for the Weissenhofsiedlung model-housing exhibition in Stuttgart in 1927.

10 F. Bless, *Rietveld 1888–1964: een biografie*, Amsterdam: Utigeverij Bert Bakker/Baarn: Erven Thomas Rap, 1982, p. 150

11 Laan, in Adriaansz *et al.*, 2001, p. 33.

12 Laan, in Adriaansz *et al.*, 2001, p. 22.

13 W. J. Paijmans and J. Molenaar, 'A Modern Villa from 1933 in 2001, "As if nothing had happened"', in Adriaansz *et al.*, 2001, p. 154.

14 For details of 24 Dutch and international references to the Erasmuslaan houses, see Theodore M. Brown, *The Work of G. Rietveld, Architect*, Utrecht: Bruna & Zoon, pp. 174–5. See also Marijke Küper and Ida van Zijl, *Gerrit Th. Rietveld, 1888–1964: The Complete Works*, exh. cat., Utrecht: Centraal Museum, 1992, pp. 134–5.

15 Another slightly later house in Blaricum (originally designed by Rietveld in 1935 for a children's writer named Hildebrand), recently restored by Bertus Mulder, is also owned by the Henrich der Keyser foundation, which plans to hire it out to government organisations and commercial companies for meetings and conferences.

16 *De werkende vrouw*, 1 (1), pp. 12–14.

17 Ten years after designing the Erasmuslaan houses Rietveld wrote in 1941:

> A cheap house (a so-called worker's house) must be a category of its own; it should not be a scaled-down middle-class house, just as this again is a scaled-down version of a 'gentleman's house'. As a result of mass production and industrialization, the product meant for the masses is no longer a replica or a reduced version of the product for the individual citizen, but rather a standard product. Thus the product intended for the individual is at best a luxury version of this basic form.
>
> (*De 8 en Opbouw*, no. IX, 1941, quoted in translation in *G. Rietveld, Architect*, exh. cat., Amsterdam: Stedlijk Museum/London: Hayward Gallery, 1971–2, n. p., caption to Fig. 66)

Chapter 6

'A man's house is his art'

The Walker Art Center's *Idea House* project and the marketing of domestic design, 1941–7

Alexandra Griffith Winton

In 1941, the Walker Art Center of Minneapolis, Minnesota, built and exhibited *Idea House*, America's first museum-sponsored, fully functional modern exhibition house, created to present ideas on home building in a domestic environment. The Walker followed *Idea House* in 1947 with a post-war iteration of this same project, *Idea House II*, which garnered national media attention and the interest of other museums. *Idea House* predates by several years both the *Art and Architecture* Case Study House project and the Museum of Modern Art's House in the Museum Garden series. In addition to the two inhabitable and completely furnished houses constructed on museum grounds, at least six other Idea Houses, intended for a suburban subdivision, were planned but never built. *Idea House I* was demolished in 1961 to make room for the Tyrone Guthrie Theatre, designed by Minnesota modernist architect Ralph Rapson. *Idea House II* was demolished in 1968 as part of a Guthrie expansion.

Bracketing the ends of the Great Depression and World War II, the Walker Art Center's *Idea House* exhibitions synthesized aspects of the production and consumption of home design, borrowing techniques of salesmanship from advertising and industry in order to convince its visitors of the relevance and importance of design to their lives. The form of this unusual sales pitch was the most potent symbol of the American Dream: the single-family house.[1] By assuming the format of the model home, *Idea House* attempted to disrupt its conventional role, encouraging viewers to borrow from a range of solutions, rather than accepting a prepackaged, standardized home design. These dwellings created a participatory consumer spectacle of the type experienced in World's Fair exhibitions and commercial model-home developments, in which visitors were introduced to a variety of modern architectural concepts, materials, and techniques, as well as the most up-to-date home appliance technology. In contrast to those types of home displays, however, the *Idea House* goods and materials were selected by museum curators. The houses themselves were designed by architects retained by the Walker, rather than commercial sponsors. While they took the conventional form of model homes, I shall argue that the Idea Houses were, in fact, polemical exercises in reform – household and museological. Aimed at activating the art museum as a relevant social and cultural institution for the widest possible population, and raising the quality of home design and technology by serving as exemplars, *Idea House* traversed the bounds of art, politics, and business in new and innovative ways. The very structure of the *Idea House* exhibitions, with their extensive didactic information and immediate physical access, encouraged visitors to involve themselves actively in the thoughtful design and furnishing of their own homes, at the same time transforming their museum experience. These projects reflect a period of American history in which the spheres of government social policy, economics, and architecture were inextricably entwined, and housing was a priority of government as much as commercial entities. Discussion of the project is complicated by its role as a museum exhibition, and its architectural and museological methods are arguably inseparable. The twin goals of providing quality home-design advice and reinventing the museum experience are what made the project popular in its day and interesting now. It is necessary to treat the houses both as exhibitions and as houses, and the interplay of commerce and the museum is perhaps essential to discussion of the project: the overwhelming commercial influence on home design and furnishings was what inspired the project in the first place.

The summer of 2000 saw the reincarnation of *Idea House II*, or at least a portion of it, inside the Walker Art Center galleries. As part of a larger exhibition called *The Home Show*, the Walker re-created the living room of *Idea House II* and opened it up for visitors to explore. The *Idea House II* re-creation joins those for the Case Study House Project (1989) and Le Corbusier's 1925 Pavilion de L'Esprit Nouveau (2000) as important modern interiors partially reconstructed within the context of a museum exhibition.[2] This generally thoughtful and considered re-creation of the 1947 living-room in a museum dedicated to contemporary art poses a number of questions about the evolving interpretations of twentieth-century design and architecture within current curatorial practice, and highlights the shifting significance of this material from 1947 to the present day.

Perhaps the most remarkable aspect of this re-creation is how much of the material from *Idea House II* is still manufactured today. The Walker's Summer 2000 calendar brochure states:

A partial re-creation of the house's main living space serves as a focal point in the exhibition galleries, featuring historically accurate materials and furnishings by such design luminaries as Charles and Ray Eames, Alvar Aalto, Isamu Noguchi, Walter von Nessen and George Nelson.

All the furnishings were acquired new from Knoll, Herman Miller, and other makers. Eva Zeisel's Town and Country dinnerware was also reintroduced shortly before the exhibition opened, in a Zeisel-authorized reproduction, and was featured in the living-room (Figure 6.1). In her essay 'The Exhibitionist House,' architecture historian Beatriz Colomina writes:

> Manufacturers have played a crucial role in promoting modern architecture throughout the century: the discourse around the modern house is funda-mentally linked to the commercialization of domestic life. In the end, all the different forms of exhibition were really advertisements.[3]

At the beginning of the twenty-first century, the fruits of this persistent promotion and advertisement of modern design were clearly evident in *The Home Show*, but it is no longer the manufacturers but the designers who are on display: 'good design' is now a branded entity, and its designers are described as 'luminaries.' While in the original *Idea House II* literature, scant mention was made of any particular designer; here they are celebrities.

Idea House II was created first and foremost by a museum as an exhibi-tion dwelling, and in re-creating it in part, it is necessary to examine that definitive aspect in greater detail. By relying on modern samples of the original furnishings, rather than now-valuable period pieces, the exhibition enabled visitors to interact freely with the furnishings and accessories within the living-room. In encouraging this close, tactile interaction between visitor and object, the exhibition shared a strong participatory element with its antecedent. However, significant additional elements of the original project's context and content were left out. No price list or manu-facturer's addresses or other references to the objects' roles as consumer items were displayed. Instead, didactic labels listed the objects' original dates and manu-facturers and, where relevant, the producers of reissued items. Viewers would have benefited from learning the prices of some of these objects in 1947, if only to target their historical perspective on the contrast between the goals of the original *Idea House* project, to promote reasonably priced modern homes and furnishings, and these same furnishings' current status as design icons. In 1947, the cost of an Eames LCW was around US$25, which would be US$185 today, while a new one costs around US$550 from an authorized retailer, and an original chair from 1947 could bring thousands at auction.[4] This is key information in helping the viewer to contex-tualize this object and its complex history, incorporating both its curatorial and commercial identities.

In its general uneasiness to engage these works as consumer items, either historically or in their current manifestation as desirable design icons, the *Home Show* installation reflected not the exemplary, consumer-oriented goals of the original project, but was instead a formally accurate display of historical design – a period room. The apparent transparency of the original *Idea House* project, in which the museum attempted to act as a conduit for good design, created a museum-sanctioned consumer spectacle that was beneficial to both consumer and manufacturer at a time when both affordable housing and maintaining a productive consumer economy were national priorities. The decision to focus on the form and objects of *Idea House II* in this re-creation, rather than its original consumer orientation, reflects both the increasing distance today between the average visitor and the architect-designed home advocated by the *Idea House* curators, and the increasing historical importance of the designers of this period.

6.1
Living-room of *Idea House II*, re-created for The Home Show, Walker Art Center, 2000.
Photo: Walker Art Center, Minneapolis

Idea House I: a groundbreaking domestic dwelling project in the American Midwest

In January 1940 the Walker Art Center, established as a private art collection in 1875, became one of over 100 civic arts centers across the United States operated under the auspices of the Federal Arts Project (FAP) of the Works Project Administration, Franklin D. Roosevelt's massive federal program to employ the scores of unemployed Americans during the Depression. Daniel S. Defenbacher, an architect by training and a veteran administrator of the FAP, was named its director. Bringing to the Walker the FAP mandate to employ artists and foster creativity and interest in the arts among the general population, he immediately reorganized the institution, radically transforming it into a center for contemporary art and design. Defenbacher reimagined the role and mission of the art museum, seeking to activate its cultural influence by rendering its projects relevant to the lives of people who did not feel welcome in a traditional museum. Recalling the philosophies of John Cotton Dana at the Newark Museum earlier in the century, he perceived the museum as 'a repository for the possessions, the glorious relics, the intimate triviata of dead and mysterious ancestors,' in stark distinction to the art center, which sought to make art in all its forms, including industrial design and advertising, relevant to 'human meaning and contemporary experience.'[5] Among his earliest and most influential projects was *Idea House*, a project that would illustrate Defenbacher's premise that, 'As a consumer, every man uses art. . . . His medium he obtains from stores, manufacturers, and builders. His composition is his environment.'[6]

In October 1940, Defenbacher wrote to a local building materials vendor to solicit in-kind contributions to the Walker for an upcoming project. In conjunction with a three-part exhibition titled *American Living*, the museum planned a fully functional, completely furnished house, as Defenbacher believed that models and drawings were no longer a sufficient means of experiencing the spatial and material innovations of modern design. This exhibition house, called *Idea House* because it was meant to present multiple ideas about home design, materials, and decoration, was designed by local architects Malcolm and Miriam Lein, and built on a plot behind the Walker on its landscaped grounds. It opened to the public in June 1941. *Idea House* ran from June through November, after which the museum planned to use the house as a classroom and laboratory for design and home decorating programs. Defenbacher explained:

> The exhibition home has been designed by architects who have been retained in the Art Center staff for this purpose. The house exemplifies up-to-date 'open-planning' and 'multiple use of space'. The major feature in planning has been to obtain the maximum spaciousness within the cubic content of the average five room house. The house will be so-called modern in appearance, but will not have the box-like character, which so

many people dislike. ... The house will be open to the public day and evening and on Sunday for six months. We will provide guards and attendants at all times. We will charge 10 cents admission to the house until our investment has been returned to us. After that, admission will be free.[7]

Targeting vendors and manufacturers of home building supplies and furnishings, Defenbacher promoted the economic and public-relations benefits of contributing goods to the exhibition, while at the same time he attempted to protect the institution from the potential taint of commercialism, writing, 'We are an educational institution interested only in giving the layman information and ideas. We are, therefore, unrestricted by the need for commercial exploitation which accompanies the average model home plan.'[8]

The Walker's choice of a single-family house, rather than a model apartment, reflected a longstanding American interest in home ownership, especially the free-standing private house in suburban surroundings.[9] *Idea House* (subsequently referred to as *Idea House I* to distinguish it from the 1947 *Idea House II*) was built at a time when the economy was just beginning to recover from the Great Depression, and there was deep general concern over America's impending involvement in World War II. The Depression years saw housing start to plunge dramatically from the boom years of the 1920s, and financial duress was so widespread that by 1933, 49 percent of the national home mortgage debt was in default and each week there were around one thousand home foreclosures.[10]

By 1934 the situation was so dire that Congress passed the National Housing Act, intended to provide some relief for both the general population and the real-estate industries. The Federal Housing Administration, founded as part of this act, sought to stimulate home ownership by offering, together with cooperating banks, long-term mortgages covering up to 80 percent of a home's value. This was in contrast to prevailing mortgage practices, which demanded from 40 to 50 percent of a home's value in down-payment, with the principal due within as few as three years. Additional home improvement and modernization loans were also available through the FHA, allowing borrowers to renovate their homes or purchase major appliances they otherwise could not afford. By 1938 the housing industry appeared to rebound, with as many as one in eight American homeowners participating in the FHA loan programs. US Census Bureau statistics indicate that homeownership increased significantly from 1930 to 1950, and Minnesota consistently ranked among the states with the highest homeownership rates nationwide.[11]

From its inception, the FHA exerted a powerful influence over the appearance of the homes it helped to finance. In a series of leaflets called *Technical Bulletins*, the FHA issued direct design and construction advice to homebuilders, with titles including *Modern Design* and *Mechanical Equipment for the Home*.[12] The former addressed the meaning of 'modern' as understood by the FHA, defining it as a primarily pragmatic use of space, an economic use of materials, and judicious application of technology. This was outlined in distinction to faddish designs with stylistic features having nothing to do with the structure or function of the house. Well-planned modern homes, the guide explained, would receive high ratings from FHA evaluators, while 'modernistic' homes would not. The latter booklet addressed new appliances for the home, including dishwashers. Another booklet, *Technical Bulletin # 4: Principles of Planning Small Houses*, prescribed building standards and design principles by illustrating sample homes, establishing standards to which FHA homes would adhere for decades. This booklet was continuously updated and expanded. In its 1940 iteration, it presented a revolutionary design that allowed for variations in plan and materials within a standardized single-storey, one-family house footprint. In spite of the innovative plan, the elevations illustrated in the guide featured conventional details, with small windows and pitched roofs. This house, which became known as the FHA 'minimum' house, was designed to provide the most efficient use of space with the greatest economy of means.[13]

Model home exhibitions were extremely popular even during the Depression, and among the types of 'average model home' projects from which Defenbacher sought to distinguish *Idea House I*, were a number of demonstration dwellings sponsored by industry and housing exhibitions at highly popular World's Fairs and expositions.[14]

At the 1939 World's Fair in New York, to cite but one example, The Town of Tomorrow showcased 15 single-family house designs sponsored by at least 56 building product manufacturers.[15] According to official fair documents, architects participating in this project were instructed that the town should appear 'neither traditional nor modernistic in design. It should be *modern*.'[16] Visitors to the Town of Tomorrow received a guide to the products featured in the houses, as a means of stimulating consumer interest and education in home design and construction, and 'assisting prospective home builders to obtain more value for their money.'[17] The estimated construction costs for the 15 designs that comprised the Town of Tomorrow ranged from around US$5,000 to over US$35,000.[18] With the average FHA home costing around US$5,199 in 1940, this range reflects an effort to provide realistic examples for middle-class consumers, as well as fantasy showpieces.[19]

Among the other exhibits of interest to homeowners were the Home Building Center, where makers of building supplies showcased their goods; the Home Furnishing Building, for the display of furniture and decorative items, and the Consumer's Building, which offered fairgoers advice on budgeting home construction and repair, as well as the Consumer's Union of the United States, Inc. display, which sought to 'dramatize the need of consumers for reliable and objective information on the products that competing manufacturers ask them to buy.'[20] In contrast, Fair president Grover Whalen promised manufacturers 'direct, planned and simultaneous contact with great masses of consumers' who would be guided and influenced by the displays. Elsewhere, visitors could experience Norman Bel Geddes' futuristic vision of domestic and urban life in America in 1960 in his popular *Futurama* exhibition for General Motors.[21]

Idea House I reflected the agenda of the FHA 'minimum house': a small house with the most logical planning and use of technology, but without extraneous decorative features, understanding 'modern' as a measure of technology and living standards rather than an aesthetic categorization. It also adapted aspects of these earlier commercial exhibitions: the permanent, functional dwelling, and the emphasis on consumer outreach, with a host of didactic materials available to visitors. However, it refocused these initiatives in a new way. Unlike these earlier model home exhibitions, in which the architect was typically chosen by the sponsor with product placement and sales as the primary goals, *Idea House I* was not sponsored directly by industry, nor was it designed to showcase specific products or materials. Rather, it was intended to introduce the concept of architectural planning and the use of modern materials to the general public in a way that would prepare them for their own building programs.[22]

Construction on *Idea House I* began in January 1941, and this rare wintertime building project in the bitterly cold Minnesota climate was chronicled in weekly updates in the local paper[23] (Figure 6.2). Built of a kiln-dried timber frame sheathed in weather-treated composite board, the house was designed with the extremes of the Minnesota climate in mind. Like the FHA 'minimum house' of 1940, the house's relatively open plan relied on sliding partitions to delineate interior spaces. While the plan of *Idea House I* was compact and open in the manner of the 'minimum house,' the exterior, with its huge windows and asymmetrical roofline, were a departure from the small windows and conventional pitched roofs of the FHA's illustrated designs. It comprised a living-room, bedroom, kitchen, guestroom/study, bathroom, and service rooms. The foyer led directly into the living area, and a glass-walled partition between this area and the living space helped to keep the cold out during the winter months. The living area featured large expanses of weather-proof windows that slid horizontally to open and close, and could be removed easily for cleaning. A separate entrance led out from the living area into the landscaped museum grounds. In consideration of the long, dark winters, the large windows allowed for maximum sunlight, while the overhanging eaves helped to keep the interior cool in the summer.[24]

The bedroom and adjacent study, which was designed to function as a guest bedroom when needed, were located off the living and dining area, away from the service rooms. They were delineated by a leather-clad soundproof sliding screen that partitioned the sitting area from the sleeping area. The kitchen exemplified efficiency and the latest in technology. Featuring stainless-steel walls and ceiling, the kitchen boasted all-electric appliances, including a Westinghouse refrigerator and dishwasher and a Frigidaire range. Adjacent to the kitchen was a utility room, a relatively new multipurpose room type that typically housed appliances such as automatic washing-machines.[25] The bathroom was placed between the living area and bedroom, and was designed to be hygienic and easy to clean, using the most up-to-date fixtures. The second floor of *Idea House I* consisted solely of an enclosed sun porch, and exploited an extensive use of glass for maximum solar exposure.

6.2

Idea House I under construction, 1941, Malcolm and Miriam Lein, architects.
Photo: Walker Art Center, Minneapolis

Stylistically, *Idea House I* reflected a general ambivalence to modernist design, which in domestic architecture was understood as the 'box-like structures so many people dislike,' as Defenbacher explained in his letter to potential vendors. It was devoid of typical modernist characteristics, such as a flat roof or use of industrial materials. However, filled with modern conveniences, hygienic appliances, and employing economical use of materials and space, it reflected the FHA definition of 'modern.' It exhibited a stylistic reticence based on the desire to appeal to the greatest number of people, and an emphasis on modernity as a measure of living standards. Additionally, the FHA considered overtly modernist homes to be risky loans, perhaps providing the Walker incentive to present a house that visitors could more realistically mine for 'ideas.'[26]

Despite its status as a WPA art center, the Walker received very little government funding for the construction of *Idea House I*.[27] With almost no budget to construct the house, Defenbacher solicited materials and goods from local businesses.[28] The majority of the low-cost, locally produced goods and materials used in *Idea House I* were donated by local suppliers. All the furniture for *Idea House I* came from a single retailer, New England Furniture. It is not clear from the exhibition archives if this was a curatorial decision based on the quality of their merchandise, or one of convenience, suggesting that, in spite of the intentions of the Walker to display the best examples of home equipment, the goods displayed to a certain extent reflected both local availability and the exigencies of a very limited budget.[29]

Many vendors sought to place sales representatives on-site for the duration of the exhibition. The Walker briefly considered hiring one or two people to provide information to visitors on all the various goods within *Idea House I*, but ultimately came up with a solution that offered businesses the opportunity to promote their wares and visitors the chance to visit the house without being overwhelmed by salespeople. *Idea House I* was extensively documented in an illustrated insert in the *Minneapolis Star and Tribune*, published in conjunction with its opening.[30] While this insert resembled an editorial feature article, it was in fact a paid advertisement organized by the Walker to coincide with the public opening of *Idea House I*. In addition to descriptions of each area of the house, the insert contained dozens of advertisements for companies and goods included in the house, including Andersen Windows, linoleum installers, mill workers, a variety of electronic houseware manufacturers, and the local electric utility, Northern States Power Company. On leaving the house, all visitors received a copy of the insert and an envelope filled with promotional literature from the vendors of appliances and goods featured inside the house. Each envelope also contained an information request form, permitting visitors to ask for even more detailed information on services and items of their choice. In this way, the visitors could view and experience the house without immediately apparent commercial intervention, yet they still had access to all pertinent information about any item or product displayed in the house, and the vendors benefited from the exposure afforded by the exhibition.[31]

The Walker's success in soliciting materials and goods for *Idea House I* was due in part to manipulation of its unique position between the consumer and producers, through which it sought to shape visitors' tastes in goods, and its willingness to use sales methods such as the advertorial format of the explanatory guide, a technique that, as Kate Forde has shown, was increasingly employed by American advertisers from the late 1920s.[32] Rather than selling goods, however, the Walker claimed it was selling its 'ideas,' and the implications of these ideas were highly appealing to businesses with real goods to sell. The museum appeared to possess what the trade desperately needed: an already established clientele, specifically interested in building modern homes. This was reflected not only in the ease with which the Walker was able to solicit materials, but also in the advertising placed by contributing vendors in the *Tribune and Star* insert. Typical of these, the local Westinghouse appliance dealer took out a full-page notice enjoining readers to visit *Idea House I* to see for themselves their latest product, the 1941 model 'Martha Washington' refrigerator:

> The *Idea House* has, and every house needs, Westinghouse for better living. On your visit to the *Idea House*, see for yourself the results of

Westinghouse engineering skill, scientific research – and modern design
. . . See the "Martha Washington" today, in the Walker *Idea House* – the
refrigerator that looks as good as it *is!*[33]

Significantly, the guide concedes that building costs rendered *Idea
House I* beyond the reach of most prospective builders. At around US$7,000 for
construction alone, without land, appliances, or furnishings, it was considerably more
expensive than the average FHA-sponsored new home.[34] The guide sidesteps this
rather substantial obstacle to its viewers' ability to build their own *Idea House*-style
homes by reinforcing that it was not meant to represent a real house, but instead
it incorporated as many ideas as possible into its design, claiming, 'This house is *not*
a model or ideal for any particular family group. It is a *House of Ideas* which may be
applied to any home of any price.'[35]

In spite of its prohibitive expense, *Idea House I* proved exceptionally
popular with the general public, and by the end of its exhibition in the autumn of 1941,
56,000 people had visited the house, of whom 9,666 requested product information.[36] There is no evidence indicating that *Idea House I* was used, as Defenbacher
originally suggested, as a laboratory for the museum's home design programs after
it closed to visitors in 1941. It is not clear from exhibition documents why the house
closed, or whether attendance was high enough to pay for building the house, as
Defenbacher had initially hoped, though World War II, which America entered
immediately following the attack on Pearl Harbor on December 7, 1941 undoubtedly
contributed to its closing. *Idea House I* was subsequently used as staff housing, and
the Walker continued to honor requests to visit the house throughout the 1940s.

Idea House II: a post-war 'House of Ideas'

Beginning in the autumn of 1945, Defenbacher, curator Hilde Reiss and Assistant
Director William Friedman began planning another full-scale domestic architecture
exhibition, *Idea House II*.[37] While *Idea House I* addressed housing issues of the pre-
war period, with its economical use of materials and space and of the latest
appliances, *Idea House II* faced a different set of housing issues. Most important was
the extraordinary post-war housing crisis exacerbated by returning veterans and their
families, and the concomitant explosion of tract housing developments of varying
quality across America.

Defenbacher's decision to continue *Idea House* project at this time was
logical and practical, considering the nationwide preoccupation with housing and
the severity of the post-war housing crisis. Millions of families and young married
couples were forced to live with relatives, temporary military housing converted
into emergency housing, and even converted chicken coops and barns.[38] The
government sought to stave off potential political instability and unrest provoked by
the housing crunch by providing substantial financial benefits to returning soldiers.

The Serviceman's Readjustment Act, commonly known as the GI Bill of Rights, took effect in 1944. Providing funds for veterans' education and affordable housing were the bill's highest mandates. Under the auspices of the FHA in 1946, the Veterans Administration established the Veteran's Emergency Housing Act, under which veterans were exempt from down-payments on certain loans. While GIs qualified for home loans, the program did not remedy the underlying housing shortage, which was exacerbated by inflation and shortages of essential building materials.[39] By some estimates, the number of housing units needed in 1946 alone exceeded the total number built from 1940–5.[40]

While *Idea House I* attempted to suggest solutions to American consumers preoccupied with economic hardship and impending involvement in war, *Idea House II* sought to prescribe housing ideas for a general public refocused on a critical housing shortage. This was coupled with a bewildering number of new construction materials, home appliances, and a surfeit of discretionary income for the first time in decades.[41] In its conception, *Idea House II* was a direct response to the rapid proliferation of standardized housing developments responding to this shortage, of which Levittown, James Levitt's factory-built housing development begun in 1946–7 is the best known.[42] These developments were popular because they were very inexpensive and quickly built. The price of the earliest Levittown home was US$6,990, against an average family income of US$4,119.[43] While a variety of exterior details and paint colors differentiated their exteriors, each Levittown house possessed identical plans. With easy payment plans and guaranteed FHA loan approval, developments such as Levittown offered convenient, quick solutions to families in need of homes.[44]

All of these elements provoked the Walker to pursue *Idea House II*. The exhibition's press release emphatically describes the urgent need for good housing design:

> The excessive demand for housing has opened flood gates for cheap construction, impossible designs, shoddy materials and indiscriminate taste. Many buyers and builders will accept anything that will approximately keep out the worst weather. Bad house architecture is more plentiful today than can be excused even by current extreme conditions.[45]

Like its predecessor, *Idea House II* was not meant to be a model home, nor a prescription for prefab development. It was, literally, a house of ideas, where visitors could come and absorb new concepts in design, building materials, furnishings and technology, and apply them where and how they wished in their own homes, preferably with the aid of an architect. As with *Idea House I*, plans to the house were never made available for purchase.

The Walker again needed funding for this next experimental and expensive program. This time, the project was made financially possible by a unique collaboration between the museum and a local bank, Northwestern National Bank, specifically its Home Institute unit. Additional funding was provided by the local gas utility, Minneapolis Gas Light Company. Northwestern Bank founded its Home Institute shortly after World War II as a response to both the critical housing shortage and rising consumer confusion over the financial costs and practical application of new building materials.[46] The Home Institute pledged to assist its members in budgeting their building projects, with a special emphasis on understanding the uses and managing the expenses of new building materials. The Institute also provided a comprehensive reference collection of over one hundred volumes on building, remodeling, and decorating, as well as an extensive collection of wallpaper, fabric, and paint samples. Interior-design specialists were on hand to assist customers in devising plans and budgets for their home projects.

The design brief for *Idea House II* was a modest house for a family of four that provided flexible use of public spaces, afforded privacy for all family members, and used readily available materials, with minimum specialized building materials or techniques. *Idea House II* was designed by Reiss, Friedman and Malcolm Lein, who together with his wife Miriam had designed the original *Idea House*. It opened to the public in September 1947 and remained on view for six months. Measuring 19,000 cubic feet, this split-level house featured an open plan, with private living spaces delineated by folding partitions. The house was built using straightforward gypsum board construction and readily available building materials such as concrete block, plywood, and glass (Figure 6.3).

The living-room was the largest and most flexible space in the house, and the museum's didactic materials referred to it as a four-in-one room: in it a family could eat, play, work, or entertain. It featured extensive expanses of WindoWall™, a prefabricated product somewhere between a traditional window and a curtain wall, which helped the small space to feel more integrated into the exterior garden. The room was furnished with the most progressive furniture designs of the day, including Eames dining and lounge chairs from Herman Miller, Knoll Planning Unit sofas, a Saarinen Grasshopper chair also from Knoll, lighting fixtures designed by Walter von Nessen, and built-in storage units by George Nelson, called Storagewall™. While many of these furniture designs are today icons of mid-twentieth-century design, in 1947 they were new, untested products by designers largely unknown to the general public. *Idea House II* inventories typically cite only the furniture manufacturers, not the designers' names.[47] Unlike *Idea House I*, numerous manufacturers supplied the furnishings. Several of these designs exploited technologies or methods developed as part of the war effort: the Eames's molded plywood furniture evolved from their work for the US Army creating splints, and George Nelson claimed that his early modular storage designs came from observing stacked ammunition storage in fighter planes.[48]

The kitchen could be opened to the living-room or cordoned off with a sliding screen. It was a compact space, featuring all the latest home appliances, including a dishwasher. While more and more households possessed these appliances, and women became increasingly important consumers of home equipment,

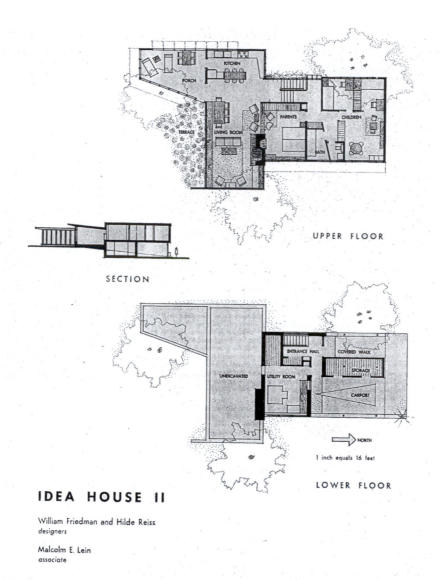

6.3
Idea House II **plan,
William Friedman
and Hilde Reiss
with Malcolm
Lein, architects.**
Photo: Walker Art
Center, Minneapolis

UPPER FLOOR

SECTION

LOWER FLOOR

NORTH

1 inch equals 16 feet

IDEA HOUSE II

William Friedman and Hilde Reiss
designers

Malcolm E. Lein
associate

there are indications that new technology could actually add to a homemaker's stress. In September 1947, the month *Idea House II* opened, an article appeared in *McCall's* titled 'So You are Learning to Cope with your Range and Refrigerator.' It advised readers on the most efficient uses of these appliances, suggesting that many were unfamiliar with how best to use them. By reinforcing the importance of a newly equipped kitchen, and emphasizing the anxiety it might cause, this *McCall's* editorial intersected with the publication's considerable consumer appliance advertising in a manner that both reinforced the role of *McCall's* as a homemaker's reference, and the advertisers' agendas of promoting goods.[49] By offering advice ostensibly free of commercial subtext, *Idea House II* sought to calm just these types of consumer anxieties.

6.4
**Children's study,
Idea House II.**
Photograph:
Rolphe Dauphin for
Walker Art Center,
Minneapolis

The living quarters were on the upper level. In one of the most significant contrasts between the 1941 and 1947 *Idea House* projects, *Idea House II* featured distinct, specific areas for children. The plan featured room for two children's sleeping areas, with folding partitions for privacy, and a shared study and play area (Figure 6.4). The house had only one bathroom, which was typical for new house construction at the time.[50]

While *Idea House II* was not especially innovative when compared to influential modern homes of this period, such as the Eames's Case Study House 8 in Los Angeles (1945–9), it was not necessarily intended to push the boundaries of modern architecture. Instead, it represented a moderate, modern home to which visitors could identify as both reasonable and attainable, using readily available home building materials, rather than the many industrial materials used in the Eames house.[51] It was also markedly more innovative than other local model homes. For example, the St Paul Home Show, just across the Mississippi river from Minneapolis, featured a model house valued at US$15,000, which was given away in a jingle-writing contest at the end of its exhibition in September 1947. With its low profile, hipped roof, and small windows, this house by contrast emphasizes *Idea House II*'s more progressive elements, such as the rambling split-level plan and sloping roof.[52]

In terms of cost, *Idea House II* was even more prohibitive than its predecessor. While original estimates were around US$11,000, the completed project came in well over three times that amount. According to a private-sector study published in November 1947, the average cost in Minneapolis of building and furnishing a typical six-room house with one bath, excluding land costs, was US$11,700. The cost of *Idea House II*, in spite of its organizers' efforts to use standard building methods and inexpensive materials, was well out of range of the average home buyer.[53]

Public reaction to *Idea House II*: 'How livable is a modern house?'

In order for *Idea House II* to succeed, either conceptually or financially, it needed a wide audience, and so the Walker launched an extensive publicity campaign with the opening of the house in the autumn of 1947. Just as in the first *Idea House*, visitors received an information packet filled with promotional materials from manufacturers featured in the house. Both Northwest National Bank and Minneapolis Gas Light Company participated in extensive direct mail campaigns, including *Idea House II* promotional stuffers in bank statements and gas bills.[54] The Walker, together with the *Minneapolis Morning Tribune*, sponsored a letter-writing competition for readers interested in experiencing life in a modern house. Four distinct family types were sought out to spend a weekend at *Idea House II*: a young married couple with no children, a couple with young children, a working couple with teenage children, and a couple with a teenage child at home and another away at college. Hundreds of contestants wrote in, describing their current living circumstances and their interest in modern housing design. The winners of the competition, all of them white and middle-class, largely reflected the homogenous population of Minnesota at the time.[55]

One of the winning entries did not meet any of these original criteria, yet made a compelling case for inclusion. Lois Miller, Helen Tully, and Dorothy Vine wrote to the Walker, explaining that the competition organizers had left out a sizable and important classification, the 'large army that falls under the three girls who share an apartment' group, and expressed keen interest in *Idea House II*. In their cheerful, forthright demand to be included in this exploration of modern living, these young professionals also articulated the growing importance of women, often with their own incomes, as active critics and consumers of modern design. As Misses Tully, Miller, and Vine wrote in their competition letter, 'We have no in-laws or teen-age children, in fact we don't even have husbands. . . . Don't you think you're overlooking a major factor in your household cross-section? We buy food and subscribe to the papers and pay our phone bills just like any family . . . and we know what we want in the way of comfortable living'[56] (Figure 6.5). Of particular interest to these women were the comfort and convenience afforded by household appliances such as dishwashers, and enough closet space and hot water to accommodate all three of them with ease – all luxuries in the post-war housing crisis.

6.5
**Lois Miller, Helen
Tully, and Dorothy
Vine in the living-
room of *Idea
House II*, 1947.**
Photo: Walker Art
Center, Minneapolis

6.5
**Lois Miller, Helen
Tully, and Dorothy
Vine in the living-
room of *Idea
House II*, 1947.**
Photo: Walker Art
Center, Minneapolis

Idea House II received a great deal of national press from both popular and trade publications. One minor mention of the project in the *New York Times Magazine* on November 2, 1947 produced over 400 requests to the Walker for information.[57] *McCalls's* secured exclusive consumer rights to cover *Idea House II*, and published an article on the house in its January 1948 issue. The article introduced the project to a nation of magazine readers, and the Walker was subsequently inundated with requests for information from readers across America. *Progressive Architecture* held exclusive trade publication rights and featured an extensive, illustrated article on it for its February 1948 issue, exposing *Idea House II* to architects and designers around the world.[58]

In the autumn of 1948, *Life* arranged for the Stensruds, a family with two young children, to live in the house for a week and document their reactions to the design, furnishings, appliances, and other aspects of *Idea House II*. The ensuing article, 'How Livable is a Modern House,' offered a frank assessment of the design program and furnishings by a stereotypically white, middle-class American family, published in a widely read general-interest magazine.[59] The lead sentence of the article indicates a healthy skepticism of modern architecture's photogenic appeal: 'Modern architecture makes handsome movie sets, offices, hotel lobbies, and photographs, but how is it for year-round living?'. With photographs of the Stensruds in their own home contrasted with their *Idea House* stay, the article voiced the family's general enthusiasm for *Idea House II*, but they indicated that they preferred adapting some of its features to their own house, to moving to an entirely new modern home.

Eager to capitalize on the press and attention *Idea House II* generated, retailers featured it in their consumer advertising. Eva Zeisel's new Town and Country dinnerware, produced by Minnesota-based Red Wing Pottery, appeared in an advertisement in a local paper for Jacobs & Co. department store. The advertising copy assumed that readers would visit *Idea House* and urged them to seek out the dinnerware: 'Red Wing's Town and Country – as featured in *Idea House II*. Look for this gay modern pottery when you visit, and see how well it fits into the modern concept of gracious, informal living.'[60] In March 1948, *Fortune* magazine contacted the Walker to enquire about using *Idea House II* in conjunction with an Oldsmobile car advertising campaign. The campaign featured sketches of 'modern-design homes' together with the latest model Oldsmobiles, both of which are described in the advertising copy as 'Futuramic.'[61] In this unmistakable reference to Norman Bel Geddes' *Futurama* pavilion at the 1939 New York World's Fair, two prevailing influences of the post-war period converge in an advertising image: the single-family suburban house and the automobile. *Futurama*, sponsored by General Motors, the parent company of Oldsmobile, propelled visitors on a massive conveyor belt across a large diorama of America in 1960, where families lived in suburban developments, and urban centers dominated by huge skyscrapers were reached by car. While no evidence suggests that either the window display or the car advertisement were ever produced, these examples emphasize the distinction between the economic climate of the first *Idea House* and the post-war environment of the second. Free from the financial constraints of the depression and the manufacturing restrictions of the war years, businesses actively sought consumers' disposable incomes through novel marketing techniques, and *Idea House II* suggested such opportunities.

While the house attracted around 35,000 visitors – far fewer than the anticipated 100,000 – it generated a great deal of local and national interest from people looking to build a house, and the Walker received hundreds of requests from visitors hoping to purchase the plans to *Idea House II*.[62] People who never visited the house saw it in the *McCall's* feature and wrote to the museum with highly specific technical questions. The museum always referred these correspondents to the *Everyday Art Quarterly* dedicated to *Idea House II*, reminding them that it was meant to be a 'house of ideas,' not a model house, and recommended the use of a trained architect in generating a house plan that was specific to individual needs and budgets. *Idea House II* closed permanently to the public in July 1948 and, like its predecessor, became Walker staff housing, until its demolition in 1968.

Museums across the country took note of *Idea House II*'s popularity, and many of Defenbacher's colleagues wrote to him inquiring about the logistical considerations of the project. Philip L. Goodwin, a New York architect, MoMA trustee, and co-designer with Edward Durrell Stone of the 1939 Museum of Modern Art building, wrote to him in 1948, asking for advice on creating a similar exhibition in New York:

In connection with the Museum of Modern Art here in New York, I have had talks with Mr. Philip Johnson on the subject of erecting a house by some well-known architect in the very small garden attached to our museum. Mr. Johnson informs me that you have done something of this kind recently with astoundingly successful results . . . Would you be good enough to confirm this, and also let me know how long the house stood in the garden, and any other details, such as cost of erection, taxes, etc.? Were you able to sell the house when you had finished with it in the garden, and what was the removal cost?[63]

MoMA did in fact pursue a similar project, and Marcel Breuer's *House in the Museum Garden* went on view from April 14 to October 30, 1949. Designed as a house for a growing family, Breuer's plan allowed for an extension to be built over the garage, providing additional space and privacy as the children grew older, and this was the version built for MoMA. Like the *Idea Houses*, Breuer's house was fully furnished and wired for electricity. Materials and contracting work were contributed in kind and listed in the MoMA bulletin dedicated to the project.[64] Much of the furniture was designed by Breuer, including what may have been the world's first remote-control television, which retailed for an astonishing US$900.[65] Furnishings and household items not designed by Breuer were supplied by the Manhattan modern design retailer, New Design, Inc., so that rather than representing a selection of goods curated by museum staff from numerous sources, the interior of the House in the Museum Garden was more closely tied to a specific retailer. Unlike the Walker, MoMA and Breuer did make plans for this house available for purchase, and the dedicated MoMA bulletin included approximate construction costs for various suburban locations around the New York City area.[66]

While many scholars consider the *House in the Museum Garden*, along with the Case Study House project in California, as true harbingers of modern home design in America, both of these projects commenced well after the Walker's *Idea House* program.[67] Despite its original popularity, the *Idea House* project is little-known today, for a variety of reasons. First and foremost, MoMA's decision to employ Breuer guaranteed the house's legacy within the history of architecture, whereas none of the *Idea House* architects ever achieved the national prominence Breuer enjoyed. Unlike the *Idea Houses*, Breuer's house survives, having been moved to upstate New York in 1950. Additionally, Breuer's house was designed along the lines of a conventional model home, as a complete house design with plans available for purchase, rather than the almost ephemeral concept of the 'house of ideas.' At least four versions of this house were built throughout the Northeast shortly after the exhibition.[68] Nonetheless, the *Idea House* project, with its fully functional, furnished houses and extensive documentation and cataloguing of items for viewers' benefit, was in all likelihood a direct model for MoMA's more famous endeavor.

Conclusion

In its conception, the *Idea House* project was intrinsically idealistic, and the very gravity of the housing situation it sought to address precluded its immediate success. Most Americans simply did not have the time or resources to hire an architect, buy land, and build a house, especially when large housing developments offered easy financing and rapid construction. Nevertheless, both houses articulated some of the most pressing issues of their time: the dire need for quality housing, improved living standards through technology and a concomitant definition of 'modern' to indicate this improved standard, and the consumer's importance to both the economy and to good design via purchasing power. As suggested by its name, *Idea House*'s real contribution to housing and museum practice took the ephemeral forms of ideas.

In discussing *Idea House II*, Defenbacher wrote that 'a man's house is his art,' implying that the average homeowner is an active producer of art simply by virtue of furnishing his or her home.[69] The consumption of construction materials, appliances, furnishings, and other household items are necessary to this creative act, and both *Idea Houses* served as exemplary illustrations of this concept. Appropriating the methods of commercial home developers and consumer goods manufacturers, the *Idea Houses* intersected the worlds of industry and art institution in a radical manner, creating a curatorial intervention in the conventional experience of the model home. These promotional techniques were not intended to sell specific goods or materials, but rather to promote a collection of ideas about homebuilding and design. The ideological refusal to make either of the *Idea House* blueprints available to the public contributed to the project's eventual obscurity, but it confirms the Walker's dual goals of providing creative and objective suggestions to the visitor/homeowner, and reimagining the nature of the art exhibition. The high attendance figures of the exhibitions and the national media interest in the houses reinforce both the severity of the housing crisis extant throughout both exhibitions, and the degree to which housing was a national preoccupation. They also suggest that the *Idea Houses* were, in fact, influential to individuals interested in homebuilding, and art institutions seeking innovative ways of both attracting visitors and displaying design.

Acknowledgements

A version of this paper was originally published in *Journal of Design History* (17: 4, pp. 377–96) and is reproduced with kind permission of the Design History Society and Oxford University Press. I am most grateful to the *Journal*'s editorial board, and particularly to Grace Lees-Maffei, for their many helpful suggestions and comments. Special thanks are due also to Jill Vetter at the Walker Art Center Archives, whose generous assistance and deep knowledge of the *Idea House* project helped to make this research possible, and to Karen Gysin, who made the Walker's archival photographs of *Idea House* available for this publication.

Notes

1 As Gwendolyn Wright has observed, Americans have long used domestic architecture, and debates surrounding it, as a means of shaping social and political agendas. The single-family house has proved the most popular and fertile icon of family life and economic success across several centuries of America history. See G. Wright, *Building the Dream: A Social History of Housing in America*, Cambridge, MA: MIT Press, 1983.

2 The Museum of Contemporary Art, Los Angeles 1989 exhibition on the Case Study houses featured full-scale reconstructions of some of them; see Elizabeth A. T. Smith, ed., *Blueprints for Modern Living: History and Legacy of the Case Study Houses* (ex. catalogue), Los Angeles and Cambridge, MA: Museum of Contemporary Art, Los Angeles and MIT Press, 1989. A full-scale reproduction of Le Corbusier's 1925 Pavilion de L'Esprit Nouveau was part of the same institution's 2001 exhibition, *L'Esprit Nouveau. Purism in Paris 1918–25*; see Carol S. Eliel and Françoise Duclos, *L'Esprit Nouveau: Purism in Paris 1918–25* (ex. catalogue), Los Angeles and New York: Museum of Contemporary Art, Los Angeles and Harry N. Abrams, 2001.

3 B. Colomina, 'The Exhibitionist House,' in R. Ferguson, ed., *At the End of the Century: One Hundred Years of Architecture*, New York: Harry N. Abrams, 1998, p. 151.

4 US Government Bureau of Labor Statistics Consumer Price Index, www.bls.gov/cpi/#data (accessed May 22, 2005).

5 As Nicolas Maffei has shown, Dana sought to reform the role of the museum through his exhibitions of industrial design, which, like Defenbacher, he felt were closer to the lives and interests of most people than painting or sculpture. See N. Maffei, 'John Cotton Dana and the Politics of Exhibiting Industrial Art in the US, 1909–29,' *Journal of Design History*, 13: 4, 2000, pp. 302–4; Defenbacher, Foreword to *Walker Art Center* (pamphlet), 1940, p. 4, in Holger Cahill Papers, roll 1107, frame 177. Archives of American Art, Smithsonian Institution, Washington, DC.

6 Defenbacher, Foreword to *Walker Art Center*, p. 10.

7 Daniel S. Defenbacher to Joseph Worshek, the Kohler Company, October 3, 1940, in Director's Files/Daniel S. Defenbacher, box 3, folder 2, Walker Art Center Archives, Minneapolis, MN.

8 Ibid.

9 See B. Kelly, 'The Houses of Levittown in the Context of Postwar American Culture,' in D. Slaton and R. Schiffer, *Preserving the Recent Past*, Washington, DC: Historic Preservation Foundation, 1995. Available at www.cr.nps.gov/nr/publications/bulletins/suburbs/resources.htm, accessed May 22, 2005.

10 R. Tobey, *Technology as Freedom: The New Deal and the Electrical Modernization of the American Home*, Berkeley, CA: University of California Press, 1996, p. 100; Wright, *Building the Dream*, p. 240.

11 Despite its goal to stabilize American home life through improved living standards, the FHA did not view all families as equally deserving of its resources. It actively participated in discriminatory lending, encouraging neighborhood racial and ethnic homogeneity by refusing to lend money in predominantly African-American or Jewish areas, claiming that the risk of bad loans was too high. These 'red lining' practices continued overtly until 1950, two years after a Supreme Court ruled that such lending practices were discriminatory and illegal, and covertly through the 1960s. For some Americans, the FHA enabled home ownership when it had been but a remote dream. For others it simply reinforced the notion that the American Dream itself could be a restrictive covenant, selectively accessible depending on race and religion. For example, in the post-war period, the FHA refused to rescind or deny loans to James Levitt's Levittown development, even though he expressly forbade the sale of Levittown homes to anyone but 'members of the Caucasian race,' although non-white domestic staff were permitted at Levittown. See *New York Times*, March 19, 1949, pp. 12, 19; Wright, *Building the Dream*, p. 248; Tobey, *Technology as Freedom*, p. 108; *Measuring America: The Decennial Censuses from 1790–2000*, US Census Bureau, US Department of Commerce, Economics and Statistics Administration, April 2002, pp. 124–8.

12 These leaflets, published as *Technical Bulletins*, were published between 1936 and 1946. Several of them, notably 'Modern Design' and 'Principles of Planning Small Houses,' were revised several times over these years. The new editions took into account changes in domestic housing design and construction.

13 'A modern house is defined as "modern" in the sense generally used. It will be likely to be found to be a house of unusual livability and convenience, but that it possesses any revolutionary qualities will rarely be surmised. . . . Such houses are modern in the elemental sense.' Federal Housing Administration (FHA), *Technical Bulletin #2: Modern Design*, rev. ed., Washington, DC: US Government Printing Office, 1940; FHA, *Technical Bulletin #4: Principles of Planning Small Houses*, rev. ed., Washington, DC: US Government Printing Office, 1940, pp. 14–15.

14 H. Searing, 'Case Study Houses: In the Grand Modern Tradition,' in *Blueprints for Modern Living*, p. 108; R. Plunz, *A History of Housing in New York City: Dwelling Type and Social Change*, New York: Columbia Press, 1990, p. 232.

15 Plunz, *A History of Housing in New York City: Dwelling Type and Social Change*, p. 233.

16 *Cultural and Social Aspects of the New York World's Fair, 1939, of Special Interest to Women*, prepared for the National Advisory Committee on Women's Participation, New York World's Fair, New York, 1939, p. 49 (italics added).

17 Ibid.

18 *Architectural Forum* 71, July 1939, p. 66.

19 'FHA says trend toward low-priced homes growing,' *Minneapolis Sunday Tribune and Journal*, June 1, 1941, p. 12.

20 The Home Building Center also reinforced the importance of electricity as a key force in modernizing the American home with a large-scale mural by Frances Scott Bradford, with electricity as its theme. *New York World's Fair Information Manual*, New York World's Fair 1939, unpaginated manual (entries are alphabetical according to fair departments).

21 *New York World's Fair Information Manual*; Whalen cited in J. Meikle, *Twentieth Century Limited: Industrial Design in* America, Philadelphia, PA: Temple University Press, 1979, p. 197: In this highly theatrical exhibition, visitors went on a bird's-eye view tour of a vision of America 20 years hence, escorted via a large conveyor belt. Bel Geddes' *Futurama* was by far the most popular exhibition at the fair, drawing an estimated 27,500 visitors daily. It also exerted a profound influence on subsequent corporate exhibitions, redefining the way in which businesses courted consumers in fair environments. See Meikle, 'A Microcosm of the Machine-Age World,' *Twentieth Century Limited*, pp. 189–210. See also R. Marchand, 'The Designers go to the Fair: Norman Bel Geddes, The General Motors *Futurama*, and the Visit-to-the-Factory Transformed', *Design Issues*, 8: 2, 1982, pp. 23–40.

22 Searing, 'Case Study Houses: In the Grand Modern Tradition', *Blueprints for Living*, p. 109.

23 A. Blauvelt, *Ideas for Modern Living: The Idea House Project/Everyday Art Gallery* (brochure), Minneapolis, MN: Walker Art Center, 2000, p. 6.

24 *Minneapolis Tribune and Star Journal*, June 1, 1941, unpaginated insert.

25 Gwendolyn Wright notes that the utility room was a recently evolved room type purposely created to house new appliances, yet by the mid-1940s it was commonly found in most new homes. See Wright, *Building the Dream*, p. 255.

26 In *Technical Bulletin #2: Modern Design*, the FHA systems of property rating and 'adjustment for nonconformity' were laid out. This booklet made explicit the FHA position on homes of 'so-called modern design' that featured extraneous features that might be vulnerable to shifts in fashion. The bulletin is quite clear that these homes would receive low ratings for 'nonconformity' to FHA-approved definitions of good design.

27 Rolf Ueland of the Minnesota Arts Council, in a memo to its Board of the Trustees, stated that the WPA was anxious about supporting the construction of an exhibition house when 'the real needs of food, clothing and shelter of so many people are still unsatisfied.' Ueland recommended that the house be funded separately from the Walker's WPA projects, and exhibition-related documents seem to bear this out, though there is no existing budget or other document to absolutely clarify the issue. Memo from Rolf Ueland to Board of Trustees, Minnesota Arts Council, October 25, 1940, in *Idea House I* Exhibition Files, box 1, folder 9.

28 Funds were so limited and the project so experimental that Defenbacher appealed to a member of the Walker family for assistance. Archie D. Walker agreed to personally take out the mortgage on *Idea House I* when the Walker was unable to get bank funding for construction on its own. See *Idea House I* Exhibition Files, box 1, folder 9, Walker Art Center Archives.

29 Some businesses did reject the Walker's petition for goods for a variety of reasons. The largest local department store, Dayton's, refused to contribute in any way because the house would be open on Sunday, a conflict with their strict policy. Kohler simply refused to answer any of the Walker's requests. See *Idea House I* Exhibition Files, box 1, folder 9.

30 *Minneapolis Tribune and Star Journal*, June 1, 1941, unpaginated insert.

31 *Idea House I* Exhibition Files, box 1, folder 9, Walker Art Center Archives.

32 K. Forde, 'Celluloid Dreams: the Marketing of Cutex in America, 1916–35,' *Journal of Design History*, 15: 3, 2002, pp. 181–2.

33 *Minneapolis Tribune and Star Journal*, June 1, 1941, unpaginated insert.

34 While the FHA loan ceiling was US$20,000, the majority of loans were for US$6,000–8,000. See Wright, *Building the Dream*, p. 242.

35 'This house is *not* a model or ideal for any particular family group. It is a *House of Ideas* which may be applied to any home of any price. Actually the house adequately fits the needs of two people with or without one young child. . . . The cost of the *Idea House* as it stands is excessive for the average builder because there are more refinements and more *ideas* in it than the average home owner would necessarily need. . . . By the selection and elimination which would naturally be applied by the individual builder the basic *Idea House* could be built at reasonable cost. The most important *idea* of the House is *spaciousness*,' *An Explanatory Guide to the Idea House*, p. 12.

36 *Idea House I* Exhibition Files, box 1, folder 9, Walker Art Center Archives.

37 In 1945, the Walker established the Everyday Art Gallery to display industrial design and objects of every day household use. Hilde Reiss, a Bauhaus-educated architect and designer, curated the gallery. Reiss, who emigrated to America in 1933, came to the Walker by way of New York, where she worked in the offices of a number of prominent architects and designers, including Russell Wright, Gilbert Rohde, and Norman Bel Geddes. She also taught under Rohde at the Design Laboratory, a WPA-sponsored school influenced by the Bauhaus. Rohde hoped the school would fill a need for an American design school that 'coordinates training in esthetics, products, machine fabrication, and merchandising.' For more on Reiss's career, see *Idea House Oral History Project, 1999–2000*, Walker Art Center Archives, pp. 22–33, 45–6. For details on the Design Laboratory, see 'WPA Established Design School,' *New York Times*, December 2, 1935, 19; J. Keyes, 'WPA Educators Blazing Trail with School in Design Industry,' *New York Times*, October 25, 1936, N5. It was at the Design Laboratory that she met architect William Friedman, with whom she collaborated on a number of projects, including a house in northern New York State built in 1939 and subsequently featured in *Architectural Record* ('Plywood and Fieldstone Used in Same House: William Friedman and Hilde Reiss,' *Architectural Record*, 85, March 1939, pp. 44–8). Friedman joined the Walker as Assistant Director of Exhibitions in 1944, and Reiss was appointed curator of Everyday Art in 1945.

38 Wright, *Building the Dream*, p. 242.

39 Ibid.

40 Plunz, *A History of Housing in New York City*, p. 145. Some blamed outdated building codes and regulations that failed to take account of new building materials and techniques developed during the war for sluggish construction rates. The Monsanto Corporation published Marcel Breuer's unrealized design addressing the anticipated housing crisis, the prefabricated Plas-2-Point house built of plywood coated with Monsanto plastic, in its eponymous magazine in 1943. By 1946, another *Monsanto* article titled, 'Can We Build Enough Homes?' called for the reform of building standards to incorporate new materials such as plywood and plastics, products produced by the company. Despite Monsanto's financial stake in the widespread acceptance and use of these products, these articles illustrate some of the many complications inherent in housing construction immediately after the war. M. Breuer, 'Designing to Live in the Post War House,' *Monsanto*, 22: 5, 1943, pp. 22–4; 'Can We Build Enough Homes?,' *Monsanto*, 26: 3, 1946, pp. 18–21.

41 As Ronald Tobey has shown, much commercial manufacturing was converted to defense production during the war, curtailing the purchase of expensive appliances. Workers instead saved their extra income. See Tobey, *Technology as Freedom*, p. 166.

42 See Wright, *Building the Dream*, pp. 251–3; see also M. Filler, 'Building Organic Form: Architecture, Ceramics, Glass and Metal in the 1940s and 1950s,' in *Vital Forms: American Art and Design in the Atomic Age, 1940–60* (ex. catalogue), New York: Brooklyn Museum and Harry N. Abrams, 2001, pp. 132–6.

43 K. T. Jackson, *Crabgrass Frontier: The Suburbanization of the United States*, New York: Oxford University Press, 1985, p. 234; US Census Bureau, Historical Income Tables – Families – Table 1. Available at www.census.gov/income/ftp/histinc/CPI-U-RS/family/f01.lst; accessed May 22, 2005.

44 In 1949, the down-payment on a Levittown home was US$90, with monthly payments of US$58. See *New York Times*, March 7, 1949, p. 21; B. Kelly, 'The Houses of Levittown in the Context of Postwar American Culture.' Many of the developments were also poorly built, eventually prompting a Senate investigation. See Hayden, 'Model Homes for the Millions: Architects' Dreams, Builder's Boasts, Residents' Dilemmas,' in *Blueprints for Modern Living*, p. 199.

45 Undated press release, *Idea House II* Exhibition Files, box 15, folder 11, Walker Art Center Archives.

46 For more on the Home Institute, see 'Bank Program for Home Planners,' *Banking*, 15: 3, 1947, pp. 58–60.

47 For a complete description of *Idea House II*, its construction materials, techniques, furnishings, and appliances, see *Everyday Art Quarterly*, 5, 1947.

48 B. Colomina, 'Reflections on the Eames House,' *The Work of Charles and Ray Eames: A Legacy of Invention* (ex. catalogue), New York: The Vitra Design Museum and Harry N. Abrams, 1997, 137–8; 'Furnishing a Post-War House,' *Monsanto*, 22 (5), 1943, pp. 25–6.

49 'So You are Learning to Cope with your Range and Refrigerator,' *McCall's*, September 1947, pp. 48–50. This is the same technique used to reinforce reader loyalty earlier in the twentieth century in women's magazines such as *The Ladies Home Journal*, as demonstrated in Jennifer Scanlon's study, *Inarticulate Longings: The Ladies Home Journal, Gender and the Promises of Consumer Culture*, London: Routledge, 1995, p. 5.

50 Blauvelt, *Ideas for Modern Living*, p. 12.

51 E. McCoy, 'Case Study House #8,' *Blueprints for Modern Living*, pp. 51–3.

52 '$15,000 Home to be given away in Jingle Contest, Part of St. Paul Home Show,' *Minneapolis Tribune*, September 28, 1947, p. 12.

53 Blauvelt, p. 14; *Minneapolis Sunday Tribune*, November 2, 1947, p. 12.

54 Daniel S. Defenbacher to Henry McKnight, Editor of *Look*, November 12, 1947, in *Idea House II* Exhibition Files, box 15, folder 11, Walker Art Center Archives.

55 According to the 1950 census, no less than 99 percent of the state's almost three million residents were white. F. Hobbs and N. Stoops, Census Bureau, Census 2000 Special Reports, Series CENSR-4, *Demographic Trends in the 20th Century*, Washington, DC: US Government Printing Office, 2002, A-25, A-5, p. 128.

56 Lois Miller, Helen Tully, and Dorothy Vine to D. S. Defenbacher, September 24, 1947, in *Idea House II* Exhibition Files, box 16, folder 5, Walker Art Center Archives.

57 Blauvelt, *Ideas for Modern Living*, p. 13.

58 M.D. Gillies, 'This House will Help You Plan Your Own,' *McCall's Homemaking*, vol. 75, January 1948, pp. 44–53; 'Idea House II for the Walker Art Center,' *Progressive Architecture*, 28: 2, 1948, pp. 39–47.

59 'How Livable is a Modern House?', *Life*, 25 (16), 1948, pp. 105–8.

60 *Minneapolis Morning Tribune*, October 16, 1947. From the *Idea House II* scrapbook, Walker Art Center Archives.

61 A. D. Thomas for *Forbes* to D. S. Defenbacher, March 11, 1948, in *Idea House II* Exhibition Files, box 15, folder 11, Walker Art Center Archives.

62 Defenbacher was distraught that *Idea House II* was not drawing as many visitors as he had hoped, writing to Henry McKnight of *Look* magazine on November 12, 1947, 'We are getting about one third of the expected attendance to *Idea House II*. Believe me, we are painfully surprised. There is nothing wrong with the house. It is a good show and excellent architecture in any league.' *Idea House II* Exhibition Files, box 15, folder 11, Walker Art Center Archives.

63 Philip L. Goodwin to Walker Art Center, November 3, 1947, in *Idea House II* Exhibition Files, box 15, folder 6, Walker Art Center Archives.

64 *Museum of Modern Art Bulletin*, 16 (1), 1949.

65 See *Science Illustrated*, 4, 1949, pp. 65–9.

66 While the Walker and MoMA were the only two American museums to exhibit full-scale, furnished and functional houses, many museums held innovative exhibitions of modern home furnishings and interior designs in the late 1940s. Some, like Alexander Girard's *For Modern Living* exhibition at the Detroit Institute of Arts in 1949, featured completely decorated room environments from modern designers such as George Nelson, the Eameses, and Florence Knoll. Still others pursued commercial partnerships to promote their projects, such as MoMA's *Good Design* exhibitions, subtitled 'A joint program to stimulate the best modern designs of home furnishing,' which featured goods available from the Merchandise Mart in Chicago. See M. Friedman, 'From *Futurama* to *Motorama*,' in *Vital Forms*, pp. 175–7.

67 In general, scholars writing about dwelling design during the mid-twentieth century appear unaware of *Idea House*. In her essay 'Case Study Houses: In the Grand Modern Tradition,' Helen Searing lays out the rich and complex history of the antecedents of the Case Study Project, both in America and Europe, and identifies Breuer's *House in the Museum Garden* as a 'museological and temporary version of the Case Study Houses,' making no mention of the earlier *Idea House* project; see Searing, 'Case Study Project: In the Grand Modern Tradition,' in *Blueprints for Modern Living*, p. 117; Beatriz Colomina, in her essay 'The Exhibitionist House,' cites the issue of *Everyday Art Quarterly* devoted to *Idea House II* as an example of the popular appeal of the exhibited interior in the middle of the twentieth century, but makes no mention of the exhibition itself. See B. Colomina, 'The Exhibitionist House,' in *At the End of the Century*, p. 141.

68 L. Hyman, *Marcel Breuer, Architect: The Career and the Buildings*, New York: Harry N. Abrams, 2001, p. 296; J. Driller, *Breuer Houses*, M. Cole and J. Verrinde, trans., London: Phaidon Press, 2000, pp. 180–9, 263.

69 D. Defenbacher, 'A Man's House is his Art,' *Everyday Art Quarterly*, 5, 1947, p. 1.

Chapter 7

Domesticity on display

Modelling the modern home in post-war Belgium, 1945–50

Fredie Floré and Mil De Kooning

In the first decade after the Second World War, several national institutions, social movements and designer organisations in Belgium organised a series of home exhibitions. Up till now none of the model homes shown on these exhibitions have been reconstructed. Moreover, until recently very little attention was paid to their history in general. This chapter is part of a research project that tries to address this lack of historical interest.[1] It states that one of the main reasons for the late development of this research area is the fact that the post-war domestic reform movement in Belgium was far less consistent than in its neighbouring countries.[2] Instead, it was characterised by a series of independent discourses on modern living. However, this is also what makes the study of model homes in post-war Belgium interesting. At first sight, many home exhibitions appear to be simple sites of communication or representation: expressions of the organiser's educational programme focused on his specific target group. It is only by confronting them with similar projects or ambitions of other, not necessarily related contemporary home educators in Belgium that they reveal their complexity and also show themselves as sites of conflict.

Put simply, this is what this chapter tries to do. By means of different kinds of archival material and magazine and newspaper articles, it 'reconstructs' several exhibition homes and interiors, built by the national government between 1945 and 1950. The main aim is not to evaluate the influence of these homes on the domestic life of its visitors; instead, the chapter confronts the model homes with the comments and viewpoints of two other important home educators: the Flemish branches of the Catholic and Socialist movements for working-class women – namely, the Kristelijke Arbeidersvrouwengilden (Christian Workers' Women's Guilds) and the Socialistische Vooruitziende Vrouwen (Socialist Forward-looking Women). This confrontation provides us with insights in the way the exhibition houses dealt with the prevailing, often opposing visions on the modern home in Belgium. More specifically, it shows that in the early post-war years the national government made significant efforts to coordinate the actions of several home educators, but was not able to form a solid, long-term platform for discussions on home culture.

The national government as moderator

After the Second World War, it took the Belgian government several years to work out a new national housing policy dealing with the estimated shortage of about 200,000 houses.[3] The main reason for this delay was an ongoing conflict over social housing between the Catholic and Socialist parties in government.[4] After years of debate, this disagreement resulted in two housing subsidy acts. The De Taeye Act, an initiative of the Catholic party was passed on 29 May 1948 and was intended to stimulate private ownership and the erection of single-family houses, preferably on separate parcels of land. The Brunfaut Act, proposed by the Socialist party in government, was passed on 15 April 1949 and was meant to embrace collective housing. However, the Brunfaut Act was never an accurate translation of the intentions of the original bill. Instead of providing the means for CIAM-inspired housing developments with, for example, several collective dwelling services, a so-called 'war of amendments' following the proposal of the bill curtailed the act's powers, so that it could only allow restricted financial support for the infrastructure and the layout of public areas in social housing projects.[5] As a result, it was mainly the De Taeye Act that, from the 1950s on, was an instrumental factor in urban development in Belgium. Without the guidance of a structuring urban programme, it became the main reason for Belgium's well-known excessive sprawl: a scattered scene of ribbon development and detached houses.

This chapter focuses on the period before these two subsidy acts came into force. In the early years after the war the initiatives taken by the national government to improve or modernise national housing culture were often related to the Institut National du Logement et de l'Habitation (INALA) (National Institute for Habitation and Housing).[6] This institution was established in 1945 and was linked to the Ministry of Public Health and the Family. INALA was conceived as a study, information and documentation centre of a series of national organisations involved with social housing. According to its bylaws, it had a many-sided task. It was meant to coordinate all actions for 'better' popular housing; to stimulate the development of economic building techniques for housing projects by means of, for example, exhibitions; to encourage public education concerning 'modern' housing and to defend the rights of its partners.[7]

Between 1945 and 1947 three exhibitions took place, which clarified the role then played by INALA and by the national government in general concerning the improvement of post-war housing: 'Patrie et Civisme' ('Country and Citizenship') in Brussels in 1945, the 'Exposition Internationale du Logement' ('International Housing Exhibition') in Brussels in 1946 and the Belgian section of the exhibition 'Urbanisme et Habitation' ('Urbanism and Housing') held in Paris in 1947.[8] These exhibitions all included one or more model homes or model interiors that were meant to represent the nation's recent progress in domestic culture or social housing, to educate the public in 'good' or morally sound living, and to create opportunities for architecture, design and building experiments. These noble goals were often glorified in the daily press. However, when we confront the model homes with the views and comments of other contemporary home educators, a far more problematic picture emerges.

'Patrie et Civisme'

The first post-war exhibition in Belgium that drew attention to housing issues was 'Patrie et Civisme', organised by the Mission Militaire Belge (Belgian Military Mission) under the aegis of the Belgian Ministry of Information. It was held in the Brussels department store Au Bon Marché in 1945.[9] The exhibition consisted of a series of suggestive presentations focusing on the efforts made by the government for the citizens' benefit and also on the duties of the citizens in relation to their country.[10] The *salon d'honneur* glorified the Belgian efforts during the war. The two remaining sections represented the national art industry in relation to national industry in general and the relationships between Belgium and its allies. The subsection 'l'Habitation' ('the Home') was probably part of the art industry section and was designed and supervised by the Belgian modernist architect Louis-Herman De Koninck, who was also a member of the advising technical committee of INALA.[11] Among other things, 'l'Habitation' contained a model apartment, designed by De Koninck in collaboration with architect Marcel Schmitz and Au Bon Marché (Figure 7.1).

The design of the 1945 model home corresponded with De Koninck's pre-war modernist views on functional planning and design, and expressed his continuing interest in prefabricated building techniques. De Koninck believed that 'the plan of a house must be developed around its equipment which has been defined and characterised beforehand'.[12] The core of the 1945 model home, for example, was a specially designed, prefabricated sanitary block, called Ductex, which contained all plumbing needed for the kitchen and bathroom appliances, including the boiler (Figure 7.2). Thanks to this invention, the technical installation of a home was simplified to merely connecting the bathtub, kitchen sink, toilet, etc. to the Ductex bloc. Apart from promoting this time-saving and -organising construction element, the model home also continued De Koninck's interwar plea for labour-saving furniture design. The comfort of the housewife in the exhibition apartment was ensured by the installation of the innovative modular CUBEX kitchen, designed by De Koninck.[13]

7.1
**Architects Louis-
Herman De
Koninck and
Marcel Schmitz in
collaboration with
Au Bon Marché,
kitchen of the
model apartment
in 'Patrie et
Civisme', Brussels,
1945.**
Photo: *Rythme,*
s.n., September
1949, p. 45

The main difference between the housing ideals presented by De Koninck in 'Patrie et Civisme' and his pre-war modernist discourse on 'good' homes was that the 1945 model apartment was explicitly imbedded in an overall plea for the reconstruction or affirmation of national pride, human dignity and public morality. In an article of 1945 called 'L'habitation et le civisme' ('The home and citizenship'), De Koninck stated that 'good' habitation was a fundamental civic duty and that the improvement of the home and the dignity of the 'domestic existence' would enhance morality in general.[14] The model apartment did not look fundamentally different from the pre-war homes designed by De Koninck, but, thanks to its patriotic associations, it carried out a supplementary message: improving your home is improving the nation.

We were not able to find specific comments of the Kristelijke Arbeidersvrouwengilden or the Socialistische Vooruitziende Vrouwen on this early post-war model home, but newspaper reviews clearly show that a political incident involving the opposing views of the Catholic and the Socialist movement on the royal family and on the return of King Leopold III, severely coloured the perception of the exhibition. The incident was triggered by the fact that 'Patrie et Civisme' did not make any reference to the Belgian dynasty. According to the Catholic newspapers, this was unacceptable. For example, this was the case with *La Libre Belgique* which, without a lot of explanation, depicted the subsection of the home as a kind of commercial

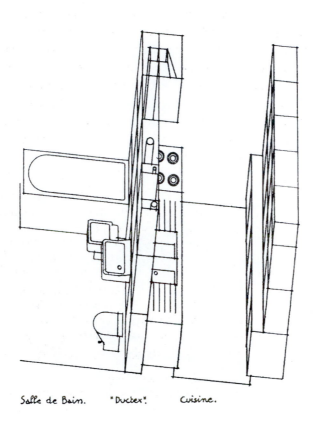

Salle de Bains.   "Ductex".   Cuisine.

7.2
Architects Louis-Herman De Koninck and Marcel Schmitz, drawing of the Ductex sanitary block.
Photo: *La Maison*, no. 3, March 1946, p. 74

fair.[15] Socialist newspapers, on the other hand, praised the 'common sense' of the exhibition organisers and the skills of the modernist designers involved.[16]

'Exposition Internationale du Logement'

One year later, in 1946, a larger official exhibition took place in Brussels, this time entirely focused on housing and the 'modern' home: the 'Exposition Internationale du Logement'.[17] This event was the first public exhibition from INALA and was supported by the Belgian Ministry of Public Affairs. The exhibition closely followed INALA's objectives: studying national habitation problems, promoting economic building techniques and educating public opinion concerning 'good' homes. In order to discuss possible solutions for the housing shortage in Belgium, a series of national and international building firms were invited to construct and fully furnish a prefabricated dwelling with two bedrooms. Although INALA offered no payment to the participants, the call was successful. The exhibition turned out to be a large experimental building site with about 45 detached single-family houses. It was situated in the Parc du Cinquantenaire in the centre of Brussels, a public park that, since the beginning of the twentieth century, had been used as a location for trade fairs and all sorts of popular festivities. Apart from the national entries, such as the ACIA house designed by De Koninck, Dutch, Swiss, British and Finnish building firms also participated in the event. Although the exhibition was often presented as an experiment in construction, it was also part of the educational programme of INALA. 'We should teach our people how to live,' Joseph Paquay, the secretary of the institution stated: 'Exhibitions like that at the Cinquantenaire already allow us to educate them by showing them, furthermore, that it is possible to construct good houses using other techniques than those we traditionally apply.'[18]

Although not as strongly as in 'Patrie et Civisme' the theme of the home in the 'Exposition Internationale du Logement' was linked up with issues of national pride and public morality. In a contemporary interview, the secretary general of the INALA declared that he had no doubt that, in comparison with the foreign exhibitors, 'the national industry would show itself once again to be capable of fighting with success for peaceful realisations'.[19] Physical references to traditional building, such as the wooden porch with thatched roof giving entrance to the Belgian section, were probably intended to present the prefabricated houses as part of a long and valuable national history of housing. In the exhibition catalogue, the architecture and design critique Pierre-Louis Flouquet furthermore referred to the 'courage' and 'civil virtue' that were necessary to sacrifice the 'redundant' aspects of the house in favour of the 'essential' ones[20] (Figure 7.3).

The 'Exposition Internationale du Logement' did not have the intention of presenting a selection of 'ideal' houses. These models rather formed an incomplete

7.3
Entrance to the Belgian section of 'Exposition Internationale du Logement', Brussels, 1946.
Photo: *Exposition Internationale du Logement* (catalogue), Brussels: Art et Technique, 1946, p. 4

set of samples of prefabrication systems available on the market and suitable for housing. For the layout of the exhibition, INALA was able to engage several reputable Belgian modernist architects and urban designers: Jean-Jules Eggericx, Maxime Wynants and Huib Hoste. Furthermore, two experimental houses designed by De Koninck were built in the park. The whole event became the subject of a lively discussion in professional circles on the use of prefabrication techniques for the restoration of the national housing patrimony.[21] However, the exhibition also brought about a vivid and critical response from outside the worlds of architects, builders and governmental institutions. For example, the Kristelijke Arbeidersvrouwengilden and the Socialistische Vooruitziende Vrouwen separately expressed more or less the same complaints. Rather than as building experiments, they evaluated the exhibition pavilions as architectural models for working-class housing.[22] They stated that most of the houses in the park were unfit for this purpose. 'Immediately we have the impression of standing in front of emergency houses, in the sense of temporary houses,' Gerina wrote in the magazine of the Kristelijke Arbeidersvrouwen, 'although almost all firms praise the durability of their housing types. We leave the durability of the materials undiscussed, but we cannot imagine how a family can live comfortably in such a house for 25 to 30 years.'[23] The Kristelijke Arbeidersvrouwen and Socialistische Vooruitziende Vrouwen stated that the model houses often lacked the indispensable cellar or attic, and that there was not enough storage room and sleeping accommodation. Therefore, they concluded that most of the pavilions were better suited as holiday or weekend bungalows than as working-class houses. 'These prefabricated houses could be very interesting for those who already possess a house and have the necessary means to build in a short time a residence somewhere outside the city,' Mathilde Schroyens of the Socialistische Vooruitziende Vrouwen wrote.[24] Her article on the exhibition was illustrated with a collage of pictures and the floor plan of De Koninck's ACIA pavilion: a one-storey steel construction with a saddle roof (Figure 7.4). Although both women's organisations praised the built-in cupboards, this house also contained all the 'deficiencies' mentioned earlier. It did not have a cellar or an attic. The storage (including a coal-shed) was smaller than 4m^2 and there were only two bedrooms. According to Schroyens, only the Swiss exhibition houses were acceptable: 'However, it must be said that the Swiss pavilions which we can see in the exhibition, are real houses, which easily can be inhabited by a family of six persons and which also have an attic; therefore they are also the most expensive ones.'[25]

The fact that both women's organisations published more or less similar reviews of the exhibition did not imply that their visions on 'modern' domestic living were identical. The Kristelijke Arbeidersvrouwen and the Socialistische Vooruitziende Vrouwen did support the housing policy of respectively the Catholic and the Socialist party in government. This was also apparent in their comments on the 'Exposition Internationale du Logement'. For example, the Christian women's organisation did not question the suburban character of the pavilions. The Socialistische Vooruitziende Vrouwen, on the other hand, did have some criticisms. Schroyens wondered where

7.4
**Building firm
Bouchout &
Thirion Réunis in
collaboration with
architect Louis-
Herman De
Koninck, the ACIA
pavilion on the
'Exposition
Internationale du
Logement',
Brussels, 1946.**
Photo: Louis-
Herman De Koninck
archive, AAM,
Brussels

the presented prefabricated houses would be built: 'Near to the city there are not enough available lots left to build many large garden districts, and not everyone can settle themselves far from the city.'[26] Therefore, in her opinion a 'good' housing policy should also take into account the possibilities of collective housing: 'the comfort possible in a house can also be considered for an apartment block. However here one should make sure there is space and opportunity for recreation for the children.'[27]

In spite of their different political backgrounds, in the end both women's organisations came to the same conclusion. They stated that more women should be represented in the national housing bodies. 'Thus it will be the task of the architects to build the new houses', Schroyens resumed, 'but we should insist that in the bodies which will be engaged in housing, women should be admitted, practical women, so that, in these new houses, all the small and big mistakes which we immediately found in these modern prefabricated houses, will be excluded.'[28] An article in the magazine of the Kristelijke Arbeidersvrouwen took a similar position: 'With women as advisors for the design of housing plans, no attic, cellars, storage rooms, coal-sheds, washhouses, and even kitchens would be forgotten, as lately in the housing exhibition in the Parc du Cinquantenaire.'[29] A year earlier, Louis-Herman De Koninck had already made a similar proposition, but he only referred to 'female architects': 'it would certainly be advisable to see a lot of female architects enter the services whose competence concerns the study and the inspection of housing conditions. These are tasks for which common sense and female perseverance are of special value.'[30]

The Belgian section of 'Urbanisme et Habitation'

The criticisms of the 'Exposition Internationale du Logement' expressed by the organisations for working-class women were not left unnoticed. The Belgian section of 'Urbanisme et Habitation', an international exhibition organised by the French Ministry of Reconstruction in the Grand Palais in Paris in 1947 clearly illustrates this.[31] 'Urbanisme et Habitation' was led by Commissioner General Paul Breton, one of the most important organisers of the Paris-based Salons des Arts Ménagers, and was meant to stimulate the interest of French citizens in the vast post-war reconstruction process. At the same time, the exhibition aimed at facilitating the international exchange of know-how regarding housing and urban planning.[32] As well as Belgium and France, Denmark, Greece, Iceland, Italy, Mexico, Poland, Czechoslovakia, the South-African Union, Sweden and Switzerland also participated. Most of the foreign presentations were situated on the ground floor of the Grand Palais, except for Sweden, which showed a series of model houses in the gardens of the palace.[33] More housing prototypes but of French origin were built on the Cours la Reine and along the banks of the Seine. France also presented several theme sections in the 'galleries' of the palace.

As with most of the foreign sections on the ground floor of the Grand Palais, the Belgian section was accessible via the long and monumental alley in the centre of the exhibition space. With a surface of 1,150m², it was the largest foreign section of 'Urbanisme et Habitation'. According to the then Belgian Minister of Economic Affairs, Duvieusart, the aim was to 'take the opportunity of this international comparison of problems and methodologies to begin a complete inventory of the housing system in Belgium and of the means which we can apply immediately and gradually in order to pass the crisis'.[34] The Belgian government provided a considerable budget for this ambitious plan: about 20 million Belgian francs.[35] Probably this was not only to contribute to a fruitful international exchange of know-how, but also to intensify diplomatic relationships with France and to enhance the export possibilities of Belgian products.[36] Two commissioners general supervised the Belgian section: Albert De Smaele, a former Minister of Economic Affairs, and Emile Vinck, vice-president of INALA and former member of the executive committee of the 'Exposition Internationale du Logement' in 1946.[37] The Secretary General of the Belgian section was Joseph Paquay, who was also secretary of INALA and the former secretary of the housing exhibition in Brussels in 1946.

The Belgian section of 'Urbanisme et Habitation' was not only for French or other foreign visitors or professionals. From the beginning, it was also meant to be an educational event for Belgian citizens. Therefore, during the exhibition the organising committee arranged an extensive shuttle service between Belgium and Paris. Switzerland and Italy also planned guided tours from their home country, but not to the same extent. 'Belgium in particular created a special auto car service that every day brought to the Grand Palais several hundred members of the universities, the building unions, organisations of housekeepers, architects and affiliates of youth movements,' Paul Breton stated in the exhibition catalogue.[38] In addition to the shuttle service, the organisers of the Belgian Section also thought of a second way to enhance the educational 'return' of the national section's presentation to the Belgian population. After the Paris exhibition, the Belgian section was transported to the Grand Palais de Coronmeuse in Liège, where it was shown from 27 September until 26 October 1947.[39]

To construct properly an overview of housing problems in Belgium and of their possible solutions, INALA established 12 technical commissions, which for a period of five months each had to study a different topic, such as: 'urban development', 'statistics', 'scientific research in relation to the building industry', etc. These commissions included architects, urban developers, engineers, representatives of the national housing bodies, politicians, and also representatives of several Flemish and Walloon, Christian and Socialist women's organisations. There was even a separate 'advisory female commission' which was meant to study all the model homes in the Belgian section in relation to housework, comfort and the health of the family.[40] This commission had 29 members and included several representatives of the Socialistische Vooruitziende Vrouwen and the Kristelijke Arbeidersvrouwen. Although not all commissions were particularly large, in total more than a hundred members of different social or professional groups were involved in the preparation of the event. The commission system was somewhat unwieldy, but created a surprisingly open platform for a wide range of post-war home educators. This kind of cross-professional forum would not occur again.

The Belgian section of 'Urbanisme et Habitation' offered a broad view of the national housing problems. It focused on the individual house as well as on questions of urban planning, and consisted of fifteen successive subsections, such as 'la vie au foyer' (life at home), 'plans concours' (competition plans), 'prix de revient' (cost price), 'nombre d'habitations' (the number of houses), 'urbanisme' (urbanism), etc. A fully furnished model apartment occupied the centre of the national presentation (Figure 7.5). It illustrates how the complex structure of preparatory commissions was able to create a temporary consensus between the different 'housing educators' involved.

The model apartment was designed by Louis-Herman De Koninck in collaboration with his daughter Monique De Koninck and Jacques Donnay. However, these three architects did not have free play. For example, they had to justify their decisions and designs to the 'social commission' of the exhibition, which included representatives of the Socialistische Vooruitziende Vrouwen and the Kristelijke Arbeidersvrouwen and their Wallonian francophone counterpart organisations.[41]

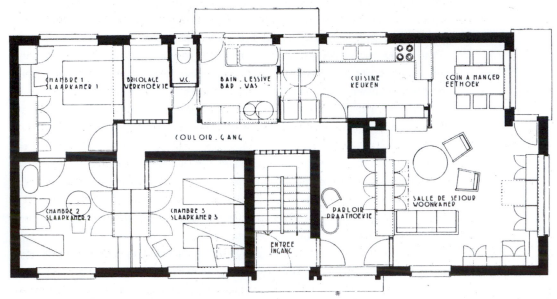

Plattegrond van de afbeelding der modelwoning. Architekt : De H. L.-H. De Koninck. — Medewerkster : Mej. M. De Koninck. — Assistent : De H. J. Donnay.

One of the tasks of this commission was to make sure that the model apartment would show a 'realistic' image of a modern home of an average family of six persons. Similar to the 1946 ACIA bungalow, the model apartment had a rectangular floor plan, based on a square screen, and was equipped with a Cubex kitchen and several built-in cupboards. However, it also had a utility room, a relatively large entrance hall, three bedrooms and a cold room for storing food, features that indirectly replied to the critique of the women's organisations after the 1946 Brussels housing exhibition. In general, the Socialistische Vooruitziende Vrouwen and the Kristelijke Arbeiders-vrouwen were pleased with the design of the 1947 model apartment.[42] They pointed out that the apartment was too expensive for the working classes, but they were confident that a thorough reorganisation of the national building industry would easily solve this problem.

Parallel discourses

With the Belgian section of 'Urbanisme et Habitation', the post-war efforts of the national government to coordinate a debate on 'good' housing led to a rare moment of consensus between several important 'housing educators'. However, this unanimity was short-lived. From the late 1940s, many home educators developed an individual programme to influence the nation's home culture. This situation was reflected in the housing exhibitions and model homes of the following period.

7.5
Architects Louis-Herman De Koninck, Monique De Koninck and Jacques Donnay, floor plan of the model apartment in the Belgian section of 'Urbanisme et Habitation', Paris, 1947.
Photo:
Internationale Tentoonstelling Urbanisme et Habitation. Belgische Afdeling. Parijs 1947 (catalogue), Brussels: Art et Technique, 1947, p. 38

Most of these model homes did not take into account any other ideology than that of its organiser. Contrary to some of the early governmental exhibition homes, they did not function as a means to negotiate with other home educators.

In the late 1940s, a new national housing policy, based on the De Taeye Act and the Brunfaut Act, became valid. After that, the national government mainly organised housing exhibitions consisting of one or two fully equipped model homes in a recently finished housing project built with state financial support. In 1949, for instance, the Institut National de La Promotion de L'Habitation (National Institute for Housing Promotion) – an institute that succeeded INALA – organised such an exhibition in Couillet, in a new project of the Société Nationale des Habitations et Logements à Bon Marché (National Society for Affordable Housing and Homes).[43] Throughout the 1940s and 1950s, similar events took place regularly. They were believed to be instrumental in the spreading of 'good' living ideals among the lower and middle classes.

In the meantime, the Kristelijke Arbeidersvrouwen developed their own campaign to influence post-war housing culture in Belgium.[44] For example, in 1949, together with their recently established male counterpart, the Katholieke Werkliedenbonden (Catholic Workers' Unions), they organised the travelling exhibition 'De Thuis' ('The Home') on the 'modern' design of working-class housing. The exhibition was the sequel to a 1939 exhibition by the Kristelijke Arbeidersvrouwen called 'Modern Gezinsleven. Wij Bouwen een Nieuwen Thuis' ('Modern Family Life. We are Building a New Home').[45] In 1949 it took place in five Flemish cities and had in total more than 45,000 visitors.[46]

The 'ideal' homes presented in 'De Thuis' were primarily characterised by a financial and organisational pragmatism and by the explicit representation of Christian family values. Having gone through an introductory section depicting the vital importance of a 'good' family life and a plea against unhealthy urban living, the visitors were told that the establishment of single-family houses in the suburbs was the best way to solve the housing shortages after the war. To convince the public that a modern, comfortable home was an 'accessible' dream, the exhibition further provided practical advice on how these new homes could be built and furnished with a modest income. The Kristelijke Arbeidersvrouwen and the Katholike Werkliedenbonden informed on the new housing policy and presented model rooms with designs for inexpensive contemporary furniture. It was made clear that the interior of the house was to be a place of personal investment of every member of the family. Therefore, 'De Thuis' also stressed the importance of DIY. Fathers, mothers and children were encouraged to make some of the furniture or carry out home decoration themselves.

Far more than the early post-war housing exhibitions, 'De Thuis' was focused on the reality and availability of 'modern domesticity' for the working class. It mainly promoted these aspects of contemporary living, which would simplify household tasks in a tangible manner or provide more living space within traditional urban or suburban dwellings. For example, a life-sized model of an attic room showed how the often-unoccupied space under a saddle roof could be changed into a boy's room. In the periodicals of the Kristelijke Arbeidersvrouwen and the Katholike Werkliedenbonden it was implied that this kind of transformation should be the work of the parents in collaboration with the sons.

While the Kristelijke Arbeidersvrouwen and the Katholike Werklieden-bonden were rapidly gaining influence, other home educators began to organise themselves independently. In 1950 Formes Nouvelles (New Forms) was established: the first post-war Belgian designer's organisation aimed at promoting 'good' contemporary living. The formation of this group coincided more or less with the participation of several of its founder members in the exhibition 'Logis 50' ('House 50') organised in 1950 by the province of Brabant[47] (Figure 7.6). This event took place in a huge army tent on the Porte de Namur, a busy urban intersection in Brussels. It was meant as a reaction against the inadequate quality and the 'bad taste' of the national furniture industry, and wanted to show alternatives to the growing import of modern, mainly Scandinavian furniture. The organisers of 'Logis 50' intended to prove that it was possible to sell good-quality objects made by Belgian craftsmen, artists and industrial manufacturers at reasonable prices. To do so, the exhibition aimed at 'improving' the

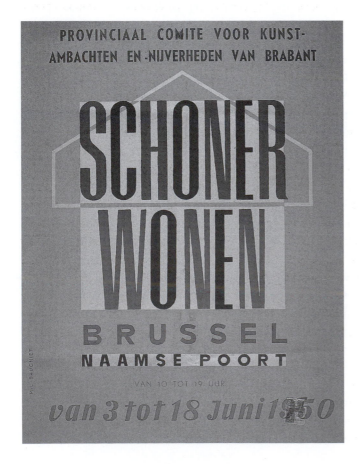

7.6
Poster (Flemish version) of 'Logis 50' or 'Schoner Wonen', designed by Marcel-Louis Baugniet.
Photo: AMVC, Antwerp

taste of a broad public of consumers, producers and distributors. However, contrary to the exhibitions of the Kristelijke Arbeidersvrouwen and the Katholike Werklieden-bonden, this educational ambition did not restrain the experimental character of the event. While 'De Thuis' first and foremost concentrated on the realistic and the pragmatic character of 'good' housing advice, 'Logis 50' became an important, open laboratory for the design experiments of the Belgian avant-garde. Along a curved path of glass slabs stood various model rooms – mainly living-rooms and bedrooms – presenting unedited work of young designers such as Raymond Van Loo and Aimée Huysmans. To stress the importance of the designers' creative input, several proto-types of chairs and other utility objects were shown separately, with clear reference to their inventors. In the early 1950s, Formes Nouvelles continued to create similar opportunities for young designers and avant-garde producers to show their work. Its actions were of fundamental importance to the revival of Belgian furniture design in the Fifties.

Conclusion

This study of the early post-war housing exhibitions organised by the Belgian govern-ment reveals a set of independent home educators with different political agendas, concerns and interests. It illustrates the attempts of INALA to engage these educa-tors in an open debate. At first, these efforts showed positive results. The Belgian section of 'Urbanisme et Habitation' was based on the fruitful collaboration of repre-sentatives of several influential organisations. It revealed a shared concern for a 'good' home culture as a fundamental aspect of the nation's identity and represen-tation. This concern was strong enough to bridge the sometimes-fundamental ideological differences of the organisations involved. The presentation of the 1947 model apartment within the Belgian section tellingly illustrates the efforts made to reach a consensus. For example, while the typology of the apartment seemed to underline the importance of collective housing, two preceding subsections somewhat nuanced this message. One of them, 'plans concours', contained small-scale models of other 'good' housing types, among which several single-family houses. Another subsection, 'la vie au foyer', consisted of a series of collages, each presenting one aspect of family life in the model apartment. The collage 'les loisirs familiaux' (the family's leisure) showed a traditional family of two parents and two children relaxing in the living-room. The background was characterised by large-scale windows looking over a terrace and adjacent garden (a fragment of a picture of the modernist Canneel house designed by De Koninck).[48] So, instead of reinforcing the reference made to collective housing, this collage rather referred to the ideal of the single-family house in green surroundings.

The success of the Belgian section of 'Urbanisme et Habitation' in balancing different views on 'good' housing was not continued. Since the late 1940s the national government chose to focus on the execution of the new housing policy.

Its housing education lost its experimental character and mainly concentrated on the public presentation of new social housing projects. At the same time, other home educators began to organise a more independent promotion for 'good' homes. As a result the model home changed from a complex framework of communication to a medium carefully isolated from foreign ideologies. From the 1950s, housing exhibitions in Belgium embracing a range of perspectives on the domestic sphere were only rarely to be found. Most of the model homes were rather straightforward expressions of the organiser's ideological programme. This trend continued until most educational efforts regarding modern living were overshadowed by less noble and increasingly consumer-oriented messages. The discussion in this chapter of some of the early post-war model homes, not as glorious moments in the history of popular education, architecture or design, but as sites of a struggling negotiation between several home educators, reminds us of the gravity with which the public communication of domestic issues used to be staged and perceived, an aspect that is often neglected in today's retrospective exhibitions on design and modern living in Belgium.

Notes

1   This chapter arises from doctoral research being conducted by Fredie Floré at the Department of Architecture & Urban Planning, Ghent University, supervised by Mil De Kooning. The working title of the thesis is: *Lessen in Modern Wonen? Een architectuurhistorisch onderzoek naar de communicatie van modellen voor 'modern' wonen in België. 1945–58* (Lessons in Modern Living? An architectural-historical study of the communication of models for 'modern' living in Belgium. 1945–58).

2   Research is currently being conducted in two Flemish universities on the history of post-war home culture in Belgium. Since 1999, a study has been underway at the Department of Architecture & Urban Planning, Ghent University, concerning design production and home information in Belgium after the Second World War. So far, this study has resulted in two books, various lectures at international academic conferences and various articles in national and international journals. The doctoral research being conducted by Fredie Floré also fits into this project. In addition, in 2003 a FWO research project was started at the Catholic University of Leuven which is also related to the history of home culture. This study, supervised by Leen Van Molle, Hilde Heynen, Veerle Draulans and Patrick Pasture, focuses on the 'social interpretation of architectural views on "living" in Flanders 1920–70'.

3   As there was no official code defining the difference between a 'healthy' and an 'unhealthy' dwelling in Belgium, the estimated housing shortage after the Second World War differs according to the source. However, it was generally stated that at least 200,000 new houses had to be built. See L. Goossens, *Het sociaal huisvestingsbeleid in België. Een historisch-sociologische analyse van de maatschappelijke probleembehandeling op het gebied van het wonen* (unpublished Ph.D. thesis), Leuven: Catholic University of Leuven, 1982, p. 4.2.–2.

4   The Catholic party was called CVP (Christelijke Volkspartij) or PSC (Parti Social Chrétien). The Socialist party was called BSP (Belgische Socialistische Partij) or PSB (Parti Socialiste Belge).

5   The content of the Brunfaut Act and the development of the 'war of amendments' are described in Goossens, op. cit. CIAM stands for Congrès Internationaux d'Architecture Moderne (International Congress of Modern Architecture).

6   As Belgium is a bilingual state, many national institutions and organisations have both Flemish and French names. For simplicity, only the French names are used in this text, and the Flemish synonyms are given in the endnotes. The Flemish synonym of Institut National du Logement et de l'Habitation is Nationaal Instituut voor Woning en Huisvesting.

7   The tasks of the institution are described in article 3 of the bylaws of INALA. This article is cited in P.-L. Flouquet, 'L'Institut National du Logement et de l'Habitation et l'Exposition Internationale du Logement. Interview de M. Albert Van Billoen', *La Maison*, no. 8, November 1945, pp. 238–9, 267.

8   The Flemish synonyms of 'Patrie et Civisme' and 'Exposition Internationale du Logement' are respectively 'Vaderland en burgertrouw' and 'Internationale Tentoonstelling van Woningen'. See F. Floré, *Lessons in Modern Living. Source Book on Housing Exhibitions in Belgium 1945–58*, in the series *Vlees en Beton*, no. 64, Ghent: WZW Editions and Productions, 2004.

9   The exhibition was held from 20 July until 1 September 1945.

10 See V. Bourgeois, 'Urbanisme, architecture et civisme', *La Maison*, no. 5, August 1945, p. 137.

11 C. Mierop and A. Van Loo (eds), *Louis Herman De Koninck. Architecte des années modernes*, Brussels: AAM, 1998, p. 282.

12 L.-H. De Koninck, 'L'équipement moderne des habitations', *La Maison*, no. 3, May-June 1945, pp. 85–9.

13 The CUBEX kitchen was presented for the first time at the third CIAM congress in Brussels in 1930.

14 See L.-H. De Koninck, 'L'Habitation et le civisme', *La Maison*, no. 4, July 1945, pp. 144–6.

15 See 'Une pseudo-exposition de la patrie et du civisme', *La Libre Belgique*, 20 July 1945, s.p. For a review in a Flemish Catholic newspaper, see, for example 'Vaderland en Burgertrouw', *De Nieuwe Standaard*, no. 200, 20 July 1945, p. 2.

16 See, for example, 'Patrie et Civisme', *Le Peuple*, no. 167, 21 July 1945, p. 1. The designers of the exhibition in general were architect Victor Bourgeois, Joris Minne, Decock and Camille Broodcorens.

17 The exhibition was held from 18 May until September 1946.

18 J. Paquay, 'Problèmes actuels de la reconstruction', *L'Ossature Métallique*, nos. 5–6, May-June 1946, pp. 101–9.

19 P.-L. Flouquet, op. cit., pp. 238–9, 267.

20 See P.-L. Flouquet, 'Een wandeling doorheen de tentoonstelling', *Internationale Tentoonstelling van Woningen* (catalogue), Brussels: Art et Technique, 1946, pp. 7–9.

21 The use of industrial techniques for the construction of houses was again a topical subject after the Second World War. In the first post-war years, many architectural and building magazines in Belgium, such as *Architecture Urbanisme Habitation, Het Bouwbedrijf, Le Document, La Maison, L'Ossature Métallique*, published articles on prefabricated housing.

22 Mathilde Schroyens of the Socialistische Vooruitziende Vrouwen believed it was justified to evaluate the exhibition in that way because the administrative board of INALA consisted mainly of representatives of organisations dealing with working-class housing. See M. Schroyens, 'Eerst en vooral een goede woning', *De Stem der Vrouw*, no. 9, September 1946, p. 2.

23 Gerina, 'Een woningententoonstelling te Brussel', *Vrouwenbeweging*, s.n., June 1946, p. 15.

24 M. Schroyens, op. cit., p. 2.

25 Ibid.

26 Ibid.

27 Ibid.

28 Ibid.

29 'Onze moeders als architecten', *Vrouwenbeweging*, s.n., September 1946, p. 20.

30 L.-H. De Koninck, 'L'habitation et le civisme', *La Maison*, no. 4, July 1945, pp. 144–6.

31 'Urbanisme et Habitation' took place from 10 July until 17 August 1947. The exhibition was patronised by the Comité Français des Expositions. See *Exposition Internationale de l'Urbanisme et de l'Habitation* (catalogue), Paris: Ministère de la Reconstruction et de l'Urbanisme, 1947.

32 See *Exposition Internationale de l'Urbanisme et de l'Habitation* (official programme), Paris: Ministère de la Reconstruction et de l'Urbanisme, 1947. See also P. Breton, 'Ce que fut l'Exposition Internationale de l'Urbanisme et de l'Habitation', *Urbanisme et Habitation* (catalogue), Paris: Commissariat Général de l'Exposition Internationale de l'Urbanisme et de l'Habitation, 1947, pp. 5–7. Both publications are preserved in the *Centre des Archives Contemporaines*, Fontainebleau, no. 19850025, article 31.

33 Switzerland also constructed a model house in the gardens of the Grand Palais, but the main part of its presentation was situated on the ground floor of the palace.

34 J. Duvieusart, 'Boodschap van de H. J. Duvieusart, Minister van Economische Zaken en Middenstand', *Internationale Tentoonstelling Urbanisme et Habitation. Belgische Afdeling. Parijs 1947* (catalogue), Brussels: Art et Technique, 1947, pp. 6–7.

35 'Exposition Internationale de l'Urbanisme et de l'Habitation. Sections Etrangères' (unpublished report), Centre des Archives Contemporaines, Fontainebleau, no. 19850025, article 26, box 1, s.d.

36 For example, the importance of the Belgian participation in 'Urbanisme et Habitation' for exports was mentioned in 'Expositions de Paris et Milan 1947. Avant-projet de thème' (unpublished report), Centre des Archives Contemporaines, Fontainebleau, no. 19850025, article 30, s.d.

37 Emile Vinck was also president of the Société Nationale des Habitations et Logements à Bon Marché or Nationale Maatschappij voor Goedkope Woningen en Woonvertrekken (National Society for Affordable Housing and Homes) and head of the Union des Villes et Communes Belges or Vereniging van de Belgische Steden en Gemeenten (Union of the Belgian Cities and Districts).

38 P. Breton, op. cit., pp. 5–7.

39 See *Urbanisme et Habitation. Liège, 27 septembre–26 octobre* (folder), 1947.

40 See 'De raadgevende vrouwelijke commissie', in *Internationale Tentoonstelling Urbanisme et Habitation. Belgische Afdeling. Parijs 1947* (catalogue), Brussels: Art et Technique, 1947, pp. 59–60.

41 For example, Philippine Vande Putte of the Kristelijke Arbeidersvrouwen, Angéline Japsenne of the Ligues Ouvrières Féminines Chrétiennes (Christian Workers' Women's Guilds) and Jeanne Vanderveken of the Socialistische Vooruitziende Vrouwen were members of the 'social commission'. See 'Sociale commissie', in *Internationale Tentoonstelling Urbanisme et Habitation. Belgische Afdeling. Parijs 1947* (catalogue), Brussels: Art et Technique, 1947, pp. 57–8.

42 For example, see G. V., 'Avec les Femmes Prévoyantes à Paris. L'Habitation Rêvée', *La Femme Prévoyante*, no. 8, August 1947, pp. 5, 7; W. V., 'De S.V.V. te Parijs. De gedroomde Woning', *De Stem der Vrouw*, No. 11, November 1947, p. 5; A. Japsenne, 'du bonheur sur 93 m2', *Vie Féminine*, s.n., December 1947, pp. 4–5.

43 The Flemish synonym of Institut National de La Promotion de L'Habitation is Nationaal Instituut tot Bevordering van de Huisvesting. This institute replaced INALA in March 1949. The Flemish synonym of Société Nationale des Habitations et Logements à Bon Marché is Nationale Maatschappij voor Goedkope Woningen en Woonvertrekken. For more information on the exhibition in Couillet, see F. Floré, op. cit.

44 See also F. Floré, 'Promoting Catholic Family Values and Modern Domesticity in Post-war Belgium', in H. Heynen and G. Baydar (eds), *Negotiating Domesticity. Spatial Productions of Gender in Modern Architecture*, London: Routledge, 2005, pp. 83–102.

45 *Wij bouwen een nieuwen thuis* (catalogue), Brussels: KAV, 1939.

46 In 1949 'De Thuis' received the following numbers of visitors: 12,753 in Antwerp, 11,077 in Bruges, 7,773 in Ghent, 7,054 in Hasselt and 6,921 in Aalst. This information is based on the archives of the Kristelijke Arbeidersvrouwengilden, KADOC, Leuven.

47 The Flemish title of 'Logis 50' was 'Schoner Wonen' (Living More Beautifully). The exhibition was organised with the support of the Ministries of Economic Affairs and of Reconstruction. It took place from 3 to 18 June 1950. See F. Floré, op. cit.

48 See M. Dubois, 'La Maison Canneel', in Mierop and Van Loo (eds), op. cit., pp. 138–63.

Chapter 8

Kettle's Yard
Museum or way of life?

Sebastiano Barassi

In 1966 Harold Stanley 'Jim' Ede (1895–1990) gave Kettle's Yard to the University of Cambridge. With its meticulously designed display of art, furniture, everyday and found objects, the house represented Ede's 'masterpiece', a work of art in its own right that summed up his philosophy and way of life (Figure 8.1).

The memorandum outlining the conditions of the gift stated that its purpose was 'to establish a permanent Collection in which the said contents and works of art will be maintained together for exhibition in their present setting'.[1] Ede continued to live in the house with his wife Helen until 1973, caring for it on behalf of the university (Figure 8.2). Thinking of Kettle's Yard more as an artwork than a museum, on his departure he expected it to be preserved and run exactly as it was during his tenancy. He selected a resident curator, left very detailed written and photographic records of the position of each object and occasionally sent 'spies' to keep him informed on the state of house and collection. Throughout his final years he remained in close touch with his successors, eager to remind them that he expected the same level of commitment from them as he had shown and referring to the job as a 'mission'.

But would these ever be achievable goals? Could a place so closely associated with its creator and his very characteristic lifestyle retain its meaning and value in his absence? And was it in any way possible for Ede's creation to maintain its vitally important domestic and informal feeling after it had become a museum proper?

8.1
**Harold Stanley
'Jim' Ede, c. 1975.**
Photo: George
Kennethson,
copyright Kettle's
Yard, University of
Cambridge

The beginnings

Ede created Kettle's Yard in the second half of the 1950s, with the aim of offering an alternative model for the enjoyment of art to that traditionally found in museums and galleries. Born in Cardiff in 1895, in his youth he had studied painting in Newlyn, Edinburgh and London, aspiring to become an artist. Having abandoned this early ambition, in 1921 he joined the National Gallery of British Art (the Tate's official title), where he worked as a curator until 1936. Ede's arrival coincided with the early stages (still rather conservative in taste) of the gallery's concern with modern international art, a shift to which he somewhat contributed and that matched his own growing interest in contemporary developments.

Despite an occasionally uneasy relationship with senior staff, the position at Millbank gave Ede access to some of the great artists of the time, including Pablo Picasso, Joan Miró, Constantin Brancusi and Marc Chagall, whom he met during his frequent visits to Paris. Moreover, in those years Ede, who was also assistant secretary of the Contemporary Art Society, established close and often life-long friendships with a number of emerging British artists such as Ben and Winifred Nicholson, Barbara Hepworth, Henry Moore, Christopher Wood and David Jones. All these relationships were crucial for the development of his taste and collection, a fact that he liked to emphasise by referring to himself, not without a hint of affectation, simply as 'a friend of artists'.

8.2
**The exterior of
the house.**
Photo: Paul Allitt,
Kettle's Yard,
University of
Cambridge

Yet Ede was not merely excited by contemporary aesthetics. It was the whole lifestyle of the artists he met that attracted him. He admired the incessant travelling of Ben and Winifred Nicholson, between their austere homes in Cumberland and Switzerland, and the sophistication of London and Paris. And of a visit to Brancusi's atelier, he wrote:

> All the elements were there, collected in his studio, almost as though it were nature's workshop. There I found air and light, and the poise and the rhythm of his carvings . . . The only dark thing in all that world was Brancusi's eyes, they were like wet pebbles on the sand, everything else was finely powdered over, his grey hair and beard, his face, his clothes, the tall columns of eternal movement.[2]

The contrast with what Ede perceived as the stuffy atmosphere and uninspiring display style of the Tate could not have been sharper. He saw every detail of Brancusi's studio as vital, deriving from the interaction of artworks, the chance variations of light and space, the all-over whiteness and the attention to apparently insignificant details. These notions remained with him for the rest of his life, and the atelier would become an openly acknowledged influence on Kettle's Yard.

While at the Tate, Ede lived with Helen in a Georgian townhouse, 1 Elm Row, Hampstead, that became an 'open house' for like-minded people and showcased his growing collection. The main attraction was the Gaudier-Brzeska estate, acquired in 1927, which was displayed alongside works by Ede's friends and other artists such as Alfred Wallis. Visitors to Elm Row included Georges Braque, Sergei Diaghilev, Vaslav Nijinsky, Donald Winnicott, Naum Gabo, Henry Moore, the Nicholsons, David Jones and Helen Sutherland.

It was particularly through his friendship with Jones and Sutherland, a fellow collector, that Ede matured the views on beauty, faith and the ritualism of daily life that would later shape Kettle's Yard. Eager to go beyond the confines of the Methodist Church within which he had been raised, he developed an eclectic approach to the spiritual, animated primarily by a theosophical belief in establishing an individual relationship with God, without the mediation of an organised religion. Over the years he explored and assimilated ideas not only from Catholic thought, but also from Oriental philosophies (especially Buddhism and Hinduism) and Christian Science, to which he was introduced by the Nicholsons, and whose notions of finding beauty and fulfilment in things such as shadow, light and subtle spatial arrangement particularly appealed to him.

One of the most admired pieces at Kettle's Yard is a spiral made of pebbles that resembles a mandala, the Buddhist ritual figure that serves as a representation of the universe and object of contemplation (Figure 8.3). It exemplifies one of the key ideas that Ede elaborated in the 1920s: the role of natural objects as tokens of the Divine perceptible in everyday life. This notion was deeply rooted in the modernist milieu of Hampstead (in particular in the work of Barbara Hepworth and Henry Moore) and allowed Ede to expand more conventional ideas of what constitutes 'art'. Throughout his life he collected shells, pebbles, bones and other natural objects, with some being sent by friends from all over the world. Many of these became key elements of the display at Kettle's Yard, acquiring so much relevance that Ian Hamilton Finlay once described the house as the 'Louvre of the Pebble'.[3]

In Ede's vision, the search for the Divine in humble objects required much dedication, for he believed that:

> We find a perfect pebble once in a generation and once in a continent perhaps [. . .] Perfection in nature varies for each person – it is something created between the thing experienced and the person experiencing. Yet I know when I meet perfection immediately. I will discard 10,000 pebbles in my search for one whose outward shape exactly balances my idea of what a pebble is, and I do not believe that this discarding is arbitrary – we all know by some unwritten law what is a well-shaped egg. As we contemplate the egg we feel the mystery of the universe – like many artists in history – its shape is so complete and satisfying. It is perhaps strange that great sculptures should have many of the qualities which are to be found in pebbles – the smoothly rounded forms – the sense they have of evolving; the pebble out of the action of the elements and the statue out of the power of the human mind which has acted upon its nature, just as sand and water have acted on the pebble.[4]

8.3
The pebble spiral, Henri Gaudier-Brzeska's Toy (Torpedo Fish) and various found objects.
Photo: Paul Allitt, Kettle's Yard, University of Cambridge

The years spent in London represented for Ede an important formative spell, allowing him to understand fully the role of works of art and everyday/natural objects (and the conversations between them) to enhance our daily lives. As important, it was by regularly opening his house to kindred spirits that he developed the notions of social interaction that would play such a central role in the realisation of his 'mission'.

The birth of Kettle's Yard

Following a string of personal and professional problems, in 1936 Ede resigned from his Tate post, beginning an early retirement at the age of 41. Over the next twenty years he lived with Helen in Tangiers, the United States and the Loire Valley, collecting little but continuing to write on art and to review books and exhibitions. By the mid-1950s, however, advancing age and the desire to be nearer their two daughters eventually drove the couple back to England.

It was at this time that the need for a permanent home for the collection became foremost in Ede's mind. In a 1956 letter to David Jones he remarked:

> It would be interesting to be lent a great house on the verge of a city – or a place of beauty in a town (Cambridge I have in mind) and make it all that I could of lived in beauty, each room an atmosphere of quiet and simple charm, and open to the public (in Cambridge to students especially) . . . Helen and I would live in a bit of it – the rest would look lived in and its special feature would be I think one of simplicity and loved qualities.[5]

In his plan this would become:

> A *living place* where works of art would be enjoyed, inherent to the domestic setting, where young people could be at home unhampered by the greater austerity of the museum or public art gallery and where an informality might infuse an underlying formality.[6]

Once in Cambridge, the search for a suitable site proved quite difficult, continuing until Ede found four condemned cottages in the area locally known as 'Kettle's Yard'. During the following months he restored and remodelled the derelict buildings with the help of a local architect, moving in with Helen in early 1957. The house, conceived from the start to be open to the public on weekday afternoons, was soon ready to receive visitors, initially mostly undergraduate students.

One of the founding principles of Kettle's Yard was Ede's belief that an informal domestic environment would be much more conducive to a positive aesthetic experience than the supposedly neutral atmosphere of a museum. Animated by an essentially formalist approach, he explained:

> I am not particularly interested in the dates of artists or in the names or what school they belong to, but I am interested in the force of life which pushes them into expression, either in a picture, statue, music or some other form of activity.[7]

Ede advocated the enjoyment of art in the context of daily life and rejected established taxonomies and display techniques, refusing, for example, to use vitrines and labels or to hang pictures chronologically. Instead, he installed works relying on purely aesthetic principles, in usually private spaces such as bathrooms, and not only at eye level but also near or on the floor, to invite visitors to sit down and take more time to look. Paintings, sculptures, drawings, prints, furniture, glass, ceramics, textiles and other objects were positioned with great care, weighing up their relationship with each other, with the architecture and with the natural light entering the enlarged windows. Thus Ede devised exceptionally beautiful, yet subtle, visual constructions based on the play of light and shadow, and animated by entrancing conversations between objects (Figure 8.4). As the *Cambridge Review* put it, he had created an 'antimuseum'.[8]

To enhance the feeling of domesticity and informality, Ede welcomed visitors personally, offering them either a tour or to wander freely around the house. In fact, the overall care of Kettle's Yard fell largely on him, which he enjoyed because it gave him full control over his creation and the opportunity to establish routines reflecting his belief in St Augustine's doctrine of the divine nature of everyday tasks. This notion dovetailed with his idea of art as a means to spiritual growth, which in the 1950s was revitalised by new friendships with two American artists, William Congdon and Richard Pousette-Dart, who were both deeply concerned with religious matters.

8.4
**Light-play: two
works by
Constantin
Brancusi and the
Bechstein piano.**
Photo: Paul Allitt,
Kettle's Yard,
University of
Cambridge

Building on this background, Ede developed a vision of aesthetic fulfilment as the starting point of a journey that could lead one to higher values, and ultimately God. To achieve this, he systematically pursued a very modernist kind of formal purity that, by appealing to the inner feelings of visitors, was designed to induce in them a contemplative mood. Ede wished Kettle's Yard to become a place where people could find inner peace and tranquillity, and often referred to it as a 'work of devotion' or a 'house of prayer'. This desire to connect the aesthetic with spiritual enlightenment especially informed his concern with the play of light and shadow, which is apparent in the 1970 extension to the house, designed by Sir Leslie Martin and David Owers, closely following Ede's instructions and responding to his agenda. In the new building lighting comes predominantly from skylights, with an emphatic and symbolic use of natural light reminiscent of the complex web of signifiers found in Gothic cathedrals (Figure 8.5).

The use of visual language to initiate a process of spiritual revelation was for Ede what ultimately characterised good art itself. He generally favoured the work of artists who aimed at exploring reality through the rejection of naturalism and the adoption of great formal clarity, and in *A Way of Life*, the book that charts the genesis of Kettle's Yard, he wrote that 'nothing is lost by simplification, everything is gained'[9] – a notion that underlies his great appreciation of the art of, among others, Constantin Brancusi.

At the foundation of Ede's approach was the concept of balance, which in his vision related to both artistic and spiritual fulfilment, and informed not only his aesthetic choices but also the way in which the house was lived in and looked after. This is a crucial notion for the understanding of the meaning and ethos of Kettle's

8.5
Ben Nicholson's etching Porta San Gimignano lit through a skylight.
Photo: Paul Allitt, Kettle's Yard, University of Cambridge

Yard, and it is also a useful one to explain how the whole project became for Ede, in his words, a way of life. From this perspective, his treatment of the house as a work of art in its own right should come as no surprise. Ede made this point on numerous occasions, by comparing the place to a piece of music or a painting, in which each part is significant on its own, but much more important in terms of its contribution to the whole arrangement.

Eventually, Ede's spirituality also played an important part in his determination to hand Kettle's Yard over to the University of Cambridge. He argued that:

> A man's way of life should expand, his house and his possessions increase as he himself spreads out into the world, a fitting home for family and friends and his ever widening receptivity as slowly his spirit grows within him. Then as that spirit finds liberty, its material spirit becomes less and less important and gradually falls away. During this time he should shed his worldly possessions and as he needs less space to live in, shrink to smaller houses until he has no more than will comfortably fit him for his death.[10]

Life after Ede

With their eighties approaching, in 1973 Jim and Helen left Cambridge and moved to Edinburgh, where they would spend their final years. From that moment Kettle's Yard remained under the sole responsibility of the university. In spite of minor disagreements, Ede was pleased with this arrangement, because he believed that the house, with its elaborate network of visual and emotional strategies, represented a perfect complement to more scientific academic teaching. Tellingly, in 1970 he had concluded the introduction to the first guidebook declaring that 'there should be a Kettle's Yard in every university'.[11]

Thinking of himself as an artist rather than a collector or curator, throughout his tenancy Ede had treated the house as 'a painting . . . which in all honesty . . . only *he* could make with the available material'.[12] Even after the hand-over to the university, he had battled fiercely to retain total control over the realisation of his vision, systematically rejecting any external interference. This had generated more than a little anxiety among Cambridge officials during the building and furnishing of the 1970 extension. Inevitably, the situation was complicated further by Ede's departure, which came with the demand (to him legitimate in the presence of an artwork) that everything be preserved unaltered.

This set-up was to pose great problems for Ede's successors, especially because, as we have seen, retaining a domestic atmosphere was of fundamental importance to him. However, a domestic space is, by definition, alive, mobile, ever-changing. Indeed, when Jim and Helen lived in the house they offered refreshments and meals, had guests overnight and moved things around, including the works of art, whose display was not fixed until their departure. Visitors were allowed to explore objects not just visually but also, for instance, through touch, and various smells must have contributed to the creation of a domestic feeling. By all accounts the atmosphere was of the sort one would expect to find in someone's home.

Unsurprisingly, this character has proven very difficult to retain in a house that not only is no longer lived in, but which has also been condemned to immobility. This had seemed evident to some from early on, with Helen Ede and Ben Nicholson expressing their reservations already in the late 1960s. Nonetheless, following Ede's instructions the first resident curators were asked to live in an adjacent private flat created at the time of the extension, and since the early 1980s no one has actually resided on site.

When the house ceased to exist as a living space, its very nature was deeply affected. Expanding on the definition of it as a painting, a fitting analogy to describe Kettle's Yard after Ede could be that of a still life, in the sense that without its creator it became a place in which life is completely still, almost frozen. In particular, the oxymoronic implication of the expression seems to suit well the fundamental contradiction of the house, that of being a lived-in environment to be preserved intact without anyone living in it.

Incidentally, it is worth noting that Ede's idea of domesticity would hardly match most accepted definitions. In the inevitably anecdotal history of Kettle's Yard there are regular references to how he used to hide signs of his presence before opening the house to the public – a fact highlighted by the instructions left for the first keeper, which stated: 'he should be a careful host to all visitors, giving them a sense of being welcomed, and to this end it seems to me important to leave no sign of <u>personal</u> occupation during such hours'.[13] Family members have recounted how, when staying in the house, during opening hours they were expected to retreat outside or to the guest cottage, and the anecdotage also includes a reference to a chicken-wire playpen used to check the exploratory spirit of younger visitors.

Regardless of Ede's ideas on domesticity, one major consequence of his demands is that today the house has come to be perceived primarily as the expression of the taste of one individual and his age. Paradoxically, this is the opposite of what Ede had wished on the opening of the extension, when he said:

> Kettle's Yard, unlike the Fitzwilliam Museum, is in no way meant to be an Art Gallery or a Museum, nor even a special collection of works of art reflecting what might be called my taste, or the taste of a given period. It is, rather, a continuing way of life from these last 50 years, in which stray objects, stones, glass, pictures, sculpture, in light and in space, have been used to make manifest the underlying stability which more and more we need to recognise if we are not to be swamped by all that is so rapidly opening up before us.[14]

Yet today a growing number of visitors see Kettle's Yard as, or expect it to be, an art gallery or a kind of period piece, rather than a living home. This might be the inevitable consequence of it having become a fully registered museum[15] and of being presented as such in guidebooks and tourist information. However, the question does not seem to be just one of expectations: visiting rarely changes this sort of preconception, and a recurrent remark about the house is that as a domestic setting it speaks above all of absence.

Underlying all this is the implication that a significant number of visitors approach Kettle's Yard anticipating an experience similar to that offered by more conventional museums. And, to complicate matters, they visit in much greater numbers than they did in Ede's days. All this makes it very difficult to adhere to the original vision of domesticity, especially in consideration of the fact that some of today's widely accepted museological principles are in open contrast with it.

This introduces one of the key curatorial issues that Kettle's Yard presents today, that of the immobility of its displays. In Ede's vision, the addition, removal or displacement of even a single object in a room would spoil a very delicate balance. To allow his successors to preserve the place intact, he left extremely detailed instructions, which are still strictly adhered to (the only exceptions are the replacement of worn-out rugs when they become a safety hazard, objects removed for exhibitions or conservation, and the occasional introduction of works by artists shown in the adjacent exhibition gallery). In other words, today house and collection are approached and preserved more like an artwork than a museum.

While this is not particularly difficult to achieve, the immobility imposed by Ede, coupled with the changed atmosphere of the house, has some negative implications on the quality of visitor experience. Addressing them can be a difficult task, but one that lends itself to the development of creative approaches relying on the identification of areas in which Ede's ideas and today's museological practice overlap.

One relatively straightforward possibility, based on the example of similar organisations elsewhere, would be to re-create a sense of homeliness by introducing in the house everyday objects such as cooking utensils or toothbrushes. This, however, seems an unsuitable solution for Kettle's Yard, because it would not only affect Ede's displays and suggest a view of domesticity alien to him, but it would also involve rather trivial dilemmas (such as having to choose between a modern type of toothpaste or one contemporary to Ede) that seem entirely off the mark.

Another option is the temporary introduction of new artwork, usually in conjunction with exhibitions in the gallery or by commissioning interventions in the house. This has pros and cons. On the one hand, it can offer new insights into the collection and the house and regenerate the sense of contemporaneity that they supposedly had when Ede resumed collecting in the 1950s, acquiring works by relatively young and little-known artists. However, this may be an approach that does not match feelings about Kettle's Yard that were expressed as early as the 1960s. Ben Nicholson, for instance, thought that the house was too old-fashioned to be a place for contemporary art and refused to give some of his recent works for it. Moreover, the introduction of new art requires a temporary alteration of Ede's displays, which, in addition to the aforementioned ethical issues, could disappoint those visitors wanting to see the original house.

Intervening in the house, however, does not necessarily require altering the displays. One interesting experiment was made in 1998, when artists Anne Eggebert, Julian Walker and their two-year-old son Frederic were offered the chance to live in the house for a week.[16] They created new, mostly performative work and interacted with visitors, all under the gaze of 24-hour CCTV relaying images to a screen in the exhibition gallery. Unsurprisingly the project highlighted the tensions between private and exhibition spaces, and put Ede's model of domestic living to a severe test. But it also showed that the stimulation of social interaction, so valued by Ede, can be a sensitive way of regenerating the liveliness of the house and inviting its reinterpretation. Today, the programmes of educational activities, talks, concerts, fellowships and exhibitions all aim at creating 'unobtrusive' opportunities for people to use Kettle's Yard and interact with each other, thus hopefully catering for the changing needs of visitors.

Another major problem relating to visitor expectations is the provision of information on the objects on display. Ede advocated the absence of labels and wall texts as a means to create what he saw as the necessary intimacy with art. Lacking an interpretative framework, he believed, people are encouraged to bring their own thoughts and experiences to the collection. While this is often true of visitors who, once understanding the uniqueness of the place, tend to accept its idiosyncrasies, complaints about the absence of information on the walls are not infrequent. To a great extent this seems the consequence of the changing social role of art museums (and even antimuseums), which today are regarded less as temples for the cult of beauty and more as an integral part of the education system. This implies that increasing numbers of visitors go to museums expecting an active educational experience rather than the purely aesthetic enjoyment of art advocated by Ede.

This issue is addressed in two ways. On a human level, house invigilators are available to provide visitors with the information they require, which is what Ede would have done personally during his tenancy. This, however, can be an unsatisfactory arrangement for all those people who do not wish to be 'assisted' and would rather visit independently, and for all non-English speaking visitors. For them, an alternative is offered by a low-price guidebook with an introduction to the house, plans, lists of works and brief explanatory texts for each room. The combination of invigilators and guidebook seems to provide an adequate balance of informal and academic information in tune with Ede's vision.

Other aspects of the Kettle's Yard ethos and aesthetic are more difficult to reconcile with its status as a registered museum, in particular with regards to conservation standards. One significant problem is the multisensoriality of Ede's visual architectures, which were designed to stimulate more than mere visual perception. As we have seen, Ede sought the interplay of natural light with objects and architecture, treating the building as a remarkable series of sequences from dark to light, modulated by variously sized windows, skylights and Venetian blinds. Time and space awareness plays a very important role in the house, with extraordinary variations of atmosphere at different times of the day and of the year, and no set paths between rooms. In addition, Ede often allowed visitors to handle the objects on display and refused to protect them with cases or barriers, as most people would do at home.

Preserving these characteristics, which are central to Ede's vision, has major conservation implications. A number of works on paper and textiles have to be left exposed to high light levels (both direct and diffuse), the effect of which is only partly mitigated by UV film on windows and picture glazing. Light exclusion during closed hours is not realistically achievable across the building, and in any case a recent study has shown that in certain areas of the house, even considering only the periods when it is open to the public, the overall exposure of works to light is significantly above the recommended annual threshold.[17]

The question of visitors handling objects is also critical. Faced with a significant number of works without visible protection and regardless of the presence of invigilators, it is not rare for some to be tempted to touch exhibits (ceramics and sculpture appear to be the most attractive). If, on the one hand, this creates obvious conservation problems, on the other hand by asking, no matter how politely, visitors not to touch, a typical museum atmosphere ensues, which clearly clashes with Ede's intentions.

A further problem derives from the steadily increasing number of visitors. Each year, over 20,000 people visit the house, with the imaginable wear-and-tear of architecture and furnishing of a building designed essentially to be a home. The only possible answer in this case appears to be the limitation of opening times to two hours a day (three in the summer), a choice which, although in line with Ede's practice, is in contrast with growing pressures to increase access.

In conclusion

Today, Kettle's Yard remains a much admired and influential example of how art can become an integral part of daily life. Despite its idiosyncrasies, the unique atmosphere of the house remains with, and inspires, almost every visitor. This alone seems a sufficient reason to make every effort to preserve the place as Ede wished, rather than turn it into something different. However, such an approach implies that, as with many works of art made in the last 50 years, the life-span of Kettle's Yard is likely to be significantly shorter than that of most collections. In this sense, Ede left his successors much more than a building and a collection to preserve: his legacy is, above all, a challenge to make his mission meaningful in the 'here and now', and beyond.

Notes

1 H. S. Ede and the University of Cambridge, unpublished memorandum, Cambridge, 28 November 1966, Kettle's Yard Archive.

2 H. S. Ede, *Kettle's Yard: A Way of Life*, Cambridge: Kettle's Yard, 1984, p. 199.

3 Ian Hamilton Finlay on an inscribed pebble (1995).

4 H. S. Ede, unpublished typescript, undated, Kettle's Yard Archive.

5 H. S. Ede, unpublished letter to David Jones, Les Charlottières (France), 31 January 1956, Kettle's Yard Archive.

6 H. S. Ede, 'Introduction', in N. Walker, *Kettle's Yard: An Illustrated Handlist of the Paintings, Sculptures and Drawings*, Cambridge: Kettle's Yard, pp. 4–6.

7 H. S. Ede, *The National Gallery of Art, Washington, D.C.*, unpublished lecture, *c.* 1941, Kettle's Yard Archive.

8 I. Wright, 'Antimuseum', in *Cambridge Review*, Vol. 91, No. 2197, p. 174.

9 H. S. Ede, *Kettle's Yard: A Way of Life*, Cambridge: Kettle's Yard, 1984, p. 218.

10 H. S. Ede, *Between Two Memories*, unpublished autobiography, Kettle's Yard Archive, p. 212.

11 H. S. Ede, 'Introduction', in N. Walker, *Kettle's Yard: An Illustrated Handlist of the Paintings, Sculptures and Drawings*, Cambridge: Kettle's Yard, p. 6.

12 H. S. Ede, unpublished letter to Sir Frank Lee, Cambridge, 16 December 1967, University of Cambridge Archive.

13 H. S. Ede, unpublished notes, Cambridge, 1970, Old Schools Archive.

14 H. S. Ede, 'Speech on the opening of the Kettle's Yard extension, 5 May 1970', in *Cambridge Review*, Vol. 91, No. 2197, p. 174.

15 The Museum Registration Scheme (from 2004 called Accreditation Scheme) was established in 1988 by the Museums and Galleries Commission. Its main aims are to set minimum standards in museum management, collection care and public services, and to provide a shared ethical basis for all organisations involved. Over 1,800 museums across the UK have joined the scheme.

16 The project, entitled *Mr & Mrs Walker have moved*, was completed in June 1998.

17 M. Constantoglou, *Exposure to Light in the Exhibition Space: A Methodology Applied to Kettle's Yard Art Gallery*, unpublished M.Phil. essay, University of Cambridge, 2005.

Chapter 9

Two Viennese refugees

Lucie Rie and her apartment

Eleanor Gawne

The Kaiserliche Hofmobliendepot (The Imperial Furniture Collection) in Vienna evolved after the First World War from an imperial furniture store into a major museum of furniture and interior design. In addition to individual pieces of historic furniture, it now houses many room sets taken from buildings as varied as imperial palaces to bourgeois apartments. One recent acquisition which stands out, on display since 1999, are two rooms of built-in and free-standing furniture that had belonged to the potter, Lucie Rie. These rooms were originally designed in 1928 by Ernst Plischke, an architect friend of Rie, and her husband Hans, for their flat in Vienna. When the Ries were forced to leave Vienna in 1938 at the *Anschluss* (the enforced union of Austria with Nazi Germany), the interior was dismantled and shipped to London, where it was reassembled by another Viennese architect and refugee, Ernst Freud, the son of Sigmund Freud. The fittings were adapted by Freud to fit into a small house at 18 Albion Mews, W2, immediately north of Hyde Park, London, where Lucie Rie had her flat and studio (Figure 9.1). Following her death in 1995, the interior was again taken back across Europe, restored and reconstructed for display at the Hofmobliendepot.

Although there is intrinsic interest in this interior because it belonged to a famous potter and because it was designed by Ernst Plischke, the apartment also poses questions concerning the display of rooms as museum objects and issues such as authenticity. Many museums with period interiors, such as the Museé Carnavalet in Paris, display rooms that are almost wholly restored, or 'reconstructed', as well as rooms that are original and in various states of preservation, sometimes complete

9.1

Lucie Rie sitting in an armchair in her first-floor living-room, at 18 Albion Mews, London, 1940s, with some pieces of furniture designed by Ernst Plischke for her in 1928.

Photo: Crafts Study Centre, 2005

wrecks. The problems of collecting and display of period rooms has been a subject of debate, especially from the 1950s to the 1980s. Philippe de Montebello, Director of the Metropolitan Museum of Art, New York, has discussed some of these arguments about period rooms in terms of their appropriateness, their purpose and their degree of authenticity. Indeed, in the US, some museums removed their period rooms from public display after several years because in-depth research found that they were inauthentic. Montebello writes that it was only from the 1980s that curators and art historians began to re-evaluate the importance of such rooms and revised their thinking about the rooms and the information provided about them to the public.[1] In addition to these issues, Charles Saumarez Smith raises another argument against period rooms – that of the potential audience, and the expectations and knowledge they may bring. He also addresses the wider issue of how period rooms should be treated by museums generally, writing:

> artefacts do not exist in a space of their own, transmitting meaning to the spectator, but, on the contrary, are susceptible to a multiform construction of meaning which is dependent on the design, the context of other objects, the visual and historical representation, the whole environment; that artefacts can change their meaning not just over the years as different

historiographical and institutional currents pick them out and transform their significance, but from day to day as different people view them and subject them to their own interpretation.[2]

The Lucie Rie apartment also raises questions about the role of exhibiting modern movement interior design, devoid of memory-bearing clutter, within an historical setting, a museum. As Gillian Naylor points out 'The icons of modernism were designed to defy memory and deny the past.'[3]

The Viennese interior we are examining here also raises other considerations concerning the role of women as clients of modern architecture and design, the question of national identity and acquired identity, and the construction, reconstruction and display of modern design and modern craft. This chapter addresses the following questions: to what extent was this interior different from other modern interiors in the Vienna of 1928? Did Lucie Rie specifically intend to create a *gesamtkunstwerk,* commissioning an interior to better display her own ceramics? How successfully can an interior be exhibited, like an object, in a museum? How authentic is a reconstructed interior after it has been built, dismantled, crossed Europe and been reinstalled, let alone after that has happened twice?

Lucie Rie (1902–95) (née Gomperz), liked to be referred to simply as Lucie by her friends.[4] She worked within a particular craft-based strain of modernism. She studied ceramics from 1922 to 1926 with Michael Powolny at the School of Arts and Crafts in Vienna.[5] She received recognition for her work while still a student, exhibiting in the acclaimed Austrian pavilion at the Paris Exposition in 1925. She later won Gold Medals at the Brussels World Fair, 1935, and the Milan Triennale of 1935, and secured a prize at the Paris International Exhibition of 1937. She married Hans Rie, a technical executive at Böhm, a felt hat manufacturer, when she left art school in 1926. A year later her uncle, Sandor Wolf, gave the young couple an unfurnished roof-top apartment in a nineteenth-century block of flats at 24 Wollzeile, near St Stephen's Cathedral in central Vienna. Since they married, they had been living at Lucie's parents house. Lucie installed a kiln in one of the rooms of the flat and made it into her ceramics studio. In 1928, at the age of 26, Lucie commissioned a young architect, Ernst Plischke, to design the interior of this apartment. Accounts differ as to how Plischke and Lucie first met and how the commission came about. Each appreciated and liked the other's work. Cyril Frankel, a life-long friend of Lucie's, recounts that she had bought a grey swivel chair from Plischke, and when he visited the flat to deliver it, Lucie asked him if he wanted to design the whole flat.[6] There are also accounts that Plischke had, in fact, come to see Lucie to buy pots for a private house he was designing at Attersee in Austria. In his autobiography Plischke relates that that they had met at the School of Arts and Crafts in the summer of 1927. He recounts that Lucie had wanted another architect, Franz Schuster, to design her flat, but Plischke suggested he could do it just as well as Schuster.[7] John Houston writes that their friendship 'grew out of their liking for each others' work, the informal co-operation while planning her flat, and a continuing close interest in his projects'.[8]

Ernst Plischke (1903–92) had studied at the School of Arts and Crafts before training under Peter Behrens at the Academy of Fine Arts. In 1926, he completed his studies and went to work in the Atelier Josef Frank, before setting up on his own in 1928. He spent part of 1929 in New York, working in the office of Eli Jacques Kahn, but when that office closed due to the Wall Street Crash of October 1929, returned to Vienna at the end of that year. He was awarded the *Grosser Oesterreichischer Staatspreis* in 1935 before being forced to leave Austria and emigrate to New Zealand in 1939 (Plischke's wife, Anna, was Jewish, so he was unable to join the Chamber of Arts and continue practising as an architect after the *Anschluss*). In 1963, he returned to Vienna to take up the chair of architecture at the Academy of Fine Arts where he had trained.

Ernst Plischke was keen to start independent practice and intended the Ries' flat to be his first job. Lucie said of Plischke: 'For me he was the best architect in Vienna. He built pure, beautiful houses using simple lines. He taught me what was necessary and what was going on in building and sculpture. Curiously, he never criticised my work, so that I never knew whether he liked it or not.'[9] In fact, Plischke publicised Lucie's work throughout his life. This is the reason why there are many collectors of Lucie Rie ceramics in New Zealand, where Plischke lived from 1939 to 1963 – his clients in New Zealand were persuaded to buy her pots for their Plischke-designed houses.[10] Ernst and Lucie kept in contact throughout their lives by letter and telephone, and met up again in the 1980s.

Plischke worked within the Modern Movement; the interiors he designed for Lucie feature clean, geometric lines and space-saving ideas. In an interview in May 1984, Plischke discussed the influences on his work, particularly that of Le Corbusier, whose cubic geometric forms he admired, although he criticised the quality of the construction of the buildings, which to him were below the standards of Mies van der Rohe. He writes:

> It is a fact that Le Corbusier was by far the greatest influence in my educational career. I was just ready to throw it in, when in 1922 *Vers une architecture* appeared. Only in French, five years later in German. My French was certainly much too poor to read it properly and it was just the drawings that were so inspiring and I knew then, that was my way to follow him . . .[11]

As an émigré, Plischke had two careers, even two lives. In Austria, he is now recognised as one of the major representatives of the Neues Bauen (New Construction) movement. He was a member of the Austrian Werkbund and was interested in promoting high-quality design and craftsmanship. Significantly, the two-unit block of houses Plischke designed for the Werkbundsiedlung in Vienna in 1932 had Lucie Rie pots displayed in them when they were photographed for publicity purposes. In New Zealand, he was considered a 'Bauhaus man', an important émigré architect, described by Linda Tyler as a key figure in the introduction of modernism into Wellington architecture in the period following the Second World War.[12] Plischke's importance was recognised in 2003, with two exhibitions held in Vienna to celebrate the centenary of his birth – one on his furniture design at the Hof-mobiliendepot, the other on his architecture, at the Academy of Fine Arts.

The design of the interior

The design concept of the apartment's interior was probably intended to provide a *gesamtkunstwerk*, or unified whole, but was also designed for flexible use. According to Plischke, it had a peaceful and open feel.[13] He took the commission seriously and apparently measured Hans Rie's legs to ensure the proportions of the sofas and the height of the cupboards were correct. The walnut cupboards presented a continuous, unbroken front and they had versatile shelves and drawers, so clothes, cutlery and books could be stored; the fittings were designed so that they could be completely dismantled because they were screwed together rather than glued. The doors of the cupboards were of flat uniform panelling with new invisible sunk hinges. The bedroom had three walls of built-in cupboards. Individual pieces of furniture, including stools, tables and easy chairs, were also designed by Plischke especially for the flat and could be grouped according to need. The covers and curtains were made of Swedish hand-woven fabrics or of a single colour linen (the covers were apparently woven by Plischke's sister using a loom he brought specially). The floors were covered with natural coloured bouclé and their uniformity was intended to tie the rooms together. Plischke remarked on how different the flat looked from the rooms that Josef Frank designed, which mixed modern and antique pieces.[14] Plischkes' family were joiners and he had worked in the family joinery business every summer holiday, so he had a thorough knowledge of woodcraft techniques.

So, what was the cultural background provided by Lucie's family, and how might this have shaped her future outlook on design, and the choice of architect for her apartment? Lucie came from a well-to-do Jewish family and as a child had witnessed the employment of an architect to design an interior. Her father, a prosperous ear, nose and throat doctor with artistic interests, had commissioned the architect Eduard Wimmer to design furniture for his surgery and reception room, in the modern Viennese style, using simple white rectangular forms. Indeed, Lucie always maintained that Josef Hoffmann[15] was the biggest influence on her work and her own works have always been considered to be rooted in the ideas of the modern movement.[16] Writing in 1982, Peta Levi thought that her pots were above all simple: 'undoubtedly these qualities derived from an interest in architecture and form'.[17] Other influences on her work and ideas about interior design came from visits to France and Italy, and the Roman pottery in her uncle's house museum at Eisenstadt.[18] Uncle Sandor, as mentioned above, had bought the flat for them in Vienna in 1927, and was a passionate collector of antique ceramics.

Throughout her career, Lucie's work had been associated with modern movement principles. In 1951 George Wingfield Digby had remarked on her work as follows:

> [the] intimate and delicate handling of fine clay in clear-cut brown, black and white, ornamented solely with engraved, rectangular lines, is particularly suited to certain simple, architectural styles of interior decoration such as the very best English, American and Italian.[19]

Similarly, in the introduction to the catalogue that accompanied the first retrospective exhibition of Lucie's work in 1967 organised by the Arts Council, Wingfield Digby wrote 'Here was a Studio Potter who was not rustic but metropolitan; her work had no nostalgic undertones of folk art; the style was that of someone conscious of modern architecture.'[20] In 1981, Victor Margrie remarked on how her pots sprang 'naturally from a potter born into a society which had extolled the virtues of Modernism rather than as in Britain, rejecting them in favour of a tepid historicism . . .'.[21] The modernity of the rooms that Plischke made for Lucie harmonised well with her pots, a fact often remarked on by critics of her work. In a review of an exhibition of Lucie Rie and Hans Coper's work in 1956, the critic wrote of the pots:

> [their] elegant severity is extremely sophisticated and subtle. These pots, one feels, would look their best not on rough, scrubbed refectory tables, but in modern interiors where their carefully calculated shapes showing the moulding of skilled hands would contrast with and be set off by the impersonal finish given by the machine.[22]

So why, and indeed how, did Lucie bring the fittings and furniture of her Viennese apartment with her to London? John Houston writes that 'it must have taken a deal of persuasion and influence to export the whole flat in 1938'.[23] It was, of course, common enough for émigrés to bring portable possessions such as furniture or household items as reminders of their native land, or to decorate their new homes in a style that reminded them of their origins, but to ship the entire decor seems astonishing in terms of expense and the organisation required in difficult circumstances. Also, by 1938 the marriage of Lucie and Hans was breaking up (it was dissolved in 1940), and one might have thought that the interior would have had sad connotations for her. Indeed, it is useful to compare the interior with the rooms of 2 Willow Road, Hampstead, the house designed by the émigré architect Ernö Goldfinger for himself and his family in 1938. As Gillian Naylor writes, here the house 'does not, and could not, celebrate an English past, but neither does it acknowledge an inherited past, or many personal memories of either Ernö's or Ursula's pre-marital past'.[24] But in Lucie's case, she may have brought the apartment with her to preserve part of her Viennese self-identity. Even though she was starting a new life in England,

and knew that her life was just beginning, we may speculate that she still wanted to retain part of her former existence. Or there may be another explanation: Lucie's friend, Cyril Frankel, remarked that he believed Uncle Sandor provided Plischke with the money to ship everything to London, so it may have been down to these two men rather than Lucie herself that the fittings came to England.[25]

To British eyes, even in 1938, the year of the MARS Group exhibition at the Burlington Galleries, this particular ensemble of fittings and furniture must have looked both particularly modern and especially Continental. The suite Plischke designed for Lucie consisted of two main rooms – a living-room and a bedroom, (Figures 9.2, 9.3 and 9.4) plus a vestibule or anteroom, kitchen, bathroom and Lucie's pottery studio. Plischke designed the two main rooms so that they were homogenous in function and decoration. Eva Ottilinger points out that Plischke 'created an entirely modern living space . . .' which avoided 'the traditional differences in decoration between private and public rooms and traditional gender schemes, which considered the bedroom as a female sphere and the living room as a male dominion'.[26] She also notes that both rooms were used during the day, and both rooms were open for visitors. In Vienna, the living-room as photographed in *c.* 1930 shows books on the fitted shelves, and only one pot is displayed in the anteroom. John Houston writes that having met Plischke 'he doubts he would have sanctioned more than one artifact in his jewel-like conception!'.[27] When Lucie first moved to London in September 1938, she met again a friend from Vienna, Ernst Freud, in Hampstead, where she initially rented a flat at No. 24 Frognal. Lucie probably knew him through her father, who was a close professional colleague of Sigmund Freud. She asked Freud to convert a garage she had found at 18 Albion Mews into a studio and small flat, which she rented from the Church Commissioners and had got by chance. She requested him to incorporate Plischke's fittings, shelves, tables and chairs which had been shipped over from Vienna.

Ernst Freud (1892–1970) had emigrated to Britain earlier than Lucie, in 1933. Born in Vienna, he studied architecture there and in Munich, graduating in 1919 and subsequently moving to Berlin. In Berlin he designed houses and flats, commercial buildings and furniture for individual clients. His practice in London was largely concerned with domestic design, especially flats, and he specialised in conversions. Significantly, he had experience of reusing shelves and panelling taken from another room in Berlin in his own home in St John's Wood Terrace, London, in 1935.[28] Following a heart attack, he later gave up his architectural career to edit his father's papers.[29] In 1995 Lucie's living-room was described as

> retaining its 1930s elegance, its design of straight lines, natural coloured white and pale cream fabrics and dark wood softened by copious pots of flowers. It had the soothing calm of a retreat in which the only change over the years was the pile of books in the corner which seemed to grow in height.[30]

9.2
The living-room in Lucie and Hans Rie's apartment in Vienna, designed by Ernst Plischke, 1928–9.
Photo: Plischke-Nachlass/Plischke Estate

9.3 *(below)*
Another view of the living-room in Lucie and Hans Rie's apartment in Vienna, designed by Ernst Plischke, 1928–9.
Photo: Plischke-Nachlass/Plischke Estate

9.4
**The bedroom in
Lucie and Hans
Rie's apartment in
Vienna, designed
by Ernst Plischke,
1928-9.**
Photo: Plischke-
Nachlass/Plischke
Estate

Tony Birks, writing on the 'severe but serene beauty' of the flat, writes 'It is quite difficult to assess how much is the effect of the Plischke furniture and how much that of a sensitive architect – Freud – in supervising the living arrangements of his Austrian friend.'[31]

The fittings from the flat in Vienna were necessarily used in different rooms in London. John Houston notes that in Vienna the fittings were very precise and formal; in London, as adapted by Ernst Freud, they had to be grouped more informally to fit the spaces of a nineteenth-century mews house.[32] Sadly, there is no trace of Freud's adaption of the fittings in the collections of his drawings and photographs now held at the British Architectural Library, Royal Institute of British Architects. The open-fronted shelving for the display of books from the living-room in Vienna continued its function, together with some solid-door cupboards, as the showroom, or outer room, of Lucie's ground-floor workshop in Albion Mews, where she received visitors. Only some visitors were allowed beyond this room into the studio itself. Margot Coatts recounts that this studio was like an inner sanctum.[33] The shelving unit was used as a room divider; on these units, Lucie kept samples for customers to order and some of her favourite pots, many of which she could not replicate because they had happened by accident. The rest of the fittings from Vienna were reworked by Freud to fit one wall of the single large sitting-room on the first floor. On this floor at Albion Mews there was also a tiny kitchen and small bedroom, neither of which had any Viennese fittings. She also combined individual pieces of modern furniture by Plischke she had brought from Vienna, with vernacular English furniture, including a Windsor chair.

How did the flat come to make the return journey to Vienna? Plischke was a good self-publicist and had written his autobiography in 1989, and considered this first commission the creative nucleus of his work. He featured the flat in his books and was proud of this early work. Similarly, Lucie wanted very much for Plischke to be recognised in some way. One of Plischke's pupils, Alessandro Alvera, was employed to enlarge the Hofmobiliendepot museum in 1990 and it was then that Plischke asked the museum to include a reconstruction of Lucie's bedroom in the new galleries. Plischke died in 1992 and bequeathed the drawings and photographs of the apartment to the Hofmobiliendepot (they were subsequently passed on to the Plischke archive at the Academy of Fine Arts). Lucie informed the museum that she would be pleased for the fittings to be reconstructed in their original form for the museum. After Lucie's death in 1995, the Hofmobiliendepot made an offer to the estate to buy and reconstruct the interior according to Plischke's original drawings. On display since October 1999, the museum is proud to have

9.5
Design for the bedroom in Lucie and Hans Rie's apartment in Vienna, by Ernst Plischke, 1928.
Photo: Plischke-Nachlass/Plischke Estate

such a complete interior that they restored in their own workshops; it is advertised in the museum's publicity as an 'early work by E.A. Plischke' and 'as a living remembrance to an artistic friendship'. The two main rooms of the flat were put back to their earlier incarnation from 1928 to 1938, although the original pottery studio from the flat in Vienna was not re-created.

It is clear that the Plischke/Rie rooms have had two incarnations. The second, London, 'life' of the rooms, 57 years, was longer than its short first life in Vienna. One might argue, therefore, that the London 'version' was historically more significant. It is interesting to speculate whether the interiors would have been put back to their Viennese incarnation if they had been acquired by a British museum and displayed in the UK, or kept as Freud had reworked them. Perhaps the interiors in Vienna may be considered to be more a reflection of Plischke's original design intentions than of the habitat of Lucie Rie, the British potter. They may also be considered to be more a reflection of the youthful work of Ernst Plischke or Lucie as a young client, than a true reflection of the 'life' of the rooms in the 57 years they were at 18 Albion Mews.

To conclude, having described the double life of this interior, we may speculate whether the Lucie Rie rooms as displayed in the Hofmobiliendepot are 'authentic' as museum exhibits are presumed to be, or how much they should be considered a reconstruction. It is not made clear to the everyday, non-specialist visitor to the museum how much of it is 'real' or a reconstruction. We know that what we see today at the Hofmobiliendepot is based on Plischke's original designs, so is its 'authenticity' questionable? The museum in Vienna rebuilt the rooms according to the early drawings of Plischke. This implies that first versions of a design, even though they may have only a short life, are more 'important' than secondary, revised versions, which in this case, had a much longer life in Albion Mews. One might also consider whether it would have been preferable for the rooms to be preserved in a suitable museum in the UK, where it might have been associated with the life and work of Lucie Rie and Ernst Freud, rather than the work of Ernst Plischke. Clearly, the force of Plischke's personality and his significance in Austria were overriding factors in the apartment's future. The museum has also made curatorial decisions on the display of the room – for example, displaying Plischke's book collection, part of his archive, on the shelves in the Lucie Rie apartment. Despite these qualifications, the interior has found an appropriate home at the Hofmobiliendepot, and it is one of the many exciting and unexpected 'gems' to be found there.

Acknowledgements

My thanks to Charlotte Benton, Margot Coatts, Cyril Frankel, Lizbeth Gale, Wendy Garvey, Tanya Harrod, John Houston, Jolanta Kent, Monika Knofler, Jill Lever, Yvonne and Max Mayer, Eva Ottillinger, Linda Tyler, Jean Vacher, Lynne Walker and Volker Welter.

Notes

1 A. Peck and J. Parker (eds), *Period Rooms in the Metropolitan Museum of Art*, New York: Harry N. Abrams, 1996, pp. 9–10.

2 Charles Saumarez Smith, 'Museums, Artefacts, and Meaning', in *The New Museology*, ed. P. Vergo, London: Reaktion, 1989, p. 19.

3 Gillian Naylor, 'Modernism and Memory: Leaving Traces', in *Material Memories*, ed. Marius Kwint, Christopher Breward and Jeremy Aynsley (eds), Oxford: Berg, 1999, p. 91.

4 See John Houston ed., *Lucie Rie: A Survey of Her Life and Work*, London: Crafts Council, 1981 and Tony Birks *Lucie Rie*, revised ed. Marston Magna, Somerset: Marston House, 1994.

5 Michael Powolny (1871–1954), best known for decorative figurative ceramics, taught ceramics from 1912 to 1936 at the School of Arts and Crafts in Vienna. See John Houston ed., *Lucie Rie: A Survey of Her Life and Work*, London: Crafts Council, 1981, pp. 12–13 for information on Powolny's work.

6 Personal communication with Cyril Frankel, 28 April 2003.

7 Ernst A. Plischke, *Ein Leben mit Architektur*, Vienna: Locker, 1989, p. 103.

8 John Houston ed., *Lucie Rie: A Survey of Her Life and Work*, London: Crafts Council, 1981, p. 18.

9 Peta Levi, 'The Viennese potter who came in from the cold', *House & Garden*, January 1982, p. 40.

10 Personal communication with Linda Tyler, Hocken Library Gallery, University of Otago, Dunedin, New Zealand.

11 August Sarnitz and Eva B. Ottillinger *Ernest Plischke: The Complete Works: Modern Architecture for the New World*, Munich/London: Prestel, 2004, p. 258. In fact, *Vers une architecture* appeared in book form in 1923. See Darlene Brady, *Le Corbusier: An Annotated Bibliography*, New York, London: Garland, 1985.

12 Linda Tyler, 'Enemy Aliens or Cultivated Continentals: The New Zealand response to Ernst and Anna Plischke', unpublished paper presented at the Architecture Centre, Vienna, 21 March 2003.

13 Ernst A. Plischke, *Ein Leben mit Architektur*, Vienna: Locker, 1989, p. 103.

14 Ibid.

15 Josef Hoffmann was Professor of Architecture at the School of Arts and Crafts in Vienna from 1899 to 1941.

16 E. Cooper and M. Coatts, 'Dame Lucie Rie' (obituary), *The Independent*, 3 April 1995, p. 29.

17 Peta Levi, 'The Viennese potter who came in from the cold', *House & Garden*, January 1982, p. 40.

18 The museum is now called the Burgenlandisches (County Museum), then part of a Museum of Jewish Life, situated two hours from Vienna.

19 George Wingfield Digby, 'Contemporary pottery', *House & Garden*, November 1951, p. 34.

20 Arts Council, *Lucie Rie: A Retrospective Exhibition of Earthernware, Stoneware and Porcelain 1926–67*, London: Arts Council, 1967, catalogue introduction by George Wingfield Digby, p. 9.

21 John Houston ed., *Lucie Rie: A Survey of Her Life and Work*, London: Crafts Council, 1981, p. 9.

22 S. Bone, review of exhibition of the work of Lucie Rie and Hans Coper, *The Guardian*, 25 October 1956, p. 5.

23 Personal communication with John Houston, 29 March 2003.

24 Gillian Naylor, 'Modernism and Memory: Leaving Traces', in *Material Memories*, Marius Kwint, Christopher Breward and Jeremy Aynsley (eds), Oxford: Berg, 1999, p. 105.

25 Personal communication with Cyril Frankel, 28 April 2003.

26 Eva Ottilinger, 'Home again', *Crafts*, May/June 2001, p. 37.

27 Personal communication with John Houston, 29 March 2003.

28 Noel L. Carrington, 'Ernst L. Freud', *Decoration*, November 1935, pp. 22–3.

29 Charlotte Benton, *A Different World: Émigré Architects in Britain 1928–58*, London: RIBA Heinz Gallery, 1995, pp. 155–6.

30 E. Cooper and M. Coatts, 'Dame Lucie Rie' (obituary), *The Independent*, 3 April 1995, p. 29.

31 Tony Birks, *Lucie Rie*, revised ed. Marston Magna, Somerset: Marston House, 1994, p. 35.

32 Personal communication with John Houston, 29 March 2003.

33 Personal communication with Margot Coatts, 15 April 2003.

Chapter 10

The preservation
and presentation of
2 Willow Road for the
National Trust

Harriet McKay

In April 1996 the National Trust property, 2 Willow Road, Hampstead, opened to the public. I was custodian of the property from January 1996 until February 2005. The house was built in 1938–9 by the architect Ernö Goldfinger as a home for his family. The Goldfingers lived there until their deaths, Ernö dying in 1987 and Ursula, his wife in 1994. Partly as a result of Goldfinger's conviction in the 'rightness' of his design from the moment of creation, which resulted in a building very largely unchanged except where limited alterations were – very rarely – occasioned by practical need, and partly because it presented the total package of architecture, art and social life, the National Trust was able to put together a bid for acquisition headed by Edward Diestelkamp, a senior curator at the Trust's Head Office, and co-ordinated by Anthea Palmer, Historic Building's Representative, from Hughenden Manor, the Thames and Chilterns area Regional Office. The Goldfinger family responded positively to the proposal that the house and full contents be transferred to the Trust, a move made possible through the organisation's receiving the house via the National Treasury in lieu of inheritance tax, and a subsequent fund-raising campaign and grant from the Heritage Memorial Fund.[1]

  The process of acquiring Trust properties always involves the rigorous formulation of what will become post-acquisition policy, but Willow Road in particular represented a series of unknown quantities for the organisation. Not least were issues surrounding the presentation of so different a property to an audience (the National Trust's membership) dedicated to the preservation of a canon of buildings which had not hitherto included those created within modernism.[2] Also of paramount concern was the situation, unusual for the Trust, of operating from an ordinary, domestic-sized space where there would be no 'behind-the-scenes' office space for administrative, security and conservation work. How, the Trust asked, was it going to be possible to preserve the integrity of a family home that, however recently occupied, was nevertheless a historic interior and a habitus specific to a period and to a particular group of people when the presence of both National Trust staff – and indeed visitors – and the infrastructural requirements of the house's new museum status threatened to impinge on the 'authenticity' that the very nature of the project itself required? This chapter offers an account of some of the problems faced by the National Trust and summarises the decisions made, and the thinking behind these, in the early years of Willow Road's being open to the public. It will describe issues for which resolution was found, and also concerns over which no conclusion had been reached by the time of my leaving the post in February 2005.

Architecturally, the scheme at Willow Road – a terrace of three houses, constructed in reinforced concrete but faced with brick – represents a bold reworking of the British eighteenth-century terrace of which Goldfinger was a great admirer (Figure 10.1). Number 2, forming the middle of the terrace, can be read as the outcome of a combination of Goldfinger's unique *beaux-arts* rationalist training, with an understated and personal interpretation of the key tenets of modernism. The classicism of the beautifully proportioned exterior elevations is matched by immaculate detailing inside the house. Built on a very compact site and straightforwardly

10.1 *(below left)*
**Exterior of
2 Willow Road.**

10.2 *(right)*
View of the studio at Willow Road from the dining-room with works of art by Max Ernst, Robert Delaunay (left-hand side) and Amedée Ozenfant and Prunella Clough (right-hand side).

rectangular in plan, the house provides a perfect example of the adroit articulation of volume, space and light that was such a hallmark of Goldfinger's work. As a result, the house has a greater feeling of openness than its relatively limited physical space, and position in the centre of the terrace, would have otherwise allowed.

Number 2 Willow Road is also home to the art collection acquired by the Goldfingers throughout their lives there. The presence, for example, of works by Henry Moore, Max Ernst and Amedée Ozenfant is made all the more striking by virtue of their domestic setting. (Figure 10.2). Thus, the house represented for the Trust a unique opportunity to display significant art alongside the usual household effects associated with a family home, and indeed this was one of the key incentives for acquisition.

Legal ownership of the property by the National Trust was granted in July 1994, following which an extensive programme of building work was undertaken by Avanti Architects, the London-based practice, which at the time of its appointment by the Trust had already completed the successful restoration of another reinforced concrete structure, Berthold Lubetkin's iconic London Zoo Penguin Pool (1935), and also his building, the Finsbury Health Centre (1938). Avanti's brief was to adapt the building from domestic to museum status as unobtrusively as possible. It was clearly incumbent upon the Trust that repair of the building, installation of modern systems and general preparation for public opening be as discreet as possible in order that intervention into the original aesthetic and design of the house be kept to a minimum.

Running parallel with this programme of structural repair and conservation was the need to establish an administrative regime that would see the property through and beyond opening its doors. It was imperative that the sensitive work carried out by Avanti should not be squandered by lack of attention to the systems for admitting the public that were to be implemented. Any organisational structure employed for the presentation of the house to the public had to reflect this concern. Related to this, another of the key challenges at this stage was to work for and within the organisation without allowing the house and its unique identity and design to be obliterated by an avalanche of oak-leafed literature (a major success on this account was being granted unique dispensation by Head Office not to have to use NT Bembo as a standard font but rather Gill Sans), gifts and membership leaflets.[3] Likewise, the imposition of the usual systems for presenting a property to the public – ropes, barriers and signage – were not felt to be appropriate in this instance.

It was here that a tension arose: it was essential that a museum-like space for the physical and environmental safety of the collection was created and maintained. However, it was equally critical that wherever possible – while paying close attention to the security needs of both house and contents – this was not what was seen to have been done. It was vital that both the aesthetic and ambience of the property as handed over to the Trust by the Goldfinger family be honoured wherever possible. It would have been simple enough to present the property as a gallery or as a historic house. What was needed was a structure for the display of a home.

I have already referred to the fact that the preservation of the entire package that was the house and its contents was one of the arguments in favour of the acquisition of Willow Road, and it was our strong sense that the house's very particular atmosphere arose from its unique combination of ordinary domestic objects and works of art. The house also presents a rare opportunity not only to present lived-in modernism, but also to problematise the discourse around modernism through the presentation of unexpected ephemera and objects; the ornate nineteenth-century silver candelabra adorning the dining-room sideboard that had once belonged to Ernö's mother, Regine Goldfinger, provides a good example. This very particular ambience would have been severely compromised by the imposition of physical restrictions in the form of ropes and barriers. In addition, Willow Road is a house that opens up (literally unfolding in fact, with the provision of first-floor screen walls) upon exploration of its interiors. It is the detailing of these that is one of the property's chief delights. It was critical to Goldfinger's design that both physical and visual access to the spaces should not be impeded; that rooms could be viewed as a whole, but that their very skilful design be visible at close quarters too. It was over this issue that a predicament was faced as to how to balance the opposing needs to pay close attention to the requirement to control and regulate visitor numbers and flow, while also allowing unimpeded visual access.

Ultimately, however, the house itself set the terms for its presentation. The National Trust sets optimum visitor figures at each of its properties. These are calculated against projections as to likely physical wear and tear, and against the exposure to daylight per opening day. At Willow Road, shortage of space in the house itself meant that visitor numbers were going to be essentially limited in any case. If there had been any doubt about the procedural correctness of avoiding the use of barriers, the property's domestic scale was a further deciding factor. Although reasonably generous as a family home, the house is not large in terms of comfortable wide-scale public access, particularly since, until 2003, the house was only viewable by guided tour in a group. It was recognised that if areas of the property were to be cordoned off, its limited space would be reduced still further.

The outcome of these deliberations was that the public was given virtually unrestricted visual access to the house and its contents in terms of the proximity that is possible – an advantage given the detailing, which, as mentioned, deserves to be seen close to and also given the large number of small, incidental objects on display. As was often the case, however, the resolution of one problem proved to be the origin of another. In deliberately ignoring the usual physical constraints associated with the museum environment, a serious dilemma was created as to the practicability of security measures.

In lieu of physical restrictions, it was decided that, as elsewhere in the National Trust, a system of human surveillance for the house and its contents would be employed. Originally, it was believed that the use of the room steward – the Trust's equivalent of the museum guard normally employed in historic houses – would be as intrusive as the barriers that he, or she, was being used to replace.

Instead, for the guided tours, a practice whereby a member of staff accompanied each group as it toured the house, thereby acting as both sheep- and watch-dog, was adopted. In Willow Road's early days, the unobtrusive but emphatic presence of a clearly vigilant member of staff provided the means by which (and actually, very effectively) high standards of security were maintained without lessening the sense that the visiting public experiences of being in an 'ordinary' family home.[4]

The sense of entering the private, 'closed' world of a family home was further heightened, when in 2003 the arrangement was introduced whereby the public was able to visit the house between 3 pm and 5 pm without having to do so as part of a tour. This system was sanctioned by the National Trust's security department, the remit of which, among many others, is to audit physical security and opening arrangements throughout the organisation. It was agreed that several staff be present on each floor as a return to the traditional National Trust room steward system. Since by this time – that is, after seven years of having been open to the public – volunteer staff knew the house extremely well from having conducted guided tours and since, in any case, many were experts in the field, the amended system for the supervision of the property had the added benefit that questions could be asked of them by the public, providing live, accurate and on-the-spot interpretation.[5]

A key concern during my administration of the house was that both staff and visitors felt comfortable and welcome – as though 'at home' in other words – at Willow Road, something that had to be balanced against the fact that this was no longer, of course, a home. This said, and while a significant number of our visitors were familiar with modernism as an architectural movement, many others were not, and might not find it a particularly 'homely' style.[6] It seemed important, therefore, that the house and its contents be normalised, without being compromised for the wary visitor. The creation of an informal and friendly atmosphere appeared the best means by which to provide the right environment for thinking through this potentially new and mistrusted territory.[7] On the other hand, the creation of a sense of ease had to be balanced out against too much informality, and not least from the point of view of safeguarding the collection. Another challenging problem was not the threat of theft necessarily, but rather of wear and tear due to the handling of such an 'ordinary'-looking collection. Of great tactile appeal, some of Willow Road's contents are so familiar that the curious visitor could be forgiven for wanting to handle objects (Figure 10.3). The discreet and sensitive supervision of visitors by volunteer staff proved, again, to be the solution. Dovetailed with the security measures employed at the house during open hours is the system operated whereby, for half the afternoon, it is only possible to visit the house by guided tour, as already mentioned, a format that has had the added benefit of resolving another set of issues – the problems surrounding the interpretation and presentation of the house.

The informality that the National Trust has been able to adopt at Willow Road arises again from the house's unique combination, under one roof, of architecture, gallery and domestic space. A corollary of this was that it was vital that a decision be made as to just what it was that was being presented via the collection

10.3

A collection of objects on a window-sill at Willow Road.

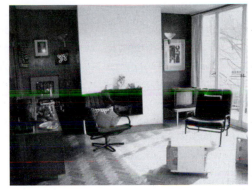

10.4 *(top right)*
View of the sitting-room at Willow Road taken in 1940.
Photo: The National Trust

10.5 *(bottom right)*
View of the sitting-room at Willow Road illustrating the 1990s' reconstruction of the room from photographs taken in 1987.

in terms of locating the building within a particular historical time-frame. Had the house that the Trust wished to open to the public simply presented art and architecture in formal terms the issue would have been less complicated. However, since the house was also to tell a family's story, it was clear that this, more personal history, would have to represent the later rather than the earlier years. A decision therefore had to be taken as to what period or moment that should be.

In order to include the weight of family history that Willow Road's contents disclose, and in order to make the most of the original acquisition remit that the house was to be presented as a holistic package, interpretation was needed to represent the longer, rather than decade-specific, history of the property. The Trust could have presented the house in its early architecturally 'pure' form by producing a facsimile of the interior of the 1940s based on the plentiful documentary evidence produced for the architectural press shortly after the family moved into their new home – for example, of the sitting-room as shown in Figure 10.4. Interpretation along these lines would, however, only have spoken of Goldfinger's architecture and design, and would have revealed very little of the family history that only becomes available through the presentation of the house towards the end of his life, as illustrated by a shot from the same position of the same room from 1987 (Figure 10.5). As discussed earlier, one of the most valuable aspects of Willow Road is the rare opportunity it affords of witnessing how a modernist architect lived in a home built, not for a client, but for his own family and for describing how, aesthetically, that might evolve in real terms across the decades.

As the year in which Goldfinger died, and also the one in which the house was – prophetically – extensively photographically documented by one of his grand-children, 1987 has become the date mark at which the house is exhibited. Aware of the dangers of arbitrary decisions as to the frozen-in-time moment, it was felt important that the collection was arranged as accurately as possible according to the photographs taken by Nick Goldfinger at that time. These were images that documented the minutiae of domestic life and not just, for example, the art collection or the furniture designs. This in itself presented a potential pitfall, however, since we were conscious that too strict a facsimile from photograph would deaden the space, robbing it of the alive and lived-in quality that was required. To offset this concern, the Trust took precautions to preserve Willow Road's contents, however ephemeral, down to the last paperclip or toothpick, the presence of which does much to mitigate against the rather static atmosphere that might otherwise have been imposed.[8]

Having decided on this policy for presentation and display, the Trust then had to decide on the best physical means for the interpretation of Willow Road's very particular juxtaposition of its more pedestrian alongside its more esoteric contents. Just as physical security measures were not appropriate in this context, neither was the use of explanatory text. This situation is nothing new to the National Trust historic house, of course, where, unlike the museum environment, it is often not possible to use labels and text since these represent an 'interference' with the visual integrity and authenticity of the space as an interior rather than as a museum piece. At Willow Road, a reasonably generously sized family home but, as explained, a rather parsimonious space when considered in terms of conducting groups of visitors around it, signage and labelling would not only have impacted on the original design, but would have adversely affected the provision of unimpeded visual access to the house for the public. This said, the nature of the house and its contents required explanation and contextualisation. Creating a regime where the house would be viewed by guided tour only for the first years of the house's new public life seemed to be the solution to both problems of interpretation and visitor regulation.

While it was envisaged that the house would attract an architecturally literate audience, it was hoped that a large number of visitors would not come from this constituency. It was always felt that one of the key points of Willow Road's importance lay in its potential, as part of the wider National Trust, to introduce new audiences to twentieth-century art, architecture and design. The provision of sympathetic, interesting information material was clearly key to visitors' understanding and enjoyment of the house. Without labels and text, the answer, again, seemed to be to rely on volunteer staff. The practice established whereby a guide leads an informal tour through the house backed – on busy Saturdays – by a security-minded steward provided the basis for an interpretation of the house, in the form of the tours offered. An unforeseen upshot and benefit that this combined approach has afforded is the 'double-act' made possible between guide and steward. The informality created by exchanges between members of staff proved to do much, lessening the deadening effect that can be the historic house tour. This arrangement often also provided an interaction with which the public could engage and which would allow tours to become discursive rather than purely didactic. It was one of the delights of offering so different a property to the public that, throughout my custodianship, Willow Road attracted a predominantly (though not necessarily chronologically) young staff, many of whom had their own professional occupations.

Partly in order to encourage repeat visits and partly to give the property another boost of energy after its sixth season of being open, public afternoons then began to admit visitors on a free-flow basis after the last guided tour was over. Although volunteer staff understandably felt the loss of the opportunity for guiding, feeling that the public experience of the house was diminished through reduced access to guided tours, the move was met very favourably by the public which was now afforded the opportunity to visit on its own terms, enquire whatever it wished of staff as to history and background, and stay for as little or as long as it wished.

We were also considerably helped in our presentation of Willow Road by the possibility of being able to screen an introductory film at the start of each tour, something that also became available for the public visiting through the free-flow part of the afternoon. The opportunity to be able to use at least some of Goldfinger's many reels of film (shot on holiday, at several of his firm's building sites, and at Willow Road itself) was too valuable to miss. Made for the Trust by a commercial production company, Uden Associates, the film is shown in a twelve-seater 'cinema' converted by Avanti Architects from one of the property's two garages. As well as providing a brief outline of Goldfinger's career and the story of the building of Willow Road, the film includes interviews with his contemporaries and colleagues. The inclusion of the film as part of the public's experience of the property allows Goldfinger's personal and professional background to be explored before the visitor enters the main part of the house and, in this way, sets the scene for a first-hand exploration of a space that was such an important and instructive building for Goldfinger's later practice.

Although invaluable as a starting point for visits, the film had another key function. The conversion of one of the house's garages into a cinema was also the outcome of a lateral approach to the problem of how to accommodate and welcome disabled visitors to a listed historic building, the central access of which is a two-storey spiral staircase. In addition to the introductory film described above, the National Trust commissioned a filmed 'tour' of the house that would be available to visitors unable to reach the first and second floors of the building as a result of the staircase-only access.[9] That the house and the organisation it represents faced a shortfall in providing greater genuine access for all has been an on-going problem, of which the staff have remained very conscious. It was hoped that working, perforce, within the restrictions imposed by listed-building status, the inclusion of this filmed

tour would at least accommodate every visitor by providing visual material and information about the house and its architect. It was rewarding when it became clear from
visitors' comments that the film has done much to add to their understanding of the
property. The implementation of the Disabilities Discrimination Act in 2004 faced the
wider historic house sector with a serious issue of concern as to how best to offer
proper, well-thought through access, but it was our hope that in proactively
addressing these problems (extending the availability of Braille guides to the house
and developing a better handling collection, for example) we would have begun the
process, raised awareness of the issues and have taken some steps to counteract
the insuperable problem imposed by the central staircase.[10]

Just as opening Willow Road to the public created a tension between the
need to preserve the house in the form in which it was handed to the Trust and the
desire to make available special provision access, so too we experienced a tension
between maintaining visual integrity and conservation needs – a theme that is
current, of course, throughout the historic house environment. The additional challenge within a twentieth-century house was that the Trust was not yet entirely sure
of solutions to the problems that could only be predicted would affect the collection
in the future. Alongside the usual predicament surrounding visitor numbers (ideally
high) in opposition to preservation concerns (in which case visitors numbers are
ideally low) Willow Road presented a number of problems that are specific to its being
a modern property. It is clearly not ideal to house a museum collection in a modernist
building designed specifically to maximise the impact of open internal space through
its large picture windows.

The most immediate question, then, was whether the house should be
shown as it was intended – as a modernist house designed to let in the light
throughout, something that would clearly be very damaging to works on paper and
textiles in particular. The UV film with which the house's windows are lined went
some way towards protecting the house and its contents but could not, of course,
protect against the extremes of heat reached through solar gain, even in a temperate
London summer, in a south-facing room with a window wall. Fortunately, as is typical
of his far-sighted attention to detail, Goldfinger included a second curtain track to
accommodate muslin sun-curtains in the south-facing areas of the house. The property relies on these to cut out the worst effects of heat and light at least. Monitoring
areas of the house most likely to be affected by light and heat will provide reliable
data that will be called on if the Trust decides that more drastic (and intrusive
measures) such as black-out curtains need, in the end, to be provided.

Elsewhere, problems have met with less obvious and even more partial
resolutions. The treads of the concrete spiral staircase at the centre of the house,
the only point of access to the first and second floors, as mentioned above, are faced
with cork tiles. From the outset, the unavoidable wear and tear they received was a
key concern. The possible solution of asking visitors to use overshoes was not
considered practical. However, the National Trust's other modernist property, The
Homewood, recently proved that requiring visitors to wear overshoes, putting these

on in a limited space and doing so alongside choreographing timed tours, is by no means impossible.[11] At the time of my leaving the Trust, nine seasons' intensive traffic up and down the stairs was beginning to show, and signs of deterioration since acquisition had become much more noticeable. It is likely that the only option will be to replace the cork tiles; simple enough in itself, it is as yet undecided as to how the Trust will tackle the attendant aesthetic issue of obvious newness. Glaringly new tiles will look very out of place besides Willow Road's otherwise slightly faded aesthetic; 'distressed' tiles will be inauthentic.

A similar problem besets the house's book collection. Goldfinger annotated his books and journals extensively. Nowadays, therefore, the Willow Road library represents not only an important element of the original contents, essential for getting the 'look' of the house right, but also an extremely important archive. Since modern book bindings often contain glues that can become harmful to the book itself over time, an extensive programme of de-acidification of the collection was undertaken to stabilise it. A further problem was that many of the books at Willow Road are paperbacks, the leaves of which become very friable with age. Possible solutions under discussion during my time in post were the removal of leaves from all books, leaving only the boards to be filled by acid-free boxes individually cut to the appropriate size and allowing the leaves to be archived, or the retiring of the whole collection into storage, its replacement being made gradually possible through the purchase of copies. Questions of the 'rightness' of inauthentic display again dog the issue. The Trust will increasingly need to tackle this and other more philosophical issues as to the house's look and feel. It may be that, with regard to these problems, there is no right or wrong, but that it is incumbent on the organisation to be transparent about the decisions it takes and, backed by research and advice from conservators and curators, be confident in the reasons for having taken them.

That these and other questions remain unanswered is not necessarily problematic, however. The challenges inherent in opening Willow Road to the public have produced a situation where, while The National Trust may not yet be sure as to every solution, it can be confident that as an organisation it has been required to think around all the issues thoroughly and sensitively. In its first decade of being open, both the house itself and the staff involved with its management needed to take time to settle with the property's new status. While a number of immediate practical and logistical decisions clearly had to be taken before opening, there was also a sense at the property that a gentle evolution would be no bad thing. New problems will appear but other issues will resolve themselves over time. The National Trust's byline is, after all, 'Forever For Everyone', and a decade is a very short span of time in Trust terms. Alongside the care and preservation of Willow Road and its contents, if the organisation can do anything to reach even a few members of the public who might not otherwise have engaged with modern art and architecture, then surely it must be doing something of value.

The challenges that were faced, precisely because they occasioned thinking, research and debate, and because solutions continued to be hard to find, have afforded the property a new life that has taken it beyond acquisition with an energy and vitality that might have been less apparent had all the answers been immediately found. One of the joys of presenting such a different house to the public within the National Trust context is that the organisation itself has been taken into new arenas of curatorial, managerial and administrative practice.

Also, the Trust has become used to having Willow Road in its midst. Convincing the organisation that it wanted to be taken to some of the places that were suggested was something that kept my post interesting and provided the house with an added vibrancy, even though risk-taking could have created the spectre of mistake-making. When Willow Road's then Regional Director, Robin Mills, saw the winter 2000 Habitat catalogue that used the property for the shoot, he sent me a friendly email which simply said 'Whatever next?'. I did not tell him that the Willow Road office was at that point fielding an enquiry from the erotic lingerie brand, Agent Provocateur, to shoot *their* next season's collection.

Notes

1 We were particularly grateful to Peter Goldfinger's support and interest in this regard.

2 The National Trust did own twentieth-century properties at the time of Willow Road's opening: Mr Straw's house, a semi-detached Edwardian property with an interior preserved from the 1920s in Worksop; Coleton Fishacre, Devon, the art-deco inspired interior designed for Rupert and Lady D'Oyly Carte; and 20 Forthlin Road, Liverpool, Paul McCartney's childhood 1950s home. None of these, however, represented stylistic modernism.

3 Associated with this was the need to navigate around ideas acceptable elsewhere in the National Trust but not in keeping at Willow Road – for example, on one occasion, a bid to use a space in the house to sell the National Trust gift range – products both aesthetically and conceptually at odds with the Willow Road design aesthetic and ethos – for Christmas.

4 Time and again during my time in post at Willow Road, it was reported by staff that visitors had remarked particularly on the sensation that they were making a clandestine visit while the Goldfinger family were out – something that, by all accounts, added to, rather than subtracted from the experience.

5 Six of the Willow Road volunteer staff have also worked regularly on the committee of the Twentieth Century Society.

6 The breakdown of visitors to Willow Road has always been roughly one-third non-National Trust members to two-thirds members.

7 Mirroring local uncertainty about Goldfinger's building Willow Road in the 1930s, the National Trust met with hesitancy about acquisition on the part of a small number of Hampstead residents in the 1990s.

8 This was an exercise that provided something of a challenge for regional conservator Linda Shelley, whose dedication and humour ran to thinking through hitherto untested 'best-practice' procedures, such as to how to conserve the original cans of tinned peaches found in the Willow Road kitchen, for example.

9 The property had its listing upgraded from Grade II to Grade II* during my time in post.

10 Following the original delivery of this chapter to the Dorich House Modern Period Rooms conference, my colleague Linda Gaskell undertook a great deal more work to make Willow Road accessible, installing hearing loops on clip-boards, so that guides are more audible, and instigating British Sign Language tours.

11 The modernist house built in Esher by Patrick Gwynne for his parents in 1938.

Chapter 11

Photographs of a legacy at the Dorich House Museum

Brenda Martin

The visitor to a twentieth-century interior displayed within a museum, such as the Frank Lloyd Wright office in the Victoria and Albert Museum in London, or the Lucie Rie interior in the Kaiserliche Hofmobliendepot (the Imperial Furniture Collection in Vienna) – the subject of Chapter 9 in this volume – does not perhaps expect to see evidence of private life. Such museums are primarily concerned with showcasing the best examples of design and the decorative arts. However, different issues are raised in the case of the 'house museum', a particular site where the modern interior has been a home. The visitor to a house museum expects to have information about the former occupants, as well as the architectural design or interior decoration. They are interested in the inhabitants as much as the interiors, and through that, how the rooms were used. The narrative of the domestic spaces and the lives lived out within them is particularly problematic, however, since domestic life within interior spaces changes over time, and the interiors themselves are often reconstructed to accommodate this, as has been remarked by other authors in this volume (Chapters 3 and 10). There is also the question of respecting the wishes of the former owners, of terms of the bequest or other instructions, such as those left by Jim Ede for Kettle's Yard, discussed by Sebastiano Barrassi in Chapter 8.

The particular challenges for the house museum focus on issues of authenticity and the conservation of a particular culture. There is also the concept of what makes an appropriate 'museum display' understood by both curators and visitors at the site of a previously private dwelling. All these considerations impact on the final story that is narrated through the display. Additional to these challenges is the problem of historicising rooms created within modernism, which by its own definition repudiated the past, drawing nothing from history. Often the original intention of a modernist interior was to create a room for the future where patterns of life would change, where even the essence of family life would change, based on the ideals of modernism which, ironically, no longer have resonance for our 'modern' society more than half a century on. Fortunately, the rooms themselves have often been documented with the aid of technology, the camera. The mainly black-and-white photographs that appear in magazines, trade and exhibition catalogues, and other publications offer images of model interiors that rarely show people. They show interiors that are impersonal, modular, insular. They give the appearance of being 'set out' like a stage set, ready for the drama of an idealised and standardised daily life. Such photographic images have been largely responsible for setting up our expectations of what we will find in actual modernist interiors, expectations that are then confounded in the physical experience of the preserved or reconstructed spaces because they contain no story of what went on in them or of the inhabitants of those spaces. However, where the inhabitants have been photographed within those interiors, the photograph can be a valuable aid to narrating their stories and their identities, lessening the problems of authenticity and stereotypes of culture that arise with a more impersonal display.

The use of photographs in interpreting the interiors of a sculptor's house, Dorich House, and in particular the domestic interiors of the top floor, are the subject of this chapter. The award of museum status to Dorich House in 2004 gave Kingston University the opportunity to rethink the presentation of this important modern studio house and its collections ten years after it opened as a public building. In the last ten years, curatorial practice has changed, and, as Lesley Hoskins has outlined above in this volume, curators have become more aware of the problems of simply creating rooms in a period style. Built in 1936 to the designs of the Latvian-born sculptor, Dora Gordine and her husband, the aristocratic Richard Hare, the architecture and interiors of Dorich House represent at the same time the universal and the singular – a unique moment of eclectic modernism in England and a very personal negotiation of that moment by the Hares.

Dorich is a conflation of the two inhabitants' first names and the intention expressed in the architectural design was to provide studios and a gallery for Gordine's sculpture, a study for Hare and a stylish modern home.[1] However, during the 1940s, the Hares, who had no children, determined to leave their growing collection of art, particularly art from imperial Russia, to the nation. Over the years, the house became an impressive treasure trove of art from all over the world containing silver, porcelain, ceramics, paintings, icons, furniture, carpets and Russian craft works, as well as being the studio for Gordine's sculpture. Following the early death of her husband, aged 59, in 1966, Dora Gordine remained a lonely 25 years in the house, adding to their already huge collection of art, both house and owner gradually sinking into old age and decline. The building was listed Grade II in 1983, and on

11.1
The Dorich House Museum in 2004.

28 February 1987, Gordine was granted permission by the Royal Borough of Kingston upon Thames for the gallery of Dorich House to be used for the 'display of sculptures and other chattels for viewing by the public'.[2] Richard and Dora's joint fervent wish that Dorich House would become a museum became an obsession during the last years of the sculptor's life, when she sought to persuade English Heritage, the Victoria and Albert Museum, and the Wallace Collection to take over the house and its art, without success. Two years after her death in 1991, Kingston University was appointed custodian of the house and its collections, thanks to the suggestion of Professor Jack Lewin, a governor of the university. Professor Lewin and his wife had been close friends of Gordine and knew her wishes and, perhaps more importantly, appreciated the risk to the house and its collections if they were left to decline further, or even sold off separately.

Immediately after Gordine's death, auctioneers removed the furniture, art and sculpture for valuation, leaving the clutter of daily life in situ, considering it to be of no value. The house was inhabited by squatters twice and in 1992 used by the BBC as a set for the film *Two Deaths,* directed by Nicholas Roeg and starring Michael Gambon and Michael Kitchen. The BBC cleared some of the rooms of 'rubbish' – in effect, the rest of the Hare's papers that had not been burnt by the squatters. When the university took on the empty shell of the house from the executors in 1993, they appointed a steering group within the university to manage the project, which included specialist external advisors from the Tate Gallery and a specialist on Russian art, as well the local councillor, James Daly, who had been a close personal friend of Gordine. A core collection of the best examples of the art and artefacts was selected and put back into storage while the fabric of the house was restored. Funds to restore the house and conserve the core collection were raised from the auction of the residue of goods. This included most of the Hares' domestic furniture, apart from a sofa made in the late 1920s in Paris, which is still awaiting restoration, and some oriental tables.

The steering group provided the forum for discussions about how best to comply with Gordine's bequest which requested that Dorich House with its collections be made available for the education and enjoyment of the public. Beside financial considerations and provisions for the mandatory health and safety regulations involved in the process of converting what had been a private dwelling to a public building, discussions focused on what period the interiors should reflect and whether to re-create the gallery and two studios as they had been in Gordine's time. From the few documents that had been saved relating to the construction and finishing of the house, it was possible to reproduce the original 1936 neutral colours that Gordine had specified (beige, pearl-grey, fawn, white) almost exactly. However, the revolving dias for the models and screens from the studio were missing. Black-and-white photographs published in *Country Life* showed the arrangement of the interiors in 1938 and these provided a guide for the opening displays.[3]

The display area for the collections was initially confined to the first two floors which, by the time of Gordine's death, had become cluttered and busy with hundreds of paintings and decorative objects crowded into every available space and on every surface, even sometimes displayed on ornate gold sconces. A decision was taken to re-create the calm and quiet ambience of the interwar period of 1936–9 for these areas, and to display as much of the core collections of sculpture and Russian art as possible through the ground- and first-floor studios and gallery, still using the halls and landings as display areas as Gordine had done in the 1930s. The large working spaces of the two studios were preserved to provide rooms for student groups, education, seminars and meetings. The decision regarding the domestic accommodation was more difficult. During their lifetimes, the Hares had been wilfully reticent about their private lives in any publicity, focusing in interviews solely on the design of their house as an artistic project and on their art collections, refusing politely to give personal details or details of their family backgrounds.[4] Much of the domestic furniture had been auctioned and the Hares' private effects were thrown away by the disinterested parties of squatters, the BBC and removal companies. It was proposed to separate the top floor flat from the rest of the public areas of the house and to modernise it for possible use as a residential facility for visiting professors and other university visitors. Interestingly, Gordine's original striking architectural designs emerged more clearly through the restoration of the rest of the building to the period of the 1930s, spoiled only by the addition of a new corporate maroon carpet in the entrance halls and stairs, which mitigated the effect of the highly polished wood floors of the Hares' time which were covered only by a narrow stair-carpet and a scattering of oriental and Asian rugs.

The house was officially opened in December 1994 and income has been generated to support free use of the house for student teaching and free access for the public. In 2004, following the award of museum status, the steering group was able to reconsider a more appropriate refurbishment of the flat. This had not become a residential facility for visiting professors as planned, but was open to the public as the private apartment of the Hares. There is presently a mixture of some original and some new furniture in the living-room and new dining furniture in the dining-room.[5] However, Gordine's original moon door feature and semicircular windows evoke the exotic nature of the original interiors. Confusingly, the bedroom and dressing-room now function as a meeting-room and display area for the neoclassical Russian furniture respectively. Thus, the rooms of the flat, furnished by the restoration architects with an uncertain brief in 1994, embody a corporate version of the domestic, made with a mixture of original furniture owned by the Hares and new furniture and rugs in the 1930s style. The proposed redisplay and refurbishment of the flat will include the restoration of the original settee, veneered with burr-walnut, with built-in bookshelves and pale-green glass sliding-doors to the cupboard sections, that stood by the fireplace, believed to have been designed by Gordine in the late 1920s.[6]

In addition to the restoration of original furniture, consideration can now be given to how best to narrate the story of the former occupants of the Dorich House museum. Ten years of research have provided a wealth of reliable information about the Hares and revealed a large archive of press photographs of the flat commissioned by Richard Hare for public consumption that provides a record of the rooms from 1939 to1955.[7] With the incorporation of some of these images into the display areas, it is now possible to illustrate the lives of the Hares as they portrayed themselves, as collectors and makers of art.

Through the many photographs now available to us, it has become obvious that Richard Hare arranged for press agencies and photographers to take pictures on a regular basis. In the absence of private papers and letters, these photographs constitute the major source material to work from with regard to the presentation of the domestic interior of the flat to complement the more public display areas of the gallery and Gordine's two studios. Four major articles were published on the interiors of Dorich House between 1937 and 1945, the result of photographers' visits. What use can these photographs be in a future re-presentation of the flat for visitors to the Dorich House Museum? Dora Gordine was happy to promote her sculpture, but less keen to reveal her private life either in public or private.[8] However, Richard Hare seems to have been keen to promote his house, his wife and their art in this very public display of their private space. Press coverage of Gordine's sculpture tended to be clustered around the time of exhibitions and was probably generated by the galleries, but the articles on the house were, it could be suggested, probably instigated by Hare as part of the building of a new dynasty for him. From his time as a student at Oxford University, he had opposed the political and patriarchal values of his aristocratic and traditionally conservative family, being more liberal and left-wing, and preferring the pastimes of music, the theatre and art collecting to the field sports of hunting and fishing, which earned the displeasure of his father and the despair of his mother.[9] The publication of his book, *The Art and Artists of Russia*, which included many of the items in his collection, and the publication in the press of articles about Dorich House and Dora Gordine, gave him and his work a validity, marking him out as a connoisseur and collector of note – which is, in fact, how the Russian community remembered him and his collection.[10] Bertha Malnik, a colleague at the School of Eastern European Studies at the University of London wrote in Hare's obituary, 'He and his wife have assembled a highly personal and utterly delightful collection of Russian art which it is hoped will be made available to the wider public it deserves.' She added that Hare had the 'impeccable taste of a born collector'.[11]

To date, there are no comments about collecting from Hare himself, except in a private letter to his American friend William Egerton, when in 1965 he wrote that it had been 'refreshing to get away from the political fixation, and to see the more edifying and enduring things in Russia'.[12] Otherwise, there are only opinions about the importance of being surrounded by beautiful things made to the press by Gordine and during her abundant telephone calls to friends. Their hundreds of ornaments and objets d'art that filled the exotic and eclectic interiors of the flat, of course reflected their personal histories. For Dora, there had been the flight from Estonia to Paris in the early 1920s, travels in China, Singapore, Malaya, Bali, India and Cambodia in the 1930s, and her experience of high bohemian society which included artists, actresses and writers such as Augustus John, William Orpen, Edith Evans and

Somerset Maugham in London from the mid-1930s onwards. For Richard, after Oxford, there had been an almost dilettante existence in the British Embassy in Paris, travels to the exotic Bali and Singapore and the collection of an equally exotic wife together with all kinds of art. Gordine was in her late 30s when she designed Dorich House and, with one bedroom and a dressing-room, there was never any question of Dorich House becoming a family home.

What narrative could be told through the new photographs of the domestic spaces? The story of a young Estonian artist and a dispossessed young aristocratic collector who took in the romance of Paris in the 1920s, the luxury and exoticism of its Chinese and Asian influences, and the modern idiom of art deco and Hollywood glamour. Richard Hare was, in his early teens, a frequent visitor to the house of a cousin of Virginia Woolf.[13] He knew Duncan Grant and the younger people associated with the Bloomsbury set. As a young boy, he was witness to the artistic milieu described so well by Christopher Reed in his book *Bloomsbury Rooms* and, despite Hare's quiet exterior, his fascination with beauty and the exotic is evidenced in his praise in letters to Godfrey Samuel of the male Balinese dancers he saw when he visited Bali in 1933 and his choice of the more erotic of Ivan Bunin's short stories as his first translations from Russian into English.[14] Obviously, then, the portrayal of the domestic interior of the Hares' flat could not be seen in terms of restrained English modernism characterised by a negation of luxury and resistance to exotic influences from abroad, or French art deco, an essentially imitative style of the antique seventeenth-century Chinese furniture that originally furnished Dorich House.

Walter Benjamin has written, 'A storyteller exists in the past. The past is not experienced as such but is lived again in the presence of collective memory.'[15] The problem with different cultural collective memories in a society is something that has beset all museum curators at one time or another.[16] But in a specific instance, such as the flat at the Dorich House Museum, what is the collective memory? What is the collective databank of experience that might contextualise Dora Gordine and Richard Hare for the general public? A continuous stream of press attention had followed Gordine's work up to the early 1960s, but in 1994 Gordine was unknown.[17] She had ceased to be newsworthy in the late 1950s and has no public presence for the present-day museum visitor. Although the Hon. Richard Hare's aristocratic family was once known to many (both his sisters were debutantes) and his knowledge of Russian art and culture was impressive, he was unknown outside academic circles. However, visitors to Dorich House never fail to experience with delight and curiosity the exotic architecture of the domestic spaces as a hidden treasure of the house, taking away the sense that they have somehow discovered it for themselves. To the relatively impersonal rooms, they add their own interpretations and associations which, of course, are many and diverse. Is it valid, therefore, lacking the space to show something more detailed and explicit such as a film, to suggest the 'romantic' story of the Hares largely through the photographs that had been taken in the past?[18] It was decided that, even with no knowledge of whose choice of shot was used – the photographer's or Hare's – these stylistic and posed photographs could be used to create context for the displays of the museum's spaces and to give an accurate indication of the personal histories of this unusual couple.

Susan Sontag, in her book *On Photography,* writes that, 'photographs are valued because they give information, they tell one what there is, they make an inventory'.[19] Of course, we know that photographs can be 'set up', cropped and manipulated, but through photographs, Sontag writes, history becomes 'a set of anecdotes'.[20] She asserts that the photograph can confer on each moment the character of a mystery, multiple meanings and invitations to fantasy. With this in mind, looking for a collective memory is perhaps the wrong approach to providing an understanding of the cultural significance of the house and its interiors, and of the lives that were acted out within them.

To demonstrate my point, we can consider the narrative of a few of the posed photographs that might be used. The first two images are double portraits of the couple at home. In Figure 11.2, the Hares are sitting in an interesting conjunction at their dining-table. Richard looks posed and concerned that the right camera angle was being used. Dora is opposite him but apart at the same time. Visually they are framed by their exoticism, symbolised in the Chinese moon doors and the seventeenth-century Chinese fresco painting sunk into a purpose-built recess in the wall. A Persian rug lies before the hearth. The dining suite is made of Chinese ebony. The wrought-iron candelabra with all its candles invites the viewer to imagine sophisticated candlelit dinners. Yet the bored ennui of Evelyn Waugh's 1930s novel, *A Handful of Dust,* seems to emanate from Gordine herself and from Hare's discarded newspaper resting near the floor. Overall, there is not a sense of domesticity, more of an aura of a sophisticated couple lacking guests.

In Figure 11.3 taken on the roof terrace of Dorich House, Hare is posed for the camera with maps and papers, perhaps before they set out for an excursion in their car with their fashionable Pekinese dog. On the table between them is a potent symbol of something important to them, old Russia – the samovar – which signifies the way these two people fitted into, and yet subverted, English traditions. The traditional English tea-set is usurped by the samovar and the tea glasses, which probably contain lemon tea. The traditional English damask tablecloth is replaced by a modern check in a rustic fabric. Even the open-air venue of the roof terrace shows clearly their affiliation to modern living, both in the modern design of a house with a flat roof and in the way they use it. With regard to the way in which the photograph is set up, the Hares don't interact with each other, she pensively gazing into her glass, he off into the distance – even the little dog sits apart in this double portrait of the couple at home.

Ludmilla Jordanova has written in her book *Defining Features* that, 'Portraits are frozen moments of elaborate processes, as such they reveal social negotiations, not individual character.'[21] This is very true of these two highly posed images which, while they are clearly contrived, may very well be capable of suggesting the mores and nuances of the way the Hares lived in the domestic spaces of Dorich House, in a way that the written or spoken word cannot.

11.2
**Double portrait of
Richard Hare and
Dora Gordine in
the dining-room
of Dorich House,
c. 1939.**
Photo: English
Heritage/NMR

11.3
Double portrait of Richard Hare and Dora Gordine on the roof terrace of Dorich House, c. 1939.
Photo: English Heritage/NMR

11.4
Photograph of Dora Gordine on the windowsill of the flat c. 1940 taken by Tunbridge Sedgewick.
Photo: English Heritage/NMR

With this in mind, we can consider a photograph of Gordine alone. For Gordine, beautiful objects and sculpture excited her, and Dorich House was for her one huge gallery with her beautiful things in it. The chestnut tree, the orchard outside the house, cooking with home-grown foods, bottling, preserving – all provided a link to nature, which Gordine loved, and to her home cultural traditions of Latvia and Estonia. To complicate matters further, whenever she spoke about her home to the press (and thereby expressly for public consumption), Dora typically made abstract pronouncements such as, 'A home for me is a centre of beauty and culture.'[22] However, lacking 'authentic' household material to display this important personal aspect of her life accurately, it is possibly better that photographs narrate this particular part of the story.

Figure 11.4 is an atmospheric photograph taken *c*. 1939 by the ballet photographer Tunbridge Sedgwick.[23] Dora is posed as a sophisticated young woman with her distinctive kiss-curl and dramatic earring in prominent view. Somehow, she seems more at ease than in the posed photographs with Richard. She sits casually on the windowsill with her right side towards the camera, by the chestnut tree which grew close the house, admiring a little Chinese dragon. The setting and pose link her to the extraordinary architecture of her home, to nature and to the art collection which is so important to her.

Another photograph, not illustrated here, shows Dora in front of a door and a wall on which is hung one of her paintings from the late 1920s – in a style which owes much to Gauguin – of the head of a Javanese girl with a flower in her hair. Gordine appears to have just come in with flowers from the garden that she is arranging in a huge Persian vase, although the flat is on the top floor and the door in the photograph is to a small semicircular balcony. The caption in *The Bystander* magazine, in which the photograph was published, gives an exotic subtext to the image. It says, '*Javanese Lady*: A Gordine portrait hangs above a Chinese mah-jong table of carved camphor wood and a seventeenth century Persian jar.'[24]

However, what is conveyed in the photograph in Figure 11.5? The Hares are still framed by the moon door which divides the two living-rooms of the flat, and they are surrounded by their collection of art, but they are engaged in the activity of caring for it. The photograph was never published; perhaps it appeared too private for public display in a newspaper or magazine of the time. This is an important image in retrospect and one that possibly gives us the best opportunity for contextualising the display in the domestic space, as it narrates the story of the Hares together, primarily as collectors. Research into the material culture of the private sphere by Daniel Miller and others has shown that, in caring for cherished objects, collectors view themselves as saviours of lost objects and disappearing worlds, and that this legitimises the time and money spent on a collection.[25] Miller and his group of researchers have also established that the articulation of history is seldom linked to an abstract linguistic manifestation and that objects themselves carry histories.[26] Dora Gordine literally lost her family and childhood home in old Russia and Richard Hare was estranged from his conservative father (the Fourth Earl of Listowel) by his political and aesthetic

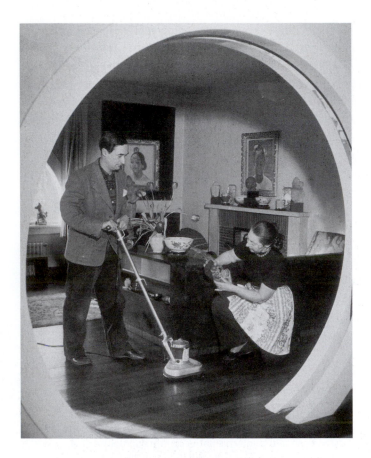

11.5
**Richard Hare and
Dora Gordine
caring for their
house and the art
collection.**
Photo: English
Heritage/NMR

beliefs. Therefore, both could be said to have a past and a future invested in their collection of art and their modern home. It could be argued that it would be more appropriate to show the Hares in their living space represented as a private museum of
memory and new identity, rather than as a space of domestic activity.

To return to Sontag's quote which notes that photographs make an inventory, we could also display photographs of the interiors as they appeared at particular
periods of the house's history, such as Figure 11.6.[27] This image of the living-room,
taken around 1949, shows a fairly cluttered interior with a display of pretty objects –
exotic oriental ornaments, glassware, sweetmeat bowls, sugar basins, tea caddies,
a favourite piece of sculpture in the centre table. There is a Gordine painting on the
wall, a Chinese screen, a Chinese lampshade, three other sculptures, an electric lamp
and a vase of garden flowers. Hare's English desk and a small white chair from the
studio in Paris in the far corner are surrounded by predominately oriental furniture.
Like a snapshot of a moment in time, this photograph can be used to show museum
visitors the location of objects in the dining-room on a particular day, and can be used
by them as a visual means of understanding the spaces that they are in. Presumably,
the room was arranged for a photographer's visit, so we cannot be sure that this was
an accurate representation of how the interior was used in everyday life. What we

11.6
The sitting-room of Dorich House, *c.* **1949.**
Photo: Bernard Howarth-Loomes, Dorich House Archives

can be sure of is that the photograph shows important things for the Hares which are privileged over other objects in the room. The little bronze by Gordine on the table, for example, appears in all the photographs of that day, taken around the house. It is moved around to appear in each shot, so some 'window-dressing' took place before the public viewing of this private space. There is very little other evidence of private life shown, except for the books on Hare's desk and in the sofa shelf. Thus, the bronzes and the books in the photograph of the living-room represent her identity as a sculptor and his identity as a scholar, reinforcing the version of their private lives that Hare wanted to appear in public.

It is also accurate to say that the art objects in the photographs were, in fact, the objects that defined this couple's relationship to each other. Susan Pearce has noted that acquiring objects for the collection of art reinforces the notion of self.[28] In this case, it is a collective 'self' of Dora and Richard as a couple, and it aligns them with the great art collectors of the day, such as Freya Stark, Gertrude Stein and Peggy Guggenheim, and perhaps with Richard Hare's ancestors, who over the years had amassed a substantial art collection, kept at his ancestral home, Kingston House in Kensington Gore, London SW3.[29] Thus, portraying the Hares 'at home' as collectors is an appropriate way of narrating a story about the construction of their identities. After Richard died in 1966, Dora's personality became quite eccentric as she took on the sole identity of collector and artist. She began to urge her friends to spend all their money on art and was frugal for herself, spending all her money on adding to the collection.[30] She also clearly felt strongly that if patrons spent money on buying her sculpture, then they too were validating her way of life and her values.

The modernity of the living room in Figure 11.6, and the identity the Hares created for themselves within it, is also apparent if one considers Benjamin's interpretation of the equivalent nineteenth-century bourgeois interior – the drawing-room – as a 'private box in the world theatre'.[31] In these photographs the Hares are not withdrawing into their 'private box', but setting it up as a stage within the 'world theatre'. In the photographs that Hare commissioned, the books and the sculpture become part of the public persona that these two people wished to present to the world through the publication of photographs of their living-room.

However, there is another comprehensive set of photographs of Dorich House taken by English Heritage without the agency of the Hares, only a couple of days after Dora Gordine's death, in order to record an artist's studio that was considered at risk. There is dust on the furniture and art, and the rooms are in chaotic disorder. The story they tell is only of 'domestic failure' and disruption by auctioneers. Two of these images are displayed at the Dorich House Museum to show the building before restoration started. The only people the author spoke to who had personal memories about the place were neighbours and old friends who knew Gordine in later life.[32] They admitted they felt uneasy and sad about Dorich House in its final years because they were unable to participate in their friend's love of beautiful things – they couldn't see them for the dark and dust. They were concerned that this version of Dorich House should not be the one to fulfil the public legacy enabled by the bequest. 'Return it to its former glory' was a phrase much used.[33] Sontag's voyeuristic approach to the past through photographs comes to mind – and, of course, the notion that cleanliness and order often serve as an indicator of moral quality, especially in the house of a woman.

Sontag observes that, 'Needing to have reality confirmed and experience enhanced by photographs is an aesthetic consumerism to which everyone is now addicted.'[34] To give a reality and cultural meaning to the experience of the visitor to Dorich House, it would seem to be possible to use Richard Hare's need for the public display of the private spaces through the agency of the press. The display of photographs of interiors that were of such significance for the identity of its owners can only add to the sum of the whole – the Hares, the architecture and interiors of the house and its two collections of art. There may be a problem in that the foregoing photographs show us a constructed scene and we cannot know what agency made this, either on their part or on the part of the photographer, and both the photographer and photographed will bring to the making of the image the cultural baggage of their times. But so does the viewer of an image, and I suggest that the element of fantasy and interpretation is a valuable negotiation of that information.

Jordanova has written about formal portraits that they do 'social and cultural work through a range of visual devices for endowing an individual with heroic qualities'.[35] In the case of the photographs of the Hares, they endow them with personal qualities. Throughout the photographs, there are potent icons and symbols of their relationship, with each other and with the art they produced and collected. In these ways, I would suggest, a careful selection of photographic images could supply a rich and complex narrative for the display within the physical spaces.

Acknowledgement

I would like to thank Professor Penny Sparke and Dr Trevor Keeble for their helpful comments in the development of this chapter.

Notes

1   For further explanation of the architectural design, see 'A House of Her Own. Dora Gordine and Dorich House (1936)' in B. Martin and P. Sparke (eds) *Women's Places: Architecture and Design 1860–1960*, London and New York: Routledge, 2003.

2   Notice R32798, Dorich House, Kingston Vale, Royal Borough of Kingston upon Thames archives. Heritage Department.

3   M. Barron, 'Dorich House, Kingston Vale', *Country Life*, 5 November 1938, pp. 456–7.

4   A freelance film-maker, Peter Schwabach, wished to make a film about Gordine, but the project was aborted when she refused to give any biographical information other than that outlined in the carefully formed press releases Hare wrote for her exhibition catalogues (undated letter from Schwabach in Tate Gallery Archives. Ref TAV/734).

5   The original dining-table in an oriental hardwood, with high-backed chairs of ebony, was probably made to Gordine's own design. The present dining-table and buffet were designed by the architect for the restoration, Diana Brown, in 1993.

6   Other art-deco style low cupboards and bookshelves from Dorich House have recently been bought back from an antique dealer who purchased them from the 1993 auctions.

7   Dorich House Archives and National Monuments Records/English Heritage BB80/2066–79.

8   Numerous interviews by the author with friends and models for Gordine revealed that they knew nothing of each other and little about Gordine's early life and background, except that she trained in Paris.

9   Interview with William Hare, 5th Earl of Listowel by the author. Dorich House archives I/18.

10 R. Hare, *The Art and Artists of Russia,* London: Methuen, 1965.

11 B. Malnik, *The Slavonic and East European Review*, Vol. XLV, No. 105, July 1967, p. 271.

12 Letter to William Egerton, Professor of Indiana University, 14 November 1964.

13 Dame Janet Vaughan (1899–1993), later Principal of Somerville College, Oxford.

14 C. Reed, *Bloomsbury Rooms*, New Haven, CT and London: Yale, 2004. For letters to Godfrey Samuel: British Architectural Library Archives SaG/8/1. Hare translated from Russian Ivan Turgenev's *Fathers and Children, Rudin* and *A Nobleman's Nest* for Hutchinson International Authors in 1947 and Ivan Bunin's *Dark Avenues and Other Stories* for John Lehman in 1949.

15 H. Caygill, *Introducing Walter Benjamin*, New York: Totem Books,1998. p. 158.

16 For discussions, see C. Saumarez Smith, 'Museums, Artefacts and Meaning' in *The New Museology*, P. Vergo (ed.), London: Reaktion, 1989 and S. Pearce, *On Collecting: An Investigation into Collecting in the European Tradition,* London and New York: Routledge, 1995, Chapter 18.

17 For a list of major articles on Gordine from 1927 to 1958 see *Dorich House Guidebook*, Kingston upon Thames: Kingston University 2004 (2nd edition) p. 24.

18 For example, as at the Goldfinger house, Willow Road. See Chapter 10 in this volume.

19 S. Sontag, *On Photography,* London: Penguin Books, 1979, p. 23.

20 Ibid.

21 L. Jordanova, *Defining Features: Scientific and Medical Portraits 1660–2000,* London: National Portrait Gallery/Reaktion, 2000, p. 164.

22 'Creating Beauty in Bronze', *Surrey Comet,* 12 February 1955.

23 Official photographer for the Sadlers Wells Ballet in the 1940s, particularly known for his dramatic photographs of the dancer Robert Helpman.

24 'Dora Gordine at Dorich House', *The Bystander,* 28 February 1940, pp. 266–7.

25 D. Miller (ed.), *Home Possessions: Material Culture Behind Closed Doors,* Oxford and New York: Berg 2001. Particularly see A. Hecht, *Home Sweet Home: Tangible Memories of an Uprooted Childhood*, p. 136.

26 Ibid.

27 Sontag, op. cit., p. 23.

28 Pearce, op. cit., p. 173.

29 The Dowager Countess of Listowel died in 1936, after which the house was demolished and the contents sold in early 1937. C. Hussey, 'Vanishing London: Kingston House Knightsbridge', *Country Life,* 20 March, 1937, pp. 300–5.

30 Interviews in Dorich House archives I/1, I/10, I/38.

31 Caygill, op. cit., p. 158.

32 Various interviews with the author. Dorich House archives.

33 Interviews in Dorich House archives I/6, I/10, I/24, I/25.

34 Sontag, op. cit., p. 24.

35 Jordanova, op. cit., p. 127.

Bibliography

Adriaansz, Elly, Molenaar, Joris and Joost Meuwissen (eds), *Leen van der Vlugt*, Amsterdam: Stichting Wiederhall, 1993.

Akkach, S. (ed.), *Camea 3rd Symposium*, Centre for Asian and Middle Eastern Architecture, University of Adelaide, 2002.

Alpers, Svetlana, 'The Museum as a Way of Seeing', in Ivan Karp and Steven D. Levine, *Exhibiting Cultures: The Poetics and Politics of Museum Display*, London and Washington, DC: Smithsonian Institution Press, 1991.

Arts Council, *Lucie Rie: A Retrospective Exhibition of Earthernware, Stoneware and Porcelain 1926–67*, London: Arts Council, 1967.

Barthes, R., *Image Music Text*, London: Fontana Press, 1977.

Bavassi, S., *Kettle's Yard House Guide*, Cambridge: Kettle's Yard, 2002.

Bauman, Z., *Postmodernity and its Discontents*, Cambridge: Polity, 1997.

Benjamin, Walter, 'The Author as Producer', in Peter Demetz (ed.) *Reflections*, New York: Schocken Books, 1986, pp. 229–30.

Bennett, T., *The Birth of the Museum: History, Theory, Politics,* London: Routledge, 1995.

Benton, Charlotte, *A Different World: Émigré Architects in Britain 1928–58*, London: RIBA Heinz Gallery, 1995.

Birks, Tony, *Lucie Rie*, Marston Magna, Somerset: Marston House, revised edn, 1994.

Blake, P., *Frank Lloyd Wright: Architecture and Space*, Baltimore, MD: Penguin Books, 1960.

Blauvelt, A., *Ideas for Modern Living: The Idea House Project/Everyday Art Gallery* (pamphlet), Minneapolis, MN: Walker Art Center, 2000.

Bless, F., *Rietveld 1888–1964: een biografie*, Amsterdam: Utigeverij Bert Bakker/Baarn: Erven Thomas Rap, 1982.

Bourdieu, P., *La distinction: critique sociale du jugement,* Paris: Les Éditions de Minuit, 1979.

—— translated by Nice, R., *Distinction: A Social Critique of the Judgement of Taste,* London: Routledge & Kegan Paul, 1984.

Breuer, M., 'Designing to Live in the Post War House', in *Monsanto*, 22 (5): 22–4, 1943.

Brown, Theodore M.,*The Work of G. Rietveld, Architect*, Utrecht: Bruna & Zoon, 1958.

Buruma, I., *A Japanese Mirror: Heroes and Villains of Japanese Culture,* London: Vintage, 1995.

Caygill, Howard, *Introducing Walter Benjamin*, New York: Totem Books, 1998.

Colomina, B., 'Reflections on the Eames House', in *The Work of Charles and Ray Eames: A Legacy of Invention* (ex. catalogue), New York: The Vitra Design Museum and Harry N. Abrams, 1997.

—— 'The Exhibitionist House', in R. Ferguson (ed.) *At the End of the Century: One Hundred Years of Architecture*, New York: Harry N. Abrams, 1998.

—— *Cultural and Social Aspects of the New York World's Fair, 1939, of Special Interest to Women*, New York: National Advisory Committee on Women's Participation, New York World's Fair, 1939.

Constantoglou, M., 'Exposure to Light in the Exhibition Space: A Methodology Applied to Kettle's Yard Art Gallery', unpublished M.Phil., University of Cambridge, 2005.

Dakers, C., *The Holland Park Circle, Artists and Victorian Society*, New Haven, CT, and London: Yale University Press 1999.

Davis, D. W., *Picturing Japaneseness: Monumental Style, National Identity, Japanese Film*, New York: Columbia University Press, 1996.

Bibliography

Defenbacher, D., *Walker Art Center* (pamphlet) Minneapolis, MN: Walker Art Center, 1940.

Ede, H. S., *Kettle's Yard: A Way of Life*, Cambridge: Kettle's Yard, 1984.

Edenheim, Ralph and Inga Arnö-Berg, *Skansen. Traditional Swedish Style*, London, Wappinger Falls, NY: Scala Books, 1995.

Eliel, C. and Duclos, F. (eds), *L'Esprit Nouveau: Purism in Paris 1918–25* (ex. catalogue) Los Angeles, CA and New York: Museum of Contemporary Art, Los Angeles and Harry N. Abrams, 2001.

Engeland, Hans and Ulf Meyer, *Bauhaus-Architektur Bauhaus Architecture*, Munich, London, New York: Prestel, 2001.

Federal Housing Administration, *Technical Bulletin #4: Principles of Planning Small Houses*, Washington, DC: US Government Printing Office, revised 1940.

—— *Technical Bulletin #2: Modern Design*, Washington, DC: US Government Printing Office, revised 1940.

Floré, F., 'Promoting Catholic Family Values and Modern Domesticity in Post-war Belgium', in H. Heynen and G. Baydar (eds) *Negotiating Domesticity: Spatial Productions of Gender in Modern Architecture*, London: Routledge, 2005.

—— *Lessons in Modern Living: Source Book on Housing Exhibitions in Belgium 1945–58*, in the series Vlees en Beton, no. 64, Ghent: WZW Editions and Productions, 2004.

Forde, K., 'Celluloid Dreams: The Marketing of Cutex in America, 1916–35', in *Journal of Design History*, 15 (3), 2002.

Gale, M., *Kettle's Yard and its Artists*, Cambridge: Kettle's Yard, 1995.

Gillies, M., 'This House Will Help You Plan Your Own', *McCall's Homemaking* 75 January, 1948.

Girling-Budd, A., 'Comfort and Gentility: Furnishings by Gillows, Lancaster, 1840–55', in McKellar, S. and Sparke, P. (eds) *Interior Design and Identity*, Manchester: Manchester University Press, 2004.

Gordon Bowe, Nicola (ed.), *Art and the National Dream: The Search for Vernacular Expression in Turn of the Century Design*, Dublin: Irish Academic Press, 1993.

Harootunian, H., *History's Disquiet: Modernity, Cultural Practice and the Question of Everyday Life*, New York: Columbia University Press, 2000.

Harrod, Tanya, *The Crafts in Britain in the 20th Century*, New Haven, CT/London: Yale University Press, 1999.

Henderson, Susan R., 'A Revolution in the Woman's Sphere: Grete Lihotzky and the Frankfurt Kitchen', in Debra Coleman, Elizabeth Danze and Carol Henderson (eds) *Architecture and Feminism*, New York: Princeton Architectural Press, 1996.

Hewison, R., *The Heritage Industry: Britain in a Climate of Decline*, London: Methuen, 1987.

—— *The Heritage Industry: Britain in the Climate of Decline*, London: Verso, 1987.

Hobbs, F. and Stoops, N., Census Bureau Census 2000 Special Reports, Series CENSR-4, *Demographic Trends in the 20th Century*, Washington, DC: US Government Printing Office, 2002.

Hooper-Greenhill, E., *Museums and the Shaping of Knowledge,* London: Routledge, 1992.

Houston, John (ed.), *Lucie Rie: A Survey of Her Life and Work*, London: Crafts Council, 1981.

Huffman, J., 'The Popular Rights Debate: Political or Ideological?', in H. Wray and H. Conroy (eds) *Japan Examined: Perspectives on Modern Japanese History*, Honolulu: University of Hawai'i Press, 1983.

Hunter, P., Robbins, D. and Suleman, R. (eds), *Linley Sambourne House, 18 Stafford Terrace, Kensington*, London: The Royal Borough of Kensington and Chelsea, 2003.

Hyman, L., *Marcel Breuer, Architect: The Career and the Buildings*, New York: Harry N. Abrams 2001.

Jackson, A. A., *Semi-Detached London*, London: Allen & Unwin, 1973.

Jackson, K. T., *Crabgrass Frontier: The Suburbanization of the United States*, New York: Oxford University Press, 1985.

Jervis, S. and Ormond, L., *Linley Sambourne House*, London: The Victorian Society, 1987.

Jordanova, Ludmilla, *Defining Features: Scientific and Medical Portraits 1660–2000,* London: National Portrait Gallery/Reaktion, 2000.

Kaufmann, E. N., 'The Architectural Museum from Worlds Fair to Restoration Village', in *Assemblage: A Critical Journal of Architecture and Design Culture*, no. 9m June 1989.

Kelly, B., 'The Houses of Levittown in the Context of Postwar American Culture', in D. Slaton and R. Schiffer (eds) *Preserving the Recent Past*, Washington, DC: Historic Preservation Foundation, 1995.

Küper, Marijke and Van Zijl, Ida, *Gerrit Th. Rietveld, 1888–1964: The Complete Works,* ex. catatalogue, Utrecht: Centraal Museum, 1992.

Kwint, M., Breward, C. and Aynsley, J. (eds), *Material Memories,* Oxford: Berg, 1999.

Lancaster, Osbert, *Homes Sweet Homes,* London: John Murray, 1939.

Lefebvre, H., *The Production of Space,* Oxford: Blackwell, 1991.

Lohse, Richard, P., *Neue Ausstellungsgestaltung,* Erlenbach-Zurich: Verlag für Architektur, 1953.

Maffei, N., 'John Cotton Dana and the Politics of Exhibiting Industrial Art in the US, 1909–29', in *Journal of Design History,* 13 (4), 2000.

Mandler, Peter, *The Fall and Rise of the Stately Home,* New Haven, CT.; London: Yale University Press, 1997.

Marchand, R., 'The Designers go to the Fair: Norman Bel Geddes, the General Motors, *Futurama,* and the 'Visit-to-the-Factory Transformed', in *Design Issues,* 8 (2), 1992.

Martin, B., *Dorich House Guidebook,* Kingston upon Thames: Kingston University, 2nd edn, 2004.

Meikle, J., *Twentieth Century Limited: Industrial Design in America,* Philadelphia, PA: Temple University Press, 1979.

Miller, Daniel (ed.), *Home Possessions: Material Culture Behind Closed Doors,* Oxford and New York: Berg 2001.

Miyoshi, M., 'Against the Native Grain', in Miyoshi, M. and Harootunian, H. (eds) *Postmodernism and Japan,* Durham, NC: Duke University Press, 1989.

MLA, *Inspiring Learning For All,* London: MLA, 2004.

—— *The Accreditation Scheme for Museums in the United Kingdom: Accreditation Standard,* London: MLA, 2004.

Monkhouse, Christopher P. and Thomas, S. Michie, *American Furniture in Pendleton House,* Providence, RI: Museum of Art, Rhode Island School of Design, 1986.

Montebello, Philip de, Introduction, in Amelia Peck and James Parker (eds) *Period Rooms in the Metropolitan Museum of Art,* Metropolitan Museum of Art: New York: H. N. Abrams, 1996.

Museums & Galleries Commission, *Registration Scheme for Museums and Galleries in the United Kingdom: Registration Guidelines,* London: Museums & Galleries Commission, 1995.

New York World's Fair Information Manual, New York: New York World's Fair Incoporated (unpaginated manual in the New York Public Library), 1939.

Nicholson, S., *A Victorian Household,* Stroud: Sutton Publishing, 1994.

—— *An Edwardian Batchelor: Roy Sambourne, 1878–1946,* London: The Victorian Society, 1999.

Nilsson, Axel, *Guide to Skansen: The Historical and Ethnographic Department of Skansen,* Stockholm: Nordiska Museet, 1911.

Nute, K., *Frank Lloyd Wright and Japan,* London: Chapman & Hall, 1993.

Oliver, P., Bentley, I. and Davis, I., *Dunroamin: The Suburban Semi and its Enemies,* London: Barrie & Jenkins, 1981.

Ottillinger, Eva B., 'Ernst A. Plischke – the Lucie Rie Apartment', Vienna: Kaiserliches Hofmobiliendepot, 1999.

Overy, P., Büller, L., den Oudsten, F., Mulder, B. (eds), *The Rietveld Schröder House,* London: Butterworth Architecture/Cambridge, MA: The MIT Press, 1988.

Pearce, Susan, *On Collecting: An Investigation into Collecting in the European Tradition,* London and New York: Routledge, 1995.

Peck. A., *Period Rooms in the Metropolitan Museum of Art,* New York: Metropolitan Museum of Art Publications, 2004.

Peter Noever, Peter, *Die Frankfurter Küche von Margarete Schütte-Lihotzky,* Berlin: Ernst & Sohn, 1992.

Plischke, E. A., *Katalog Zusammenstellung und Gestaltung Franco Fonatt,* Vienna: Architektur- und Baufachverlag, 1983.

Plischke, Ernst Anton, : Architekt und Lehrer, Salzburg: Pustet, 2003.

—— *Ein Leben mit Architektur,* Vienna: Locker, 1989.

Plunz, R., *A History of Housing in New York City: Dwelling Type and Social Change,* New York: Columbia University Press, 1986.

Porter, J. and MacDonald, S., 'Fabricating Interiors: Approaches to the History of Domestic Furnishings at the Geffrye Museum', *Journal of Design History* 3: 2–3, 1990.

——— , ——— *Putting on the Style: Setting up Home in the 1950s*, London: Geffrye Museum, 1990.

Rapaport, B. and Stayton, K. (eds), *Vital Forms: American Art and Design in the Atomic Age, 1940–60* (ex. catalogue), New York: Brooklyn Museum and Harry N. Abrams, 2001.

Reed, Christopher, *Bloomsbury Rooms*, New Haven, CT and London: Yale, 2004.

Reiss, H. (ed.), *Everyday Art Quarterly* 5, Minneapolis: Walker Art Center, 1947.

Robach, Cilla, 'Design for Modern People', in *Utopia and Reality, Modernity in Sweden, 1900–60*, New Haven, CT and London: Bard Center for Studies in the Decorative Arts, Design and Culture, New York and Yale University Press, 2002.

Russel-Hitchcock, H., *In the Nature of Materials, the Buildings of Frank Lloyd Wright 1887–1942*, Duell, New York: Sloan & Pearce, 1942.

Samuel, Raphael, *Theatres of Memory, Vol. 1: Past and Present in Contemporary Culture*, London: Verso, 1994.

Sarnitz, August and Ottillinger, Eva B. *Ernest Plischke: the Complete Works: Modern Architecture for the New World*, Munich/London: Prestel, 2004.

Saumarez Smith, Charles, 'Museums, Artefacts and Meaning', in Vergo, P. (ed.) *The New Museology*, London: Reaktion, 1989.

Scanlon, J., *Inarticulate Longings: The Ladies Home Journal, Gender and the Promises of Consumer Culture*, London: Routledge, 1955.

Shields, R., *Lefebvre, Love & Struggle. Spatial Dialectics*, London: Routledge, 1999.

Simon, R. (ed.), *Public Artist, Private Passions: The World of Edward Linley Sambourne*, ex. catalogue, London: *The British Art Journal* and The Royal Borough of Kensington and Chelsea, 2001.

Smith, E. T. (ed.), *Blueprints for Modern Living: History and Legacy of the Case Study Houses* (ex. catalogue), Los Angeles, CA and Cambridge, MA: Museum of Contemporary Art and MIT Press, 1989.

Smithells, Roger, 'Mixing to Taste', in *Daily Mail Ideal Home Book 1951–2*, ed. Margaret Sherman, London: Associated Newspapers, 1952.

Sontag, Susan, *On Photography*, London: Penguin Books, 1979.

Sparke, P., 'The "ideal" and the "real" interior in Elsie de Wolfe's *The House in Good Taste* of 1913', *Journal of Design History* 16(1), 2003.

Tanizaki, J., *In Praise of Shadows*, New Haven, CT.: Leete's Island Books, 1977.

Teasley, S., 'National Geographics of Design: Rhetoric of Tatami in 1920s and 1930s Japanese interiors', *De-placing Difference, Architecture Culture and Imaginative Geography: The Greatest of Expositions Completely Illustrated, Official Publication,* The Official Photographic Company of the Louisiana Purchase Exposition, St Louis, MI., 1904.

Thornton, P., *Authentic Décor. The Domestic Interior 1620–1920*, London: Weidenfeld & Nicolson, 1984.

Tobey, R., *Technology as Freedom: The New Deal and the Electrical Modernization of the American Home*, Berkeley, CA: University of California Press, 1996.

US Department of Commerce, Economics and Statistics Administration, *Decennial Censuses from 1790–2000*, Washington, DC: US Government Printing Office, 2002.

Vergo, Peter (ed.), *The New Museology*, London: Reaktion, 1989.

Walker Art Center, *Idea House Oral History Project, 1999–2000* (unpublished), Minneapolis, MN: Walker Art Center.

——— *Explanatory Guide to the Idea House* (brochure), Minneapolis, MN: Walker Art Center, 1941.

Walker, N., *Kettle's Yard: An Illustrated Handlist of the Paintings, Sculptures and Drawings*, Cambridge: Kettle's Yard, 1970.

William-Ellis, Clough, *On Trust for the Nation*, drawings by Barbara Jones, London: Paul Elek, 1947.

Woodham, J., 'Designing Design History: From Pevsner to Postmodernism', in *Working Papers in Communication, Digitisation and Knowledge*, Vol. 1 (1) December 2001. Available at www.aut.ac.nz/research/research_institutes/ccr/publications/workingpaper.htm; accessed 8 July 2005.

Wright, G., *Building the Dream: A Social History of Housing in America*, Cambridge, MA: MIT Press, 1983.

Wright, P., *On Living in an Old Country: The National Past in Contemporary Britain*, London: Verso, 1985.

Index